BEDFORD/ST. MARTIN'S
you get more | bedfordstmartins.com

The first completely illustrated guide to writing

Understanding Rhetoric
A Graphic Guide to Writing

Elizabeth Losh
Jonathan Alexander
Kevin Cannon
Zander Cannon

bedfordstmartins.com/
understandingrhetoric/catalog

This comics-style collaboration between rhetoricians Elizabeth Losh and Jonathan Alexander and illustrator team Big Time Attic presents the content of the composition course in a form designed to draw students in. *Understanding Rhetoric: A Graphic Guide to Writing* covers what first-year college writers need to know—the writing process, critical analysis, argument, research, revision, and presentation—in a visual format that brings rhetorical concepts to life through examples ranging from Aristotle to YouTube.

❝Highly entertaining and engaging.... It's one of the first textbooks I've seen that could be studied as a rhetorical text in a fun and enlightening way.❞

—Chris Gerben, *University of Michigan*

Reviewers

All essay submissions are reviewed blind by two external readers; those listed below are members of the active reader pool. We thank them for their critical contributions to scholarship in the field.

Linda Adler-Kassner	Lynée Lewis Gaillet	Susan Miller
Tom Amorose	Alice Gilliam	Ruth Mirtz
Valerie Balester	Maureen Daly Goggin	Clyde Moneyhun
Cheryl Ball	Angela González	Roxanne Mountford
Nicholas Behm	Lorie Goodman	Gerald P. Mulderig
Patricia Belanoff	Heather Brodie Graves	Joan A. Mullin
Patricia Bizzell	Roger Graves	Joddy Murray
Bill Bolin	Paul Hanstedt	Marshall Myers
Darsie Bowden	Dana Harrington	Gerald Nelms
Colin Brooke	Jeanette Harris	Jon Olson
Robert Brooke	Cynthia Haynes	Peggy O'Neill
Nancy Buffington	Paul Heilker	Derek Owens
Beth Burmester	Carl Herndl	Irv Peckham
Paul Butler	Brooke Hessler	Donna Qualley
Mary Ann Cain	Charlotte Hogg	Ellen Quandahl
Carol Lea Clark	Bruce Horner	Kelly Ritter
Kirsti Cole	Sue Hum	Duane Roen
Lisa Coleman	Brian Huot	Randall Roorda
James Comas	James Inman	Blake Scott
Juanita Rodgers Comfort	Asao Inoue	Ellen Schendel
Thomas Deans	Rebecca Jackson	Carol Severino
Jane Detweiler	T. R. Johnson	Wendy Sharer
Ronda Leathers Dively	Judith Kearns	Steve Sherwood
Sidney Dobrin	Martha Kruse	Donna Strickland
Whitney Douglas	bonnie kyburz	William Thelin
Donna Dunbar-Odom	Mary Lamb	Peter Vandenberg
Lynell Edwards	Donna LeCourt	Deirdre Vinyard
David Elder	Neal Lerner	Zachary Waggoner
Janet Carey Eldred	Carrie Leverenz	Kathleen Welch
Michelle Eodice	Min-Zhan Lu	Nancy Welch
Heidi Estrem	Brad Lucas	Thomas West
Sheryl Fontaine	William Macauley	Katherine Wills
Helen Fox	Tim Mayers	Rosemary Winslow
Tom Fox	Lisa McClure	Vershawn Ashanti Young
Christy Friend	Moriah McCracken	Janet Zepernick
Richard Fulkerson	Dan Meltzer	
Catherine Gabor	Laura Rose Micciche	

Member of the Council of Editors of Learned Journals

composition STUDIES

Volume 40, Number 2
Fall 2012

Editor
Jennifer Clary-Lemon

Book Review Editor
Asao B. Inoue

Former Editors
Gary Tate
Robert Mayberry
Christina Murphy
Peter Vandenberg
Ann George
Carrie Leverenz
Brad E. Lucas

Advisory Board

Linda Adler-Kassner
 University of California, Santa Barbara

Tom Amorose
 Seattle Pacific University

Chris Anson
 North Carolina State University

Valerie Balester
 Texas A&M University

Robert Brooke
 University of Nebraska, Lincoln

Sidney Dobrin
 University of Florida

Lisa Ede
 Oregon State University

Paul Heilker
 Virginia Polytechnic Institute and State University

James Inman
 University of Maryland University College

Laura Micciche
 University of Cincinnati

Peggy O'Neill
 Loyola College

Victor Villanueva
 Washington State University

THE UNIVERSITY OF WINNIPEG

SUBSCRIPTIONS
Composition Studies is published twice each year (May and November). Subscription rates: Individuals $25 (Domestic) and $30 (International); Institutions $75 (Domestic) and $75 (International); Students $15.

BACK ISSUES
Recent back issues are now available through Amazon.com for $12. To find issues, use the advanced search feature and search on "Composition Studies" (title) and "Parlor Press" (publisher). Photocopies of earlier issues are available for $3.

BOOK REVIEWS
Assignments are made from a file of potential book reviewers. To have your name added to the file, send a current vita to the Book Review Editor at asao@inoueweb.com.

SUBMISSIONS
All appropriate essay submissions will be blind reviewed by two external readers. Manuscripts should be 3,500-7,500 words and conform to current MLA guidelines for format and documentation; they should be free of author's names and other identifying references. *Electronic submissions are preferred*: consult our Web site for details. (For print submissions, submit three titled, letter-quality copies with a cover letter including the title and author contact information, loose postage sufficient to mail manuscripts to two reviewers, and a #10 SASE for the return of reviewer comments.) *Composition Studies* will not consider previously published manuscripts. We discourage the submission of conference papers that have not been revised or extended for a critical reading audience. Those wishing to submit Course Designs should first consult our Web site for specific instructions. Letters to the editor and responses to articles are strongly encouraged.

To ensure a blind review, *Composition Studies* requests
  1. The authors of the document have deleted their names from the text, with "Author" and year used in the references and endnotes, instead of the authors' name, article title, etc.
  2. With Microsoft Office documents, author identification should also be removed from the properties for the file (see under File in Word), by clicking on the following, beginning with File on the main menu of the Microsoft application: File > Save As > Tools (or Options with a Mac) > Security > Remove personal information from file properties on save > Save.
  3. With PDFs, the authors' names should also be removed from Document Properties found under File on Adobe Acrobat's main menu.

Direct all correspondence to:

   Jennifer Clary-Lemon, Editor
   Department of Rhetoric, Writing, and Communications
   University of Winnipeg
   515 Portage Avenue, Winnipeg, MB R3B 2E9
   Canada

Composition Studies is grateful for the generous support of the Dean of Arts and the Department of Rhetoric, Writing, and Communications at the University of Winnipeg.

© Copyright 2012 by Jennifer Clary-Lemon, Editor
Production and printing is managed by Parlor Press, www.parlorpress.com.
ISSN 1534-9322

www.compositionstudies.uwinnipeg.ca

composition STUDIES

Volume 40, Number 2
Fall 2012

Articles

Forging Rhetorical Subjects: Problem-Based Learning
in the Writing Classroom   9
   Paula Rosinski and Tim Peeples

Incendiary Discourse: Reconsidering Flaming,
Authority, and Democratic Subjectivity in
Computer-mediated Communication   34
   Timothy Oleksiak

Bodies of Knowledge: Definitions, Delineations, and
Implications of Embodied Writing in the Academy   50
   A. Abby Knoblauch

Reclaiming "Old" Literacies in the New Literacy Information Age:
The Functional Literacies of the Mediated Workstation   66
   Ryan Shepherd and Peter Goggin

Course Designs

Writing 302: Writing Culture   92
   Jamie White-Farnham

UWP 011: Popular Science & Technology Writing   112
   Sarah Perrault

Reviews

Remixing Composition: A History of Multimodal Writing Pedagogy, by
Jason Palmeri   134
   Reviewed by Andrew Davis

*To Know Her Own History: Writing at the Woman's College,
1943-1963*, by Kelly Ritter   138
   Reviewed by Annie S. Mendenhall

The Promise of Reason: Studies in The New Rhetoric,
edited by John T. Gage   142
   Reviewed by Abigail L. Montgomery

*From Form to Meaning: Freshman Composition and the
Long Sixties, 1957-1974*, by David Fleming 145
    Reviewed by Jacob Babb

Toward a Composition Made Whole, by Jody Shipka 149
    Reviewed by Trent M. Kays

*Conversational Rhetoric: The Rise and Fall of a
Women's Tradition, 1600-1900*, by Jane Donawerth 152
    Reviewed by Dara Rossman Regaignon

*I Hope I Join the Band: Narrative, Affiliation, and
Antiracist Rhetoric*, by Frankie Condon 155
    Reviewed by Ryan Winet

The Megarhetorics of Global Development,
edited by Rebecca Dingo and J. Blake Scott 158
    Reviewed by David Dadurka

*Words at Work and Play: Three Decades in Family
and Community Life*, by Shirley Brice Heath 162
    Reviewed by Stacy Kastner

*Feminist Rhetorical Practices: New Horizons for
Rhetoric, Composition, and Literacy Studies*,
by Jacqueline Jones Royster and Gesa E. Kirsch 166
    Reviewed by Heather Ostman

Illness as Narrative, by Ann Jurecic 169
    Reviewed by Erin Trauth

Announcements 172

Contributors 173

Forging Rhetorical Subjects: Problem-Based Learning in the Writing Classroom

Paula Rosinski and Tim Peeples

> Following a brief introduction to problem-based learning (PBL) as one type of highly-engaged pedagogy, this article examines how PBL activities in a first-year writing class and an upper-level professional writing and rhetoric class led students to develop rhetorical subjectivities. We conclude that highly engaged pedagogies, like PBL, that purposively situate students/teacher within indeterminate spaces requiring active reflection and meta-cognition are more likely to forge successful writers, writers who have more experience making a wide range of rhetorical choices, have a better sense of writing as contextualized praxis, and know to expect and value the collaborative nature of writing.

Two students, sitting side-by-side but wearing headphones and probably listening to music, write different sections of the same proposal and drop finished pieces into Google Docs. A third student sits on the ground with his laptop, organizing and reorganizing documents into different piles; he jumps up to retrieve a document from the printer but hesitates when deciding to which pile it belongs. The remaining students work in groups of two, three, or four: they conduct online research, share results and search terms, swap PDF files, rework a Web site's layout and navigation, and design a graph to support an argument. One group of students crowds around the flat screen at their table, pointing and having a slightly contentious debate about which section of video should be edited out and why. With this wide range of writing activities taking place, it is no surprise that the noise level vacillates widely. But students are engaged enough in their own work that they don't seem bothered by the outbursts of frustration or peals of laughter that erupt from different groups from time to time.

Today, it is commonplace to walk into writing classrooms in colleges and universities across the country and find scenes like the one described above. Students and teachers are regularly found during class time engaged with writing, writing technologies, and one another, and within the classroom there is a buzz of activity. If the primary aim of a writing class, at any level, is to develop effective writers, is it the development of successful writers that we are observing when we walk into the buzzing classrooms described above? Hands-on activity by itself certainly does not lead to the development of successful writers. Still, for a variety of reasons, educators in Rhetoric and Composition, as well as a growing number in higher education in general, believe strongly that learning and development are enhanced significantly through active engagement.

Engaged learning pedagogies, which come into writing classrooms in forms like service learning, project-based learning, and client projects, share features that distinguish them from other pedagogies, like lecture and discussion, and even active pedagogies like workshopping and critique, common in the fine arts. A major distinguishing factor is the way assignments in engaged learning classrooms are designed to situate students within complex, authentic contexts and often require sustained amounts of time. They also commonly require high levels of collaboration, occasionally with others outside of the classroom (see Kuh).

Problem-based learning (PBL) offers another highly engaged pedagogical option for our writing classes. PBL shares with other engaged pedagogies the features listed above, but it distinguishes itself by *initiating* learning with the introduction of an *ill-structured* problem around which all learning centers. Service-, project-, and client-based pedagogies *can* initiate learning and also be designed as ill-structured problems, thus reflecting the distinguishing features of PBL, but PBL always carries these features, making it a distinctly engaged pedagogy.

The ill-structured problem is a hallmark of and key to PBL (see Rhem; Savery). To be ill-structured does not mean poorly, casually, or sloppily designed by an instructor. Ill-structured problems are messy, real-world problems; they are dynamic, without simple, fixed, formulaic, or even "right" solutions; they require a cycle of inquiry, information gathering, and reflection that is likely iterative. PBL revolves around these carefully designed but ill-structured problems. Another hallmark of PBL is the way it initiates learning. One generally thinks of teaching and learning as a process initiated with the introduction of new content, skills, methods, et cetera. After this initial instruction, students are given instruction and time to master the new material that has been introduced. Finally, their mastery is put to the test in one fashion or another before moving on to new sets of content, skills, methods, et cetera. For instance, in most case-based pedagogies, students are introduced to new content, such as the genre of the bad newsletter in business writing, and then they are put to practicing what they have learned by writing a bad newsletter specific to a business world case. In contrast, PBL learning is *initiated* with the introduction of an ill-structured problem. The new content, skills, methods, et cetera are gathered and generated *through* the process of investigating and addressing the problem, rather than being supplied, studied, and/or practiced prior to engagement with the problem (see Amador, Miles, and Peters; Duch, Groh, and Allen). In PBL-based medical education, for instance, instruction in new areas might begin with visits to rooms with real patients. The patient in the room, along with all of his or her health details, is the ill-structured problem that initiates learning. What students learn is initiated by and contextualized within this problem.[1]

We chose to examine PBL in the writing classroom for a variety of reasons, but primary among them was to improve upon the kinds of engaged-learning already occurring at our institution[2] and in our own classrooms, from first-year composition to advanced courses in Rhetoric and Writing Studies (RWS).[3] While our experiences with PBL do not lead us to herald it as the best or even a better way to teach writing, experimenting with PBL in our actual classrooms helped make obvious, again, the impact pedagogies have on constructing students/writers—rhetorical subjects—and compelled us to reflect more critically on the student-writer subjectivities being constructed in our classrooms. Our experience leads us to the conclusion that highly engaged pedagogies, like PBL, that purposively situate students/teachers within open-ended, indeterminate, messy problem spaces requiring active reflection and metacognition are more likely to forge *successful* writers, or writers who (a) have more experience making a wide range of situated rhetorical choices, (b) have a better sense of writing as contextualized praxis that is mutually constitutive of writers, readers, texts, and contexts, and (c) know to expect, understand, and value the collaborative, messy nature of non-routine writing.

In what follows, we reflect on our process of developing and teaching PBL assignments for two writing courses: one, a required first-year composition course, and the other, an introductory course in Professional Writing and Rhetoric, required of both majors and minors. Through this assignment-based reflection, we share sample PBL assignments designed specifically for writing instruction, which is in and of itself of some value, for though there is much available in terms of literature and sample assignments for PBL, there is very little focused on writing instruction (see Pennell and Miles). However, our focus, here, is not on applying PBL to writing instruction and sharing PBL writing assignment samples, per se. Our focus is on calling attention to two central questions always involved in the teaching/learning of writing but routinely left in the shadows of either more abstract theorizing or more nuts-and-bolts instructional detailing. Through our reflective process, we call attention to the following two questions:

- "What defines a successful writer?" and
- "How can we best develop/teach such writers?"

In calling attention to these questions within pedagogy and contextualized in our own pedagogical experiences, we hope to reinvigorate explicit disciplinary, as well as local, conversations about the role our pedagogical practices—PBL in this case—play in forming writers/people/agents and the significant impact pedagogy has on the formation of rhetorical subjects.

The Subject of Writing

In *Fragments of Rationality*, Lester Faigley challenges compositionists to consider how student-writers/rhetorical subjects are called into being through pedagogy, among other social/material/cultural practices. The primary focus of argument for Faigley is the distinction and historical transition between the modern construct of the writer/rhetorical subject as the rational, autonomous individual and the postmodern construction of the fragmented writer/rhetorical subject. One iteration of this difference highlighted by Faigley is the contrast between the pedagogies advocated by Peter Elbow, on the one hand, and Kenneth Bruffee, on the other. Elbow's emphasis on helping students find their authentic voices and helping them learn ways to control language to best express those voices led Bruffee to attack, as Faigley depicts it, Elbow's pedagogy as "encouraging 'rampant individualism'" (226), a hallmark of the modernist construction of the writer/rhetorical subject as a stable, unified self. Bruffee's collaborative pedagogy, Faigley goes on to argue, emphasized "the communal nature of discourse and a view of knowledge as socially negotiated," leading to the construction of writers/rhetorical subjects who understand and practice writing (and themselves, we would add) as part of "ongoing conversations" beyond any stable, unified self (226).

Faigley's challenge to us, though, is more than historical and academic. It leads us to consider the following related questions: Are we aware of the kinds of subjectivities we're inviting students to occupy through our pedagogies? Are they the kinds of subjectivities we want or we should want students to occupy? Are they the kinds of subjectivities that will serve students well in their other college courses, as they engage in casual conversations with peers, as they enter the workplace and become practicing professionals, as they take on adult and domestic responsibilities? Are they the kinds of subjectivities that will help students become responsible, active, ethical citizens? These questions continue to be overlooked in a great deal of pedagogical scholarship, perhaps because teachers and scholars find it unsettling to consider this far-reaching implication of their classroom practice (see Couture; Russell, "Activity Theory"). While Faigley's challenge may have gone largely unheeded on a pedagogical level, other scholarship has explored, on a theoretical level, how certain pedagogies do indeed invite students to participate in learning and meaning-making in certain ways, and even affect momentarily the way students interact with the world and with others (see Ryan).

Engaged Pedagogies and (Re)Defining the Successful Writer

If compositionists and academics in the sister fields that make up the broader RWS community are to examine more closely and actively these questions of pedagogical impact on the formation of rhetorical subjects—if we are to reinvigorate explicit disciplinary and local conversations about the significant impact pedagogy has on the formation of rhetorical subjects—engaged learning is one broad pedagogical category RWS should likely investigate. Having grown up in a largely post-Freirian era, Composition Studies has long claimed high ground in discussions about engaged learning. Learning in composition, as well as most technical and professional writing classes, is and has been highly engaged. Though this term has shifted in meaning, from simply active learning (e.g., hands on) to something more complex, those of us teaching writing have long been ahead of the curve when it comes to engaged pedagogies. But taking the high ground can also mean assuming a level of invisibility, at least in the explicit conversations about engaged learning. A quick scan of the scholarship being done in this venue highlights disciplines such as psychology and education, particularly for the empirical and theoretical, as well as the sciences, where the focus is more on reports on the implementation and results of engaged pedagogies. Arguably the leader in engaged learning, at least in higher education, is the Indiana University Center for Postsecondary Research (CPR) in the School of Education, out of which come the National Survey of Student Engagement (NSSE), the Faculty Survey of Student Engagement (FSSE), Law School Survey of Student Engagement (LSSSE), and the NSSE Institute for Effective Educational Practice. Only recently (see Consortium for the Study of Writing in College, started 2007-08) have those directly related to RWS entered discussions with comparably strong, expert voices about engaged learning.

When the two of us began incorporating PBL, we began to better understand and articulate more clearly for ourselves reasons we continued to be drawn to other engaged pedagogies, like service-, project-, and client-based assignments. We had each continued to be drawn to these pedagogies in spite of the frustrations they often bring, the additional work they often require of teachers, and the fairly typical resistance teachers receive from students when such pedagogies require them to assume new (highly engaged) ways of being in school: in other words, new subjectivities. PBL was foreign enough to Writing Studies that struggling to think through its value and how to best utilize it helped us begin to rearticulate why we continued to be drawn to the messiness, indeterminacy, dynamism, and sometimes outright frustration of highly engaged pedagogies, in general, such as client-based assignments. The frustrations of project-, problem-, and client-based pedagogies have, in the end, at least, always felt worth it because we saw that our students who were engaged in such learning experiences developed ways of being that seemed a closer fit to our sense of what successful writers are like. These sorts of assignments are so authentic (often almost too real-worldly for classroom comfort) that students daily wrestle with writing as a socially contextualized, dynamic, contested, ideological, meaning-making, iterative, messy process. Within such assignments, *techne*, heuristics, strategies, and procedural knowledge are not simply bits of knowledge learned and applied transactionally. Each of these takes on a life within a specific context, the way experienced writers know they do in actual writing practice. Heuristics, theories, process strategies, et cetera become heuristic themselves, and students find themselves theorizing in context. Students are involved in more sophisticated (and dare we say, authentic) rhetorical praxis. Patricia A. Sullivan and James E. Porter define praxis as "a kind of thinking that does not start with theoretical knowledge or abstract models, which are then applied to situations, but that begins with immersion in local situations, and then uses epistemic theory as heuristic rather than as explanatory or determining" (26). As outlined earlier, all highly engaged writing pedagogies immerse students in complex rhetorical situations that often extend over more than a brief time and often require collaboration, and so they create pedagogical contexts in which students can experience, practice, and learn the *praxical* skills of writers and writing that Sullivan and Porter define. What we experienced and learned through our work with PBL, though, is that PBL's focus on *initiating* instruction and then having all learning arise out of a well crafted, ill-structured problem can heighten the immersive element of engaged pedagogies, which subsequently helps to create learning contexts in which student writers/rhetorical subjects can develop *praxical* subjectivities. *Praxical* writing subjects have developed a sense of themselves as writers who are comfortable with and confident in their ability to immerse themselves in local situations and then use epistemic theory—for example, decontextualized strategies and processes—as a heuristic for determining how to proceed and make wise writerly decisions. This is what we conceive of as a successful writer, it is what we have seen develop through and as a result of highly engaged pedagogies, and it is what we became aware of even more clearly through our implementation of PBL.

But why? What is distinct about what we are referring to as these *highly* engaged pedagogies, including PBL, that more dramatically forges these *praxical* writing subjects? We believe it stems from a change in the meaning and valuing of "engagement."

The meaning of engaged learning shifts when one moves from, say, (a) small group work aimed at ends achieved through discrete processes culminating in well-defined products to (b) immersion in messy writing problems. In the first instance—small group work—engagement is employed as a means for more effectively transferring writerly knowledge. For instance, rather than speak about and then have students individually work on revising, the small peer-group revision workshop functions as a more effective means for transferring that writerly knowledge of revising. The engagement linked to small peer-group interaction is a means to an end: more effective (e.g., experiential) transfer of learning. In the second instance—immersion in messy writing problems—engagement is no longer employed as a means for enhancing the transaction of writerly knowledge. Instead, engagement has become part of *the knowledge* being learned, as well as a context within which writers learn. Being engaged is understood and practiced as an essential part of "being a writer." The student-writer/rhetorical subject shifts from being a receiver of the transfer of knowledge through engaged/experiential means of teaching-learning (e.g., the small peer-group revision workshop) to being an active agent/writer immersed in/engaged with messy writing problems. From within this new sense of engagement, what is considered the successful writer also shifts.

One approach to defining writing success might stem from a general skills model of writing expertise (see Peeples and Hart-Davidson for discussion of the three models of writing expertise referenced here and adopted from Kaufer and Young). In this model, writing expertise is defined by the knowledge and control of general strategies (e.g., making diagrams, analogies, and means-ends analyses) that are deemed useful in and transferable to any context; the successful writer is one who can demonstrate having and effectively applying such knowledge. Another approach to defining success might stem from a contextualist model of writing expertise. In this second model, writing expertise is defined by the knowledge and control of context-/culture-specific norms; the successful writer is one who has accurately read/interpreted local norms and is able to maneuver effectively within those norms through the application of contextual knowledge. In both of these models, successful writing is relatively predictive and dependent on the application of what one has come to know in a transactional way. Engaged pedagogies *qua* active learning are valuable in both of these models because they increase motivation and the ability to transfer knowledge learned in one case, for instance, to another. In one of these two models of expertise, the contextualist model, engagement takes on an additional value, beyond enhanced motivation and practice in transfer: the creation of authentic scenarios, situations, and contexts gives students experience reading/interpreting local norms and adapting/adjusting to them. It is presumed that this experience will help students more effectively transfer such knowledge to new contexts.

A third approach to defining success might stem from an interactionist model of writing expertise. In this third model, writing expertise is defined by the sort of *praxical* wisdom and behavior earlier described; the successful writer "relies on a complex... interaction between context knowledge and general strategies that are in principle articulable and teachable" (Kaufer and Young qtd. in Peeples and Hart-Davidson 101). In this third model, successful writing is messy and less predictive. Like the general skills and contextualist models, the interactionist model values hands-on, active engagement as a means for motivation and as a crucial part of learning transfer. In addition, though, the interactionist model values hands-on, active engagement in and of itself, as something that, in and of itself, is instructive. *Through engagement*, students learn *that* writing is messy, open-ended, indeterminate, and iterative; they learn *how* to write within such contexts; and they learn to *value* the process of working through/with this messiness.

When engagement carries these new values, the goals and objectives of engagement change significantly. From the perspective of the first two models, the context for engagement is meant to be a vehicle for learning, and as such, the context should be relatively transparent. When the context itself is problematical, it should be for clearly defined instructive purposes—the problematical should be, in other words, under the control of the teacher. From the perspective of an interactionist model of writerly success, however, the problems posed by contexts—for example, the availability of resources, collaborative differences, shifting and complex matrices of power, shifting timelines, changing goals, et cetera—are themselves uncontrollable, essential, and essentially instructive characteristics of writing. From this perspective, the frustrations teachers and students have with highly engaged pedagogies, such as project- and client-based assignments, mean something very different. Teachers employing and reflecting on these pedagogies from a generalist or contextualist model perceive the problems of context as failures either of themselves, their students, or the contexts. From an interactionist perspective of writing instruction and writerly success, experiences with unpredictable, messy, and dynamic contexts are instructive, not failures.

It may or may not be an accident that many in writing have embraced highly engaged pedagogies. If an accident, we believe it is an accident that might be leading (though accidentally and, thus, not as effectively as might be the case) to the development of a different kind of student-writer/rhetorical subject, one who reflects a more *praxical*, interactionist model, for these student-writers/rhetorical subjects have experienced the messiness that is the nature of most writing. If it is not an accident, then we believe we can more effectively and powerfully develop this *praxical*, interactionist model of expertise by consciously focusing on the development of our highly engaged pedagogical practices, with attention to the changing values of engagement and the writerly experiences and qualities developed as a result.

The Forging of Rhetorical Subjects: Reflecting on and through PBL Assignments

First-Year Composition, Digital Literacies, and PBL

We designed a set of three digital literacy PBL activities—"Critiquing Search Engines," "Understanding & Using Databases," and "Documenting Digital Sources" (see Appendix for actual assignments)—for College Writing, our university's first-year composition course. Digital literacies were our focus for a variety of reasons, but first and foremost we wanted students to learn that critically engaging online research and documenting online sources is a more sophisticated, rhetorically contextualized, and messy process than a general skills model, or even a contextualist model, of writing sometimes suggests. We assumed that students often put little deliberate thought into selecting search engines and databases, since we repeatedly observed them turning to the same search engines and databases in different research situations, usually because they were the ones students learned about in high school and with which they felt most comfortable, regardless of whether or not they were appropriate or even adequate sources of information for their current research purposes. We also observed that students often failed to appreciate the disciplinary values that are conveyed through documentation standards and, instead, viewed writing citations as a kind of formulaic drudgery. Since this was our first foray into PBL, we chose to design several shorter low-stakes assignments, in the hopes that they would encourage students to embrace the activities without fear of how such an experimental pedagogy might impact their grades or standing in the course (see Anson). The low-stakes nature of these shorter PBL activities also made us, as instructors, more comfortable using this pedagogy for the first time as well.

It is easy enough to provide students with a list of numbered directions for conducting a simple search engine or database search, but in the "Critiquing Search Engines" and "Understanding & Using Databases" digital literacy activities, we wanted students to experience that how a search engine or database worked—for example, how it was designed and programmed, the search options that were or were not available, the types of sources it catalogued, the kinds of returns that were possible—could affect profoundly the activity of research and the quality of research identified. We also wanted students to learn that the practice of using research technologies is itself part of the meaning-making process, and that search engines and databases are not just mere tools for returning supposedly objective research results. We expected that immersing students in an indeterminate, messy, and open-ended research context could help them think about research engines and databases as socially and culturally constructed artifacts with biases and limitations, with intended primary and secondary audiences. And since this first-year writing course is charged with preparing students for later writing courses as well as real-world writing situations, we also wanted to disrupt what students thought should happen in writing classrooms and real writing situations by putting them in indeterminate and complex writing and research spaces. These two activities asked students to solve the problem of determining how exactly different search engines and databases functioned, and to develop strategies for deciding which ones to use for different research situations they were actually facing in their other courses (see Appendix for actual assignments).

We designed the third PBL digital literacy activity, "Documenting Digital Sources," because we wanted students to understand that there is a method behind what often seems like the madness of documentation, that this method reflects academic values and disciplinary priorities, and that such an understanding can assist one in documenting ever-evolving online sources. Janice R. Walker and Todd Taylor's *The Columbia Guide to Online Style 2/e* examines what they call "the logic of citation" and notes five principles of citation style: access, intellectual property, economy, standardization, and transparency (31-36). While Walker and Taylor's guide goes a long way to demystifying the process of writing documentation and understanding its underlying logic, we sought a more engaged way of teaching students about documentation so that they could approach it as a heuristic, not as a series of rules to follow. This last digital literacy activity asked students to solve the problem of identifying the values embodied in the different documentation features and explaining these values to an audience of high school students.

What sets each of these three PBL digital literacy activities apart from other kinds of engaged pedagogies is that they each initiated instruction with real, and in these cases, deceptively simple, problems—for example, how do different research engines and databases function? How do you decide which search engine or database to use for different research situations? What do the different components of an online citation mean? Then, all learning emerged out of student attempts to answer these questions. Initiating and sustaining all learning through real problems increased student immersion, which in turn gave students opportunities to experience and practice the *praxical* skills of writers and writing. Instead of being given abstract or theoretical knowledge about research engines, databases, and documenting online sources, students were immersed in local, meaningful situations and then had to use epistemic theory—that is, the knowledge they were creating themselves—as a heuristic for figuring out real answers to real problems.

Given that a hallmark feature of PBL is the open-endedness of the learning environment, it was interesting, but not surprising, to hear our students express disbelief that they could learn anything from these experiences. They expressed frustration at being given such open-ended assignments without clearly defined expectations for how they should respond to them and what exactly they should learn. With all three activities, students began working silently, either individually or in groups, but as they became more involved with the problems, the classrooms became animated with collaborative chatter. Students started to express surprise at the ways they tended to take certain things for granted or as givens, for example, when they realized that not all search engines returned the same results when using the same search terms, or that using different Boolean functions (or, for that matter, when they learned what a "Boolean" function actually is) returned different results; when they figured out that it was possible to determine what kinds of resources different databases collected and that there were ways to return only certain types of sources (i.e., full-text only, PDF only); or when the previously puzzling way to write a bibliographic citation finally began to make sense when they considered that the various features reflected a discourse community's concerns or values.

In their own ways, each of these digital literacy activities showed students that real engagement—the process of working in indeterminate contexts to solve real problems—is instructive *itself*. We used the "Critiquing Search Engines" and "Understanding Databases" in the middle of the term in our first-year writing classrooms, after the students had completed several shorter writing assignments but before they began longer, research-based projects. These two activities, in particular, highlighted the messy and iterative process of research and writing, because they taught students that neither search engines nor databases are objective tools and that writers need to consider their respective advantages and disadvantages on a technical as well as rhetorical level in each different research situation. What students (and in particular, at our institution, first-year students) often think should happen in a college classroom, and what they often think writers *are* and *do*, was also disrupted: instead of sitting quietly in their seats listening to a lecture and then being given explicit instructions about what kind of writing to produce in response to the assignment, students were permitted to, quite simply, decide how they were going to proceed. They were permitted, to their surprise, to physically move about inside or outside of the classroom, to ask each other questions and collaborate, or to e-mail friends or family members they thought could assist them in their inquiry, and to actually begin crafting their responses to the problem in genres of their own choosing (instead of being told, in an assignment handout, in what genre they should respond, usually outside of class time).

Their immersion and engagement in a real writing situation *itself* helped the students develop sophisticated responses to the problems they were tasked with solving. So, for example, research became for the students not a clearly delineated activity which points to the most obvious research engine or database to use, but rather an imprecise activity which requires writers to develop strategies for selecting the most appropriate research source for any given disciplinary situation, and then to revise iteratively these strategies on the spot as one learns more information either about the database, research engine, or one's research topic. Students first tried to write neat, numbered lists about how to decide which search engine to use or how to conduct effective database research, or they tried to make a list explaining which search engine or database to use in different situations. But as they themselves engaged in the research necessary to construct these lists, the impossibility of composing a series of steps to follow or writing an objective list that would cover all rhetorical situations became apparent. Students then often moved on to create more sophisticated decision-trees, but these also became too complex. Finally, most students decided upon writing responses that were rich in detail about the rhetorical, biased, and complex qualities of search engines and databases, while also emphasizing that their readers would have to make wise decisions based upon their own rhetorical and disciplinary reasons for conducting research. Supported by activity theory's claim that human actions cannot be understood outside of the wider human activity of which it is a part, the very pedagogy underlying these activities required students to take the wider human activity into account (real, student-identified research scenarios, particular research questions grounded in particular disciplines) in order to make informed research and writing decisions (see Dias et al.). So, for example, students composed humorous letters to first-year writing students, warning them not to thoughtlessly rely upon the same search engine for all occasions and encouraging them to research search engines themselves, while considering their own research purposes, before selecting a search engine to use.

We used the "Documenting Digital Sources" activity closer to the end of the term, as students were completing their long-term research project. This activity also immersed students in messy and indeterminate writing spaces and prevented them from simply regurgitating the documentation styles for online sources. Instead of being given abstract knowledge about how to document online sources, they had to use epistemic theory—that is, the knowledge they were creating themselves—as a heuristic for figuring out how to write these entries. So when confronted with the open-ended request to write an explanation to a less-experienced audience of high school students about the significance of a bibliographic citation's components, our students were often, at first, at a complete loss about how to proceed. This activity moved them from this place of certainty (all I have to do is mimic this set format, or fill in the empty spaces at the Landmark's online citation generator) to a place of uncertainty (what is the significance of these various components? why are they in this particular order? what would high school students already know about online documentation? what do I take for granted that high school students might not know?). We viewed their hesitation as a sign of a growing understanding that documenting online sources is not an isolated skill (as the filling-in-the-blank model implies), but part of a wider human activity (in this case, the activity of engaging in responsible academic discourse) that is context or disciplinary bound.

Our students first responded to this activity much like they did to the two earlier digital literacy activities: they tried to compose neat, orderly lists or explanations that would tell the high school students exactly how to compose a bibliographic citation for a digital source. But the students' efforts to write one comprehensive citation description were quickly thwarted as they were confronted with the existence of such a wide range of digital sources, with the lack of page numbers or inconsistent numbering practices, with unclear author attributions, and a plethora of other complications that arise when trying to attribute author, publisher, dates, Web addresses, and even titles to digital sources. Students ended up responding in ways similar to how they responded to the previous two activities: by writing letters, or memos, or a series of short Web pages to their audience of high school students, imploring them to think about digital citations not as a series of blanks that can be filled in mindlessly, but as one of the ways we join, participate, and extend academic discussions responsibly. For the remainder of the term, when students worked on their bibliographies, we often heard comments about how they were making decisions and choices—about which information to include, in what order, et cetera—based upon what the particular disciplinary community expected, cared about, and which information was necessary so that readers could locate the same exact resource.

This PBL activity also seemed to encourage metacognitive awareness in students because the process of articulating explicitly for a real audience why various components of an entry are significant to the academic community highlights that documenting digital sources serves a very specific purpose in academic writing. For instance, documenting digital sources increases the author's ethos and shows that the various entries are not random, but rather indicate what academic communities value in digital sources. Such metacognitive awareness also helps students identify the similarities and differences between academic, real world, and workplace writing as well (see Russell, "Rethinking Genre and Society").

Entering the Field of Professional Writing through PBL

At the same time we were exploring PBL in the first-year writing classroom, we were exploring how it might fit into and enhance some of our advanced major/minor courses in Professional Writing and Rhetoric. We designed a set of four PBL assignments—"Defining the Field," "Adding to the Conversation about Organizational Context," "Embodying Rhetoric as an Ethical Act," and "Making Space for Good Work"—for our introductory course to the major/minor. Each of the other courses within the major/minor already included some form of highly engaged pedagogy, such as client- or service-learning-based assignments. The introductory course, unlike most in professional writing, functioned as an introduction to histories, theories, and issues that defined the field, so it did not lend itself as readily to highly engaged pedagogies beyond a case study here and there. Unlike the low-stakes digital literacy activities we designed for our first-year writing course, we took it as a challenge to meet the majority of our learning objectives for this introductory professional writing and rhetoric course through PBL. Aside from a midterm and final exam, we constructed the entire course around PBL assignments. We focus, here, on the first two assignments, "Defining the Field" and "Adding to the Conversation about Organizational Context."

At the undergraduate level, in general, but particularly within an introductory course, students do not conceive of themselves as participating in defining the field to which they are just then being introduced, nor do they conceive of themselves as being able to contribute in any meaningful way to the conversations that make up the field. Students generally assume, at this level, that they will be fed the content, that all will be defined for them, and that their role is to receive definitive knowledge from another. Two of the objectives of our major/minor are that students will (a) develop their own clear definition of the field and themselves as writing and rhetoric experts within it and (b) understand their role and the role of writing and rhetoric in the shaping of the worlds in which they participate. "Defining the Field" and "Adding to the Conversation about Organizational Context" embraced those learning objectives, but quite differently through PBL than they had been addressed in prior offerings of the course. Just as it would be easy enough to supply students with clear instructions for conducting a variety of online searches, or generating accurate and appropriate citations, it is relatively easy to present students with a range of information about and within the field of Professional Writing and Rhetoric and then engage them in syntheses of the field and arguments within the field. These PBL professional writing and rhetoric assignments posed deceptively simple problems to students—"How would you define Professional Writing and Rhetoric to a group of novices?" and "What is organizational context and how does it affect the practice of Professional Writing and Rhetoric?" They then engaged students in largely self-directed problem solving that regularly included identifying, reading, and synthesizing disciplinary scholarship and, finally, drawing their own conclusions and crafting their own responses. Student learning was initiated by open-ended questions, and all learning emerged out of the students' own efforts to answer these questions.

As one might imagine, student reaction to the "Defining the Field" assignment after only one week of class was just short of either active rebellion or total paralysis (see Appendix for actual assignment). After initial vocal and kinetic resistance—for example, "You don't really mean you expect us to define the field before you've taught us anything?," "You've got to be kidding?," and looks of disgust exchanged across tables accompanied by much fidgeting—some students started asking productive, problem-solving-oriented questions: "Can we use the class text books?," "Can we ask you questions?," "Can we interview other professors and students?," and "Can we use online sources?" Somewhat surprisingly, the start of such productive questioning and writerly activity actually preceded any individual student's feelings of resolution that "Yes, he really isn't kidding" and certainly preceded any communal sense of positive resolve and proactivity. It was students' *engagement in* problem solving—in writing, in assuming the role of the active rhetorical subject—that led to positive resolve rather than vice versa. By the end of the initial class period in which the assignment was introduced, the majority of students were so engaged, and positively so, they had already surpassed the comfort level with the activity of addressing such a question—"How do you define Professional Writing and Rhetoric?"—that previous students struggled to achieve after two weeks of other teaching-learning activities. We highlight, though, that it was their comfort with *the activity of addressing* such a question that reached higher levels more quickly; they were still very much struggling over the content of their arguments, as should have been the case. On day one, the students addressing this PBL assignment were already deeply immersed in the authentic engagement of writing—of being active rhetorical subjects.

Though the students in this course were less surprised to be confronted by another problem-based assignment immediately following the completion of the first, the open-ended, ill-structured problem nature of their second assignment ("Adding to the Conversation about Organizational Context") created similar immediate and ongoing problem-solving challenges for them. In other words, feelings of resistance and disbelief were at the very least less vocal and extreme, but the socio-cognitive challenges—the writing and rhetorical challenges—were equally dramatic. We saw this, in part, as a sign of good learning very early in the course. Writers are constantly faced with new rhetorical challenges, and the expert writer not only expects that but has learned how to work through—that is, problem solve—those challenges effectively. At the very least, our students were already learning how to adjust/manage their affective response to novel rhetorical situations—that is, their PBL assignments. More promisingly, we saw them already developing, or developing-in-action, inventional and collaborative strategies and process knowledge for conducting the work writers routinely face. For example, one group of students developed inventional strategies for how to identify and keep track of resources that should be included in the project; another pair of students began designing a system, involving e-mail, Google Docs, and a free wiki, as a way to share and revise their peers' writing; several other students began generating a list of potential audiences for their organizational context project, taking complex notes on why each potential audience would be interested in such a project and how these different interests meant that the different audiences would expect different kinds of information, different ways of presenting the information, and even different navigational schemes for their project's interface.

The second PBL assignment in this class posed a new challenge: large-scale collaboration. In addition to learning about organizational context in order to address the "content problem" of the assignment, the students were experiencing the impact of organizational context building and rebuilding from the start of the project. As Linda Driskill explains, "Context can help explain what a document means, what ideas it contains, why the writer would try to express his or her ideas in a particular way, and why readers who occupy particular roles in different parts of an organization would be likely to respond to a document in particular ways" (108). In other words, writing is not successful simply because it is grammatically or structurally correct, it is successful when its writers have taken into account the organizational context and responded accordingly, for example, by defining the situation, identifying the key individuals and participants and their sometimes conflicting motivations, understanding the external influential parties, and acknowledging that there are multiple direct and indirect audiences for a given text. The students' location within the organizational context of our introductory professional writing and rhetoric classroom became a point of reflective instruction throughout and, particularly, after the completion of the assignment.

In their writing about organizational context and its relationship to Professional Writing and Rhetoric, students often reflected on their own immediate organizational/contextual experience. They would, for instance, comment on the strengths and weaknesses of their own collaborative practices with this particular assignment, as well as other class assignments, and they would begin adopting and adapting language they were learning as they studied organizational context to reflect on their own experiences and to enhance the content they were developing within their assignments. Through that reflective process, they would not only effectively learn about, write about, and revise their own writing about organizational context, but they would at some dramatic, though infrequent, moments revise elements of *their own* organizational contexts. They would, in other words, rewrite a portion of the context of their own immediate writing work and their worlds of action/subjectivity. To illustrate, one group with high motivation and strong academic skills, but that showed deep frustration early on with learning and employing digital writing technologies within the context of the classroom and the designated time of a class period, reframed their working time and space—their organizational context—to actively integrate outside resources and other spaces. They requested out-of-class time to meet with technology experts on campus, and they devised out-of-class collaborative work times in spaces beyond the classroom to work. These students learned through direct experience and engagement, accompanied by disciplinary study and reflection, about organizational context as an integral, though partially revisable, element of writing and rhetorical action. "Writing" for these students, then, was that fully-engaged, socio-cultural kind that has material consequences and impact, a lesson that is exceptionally difficult to teach in a way beyond the purely abstract. Further, "writing" for these students became a way to reinvent not only the field of Professional Writing and Rhetoric, but their own writerly subjectivities as well (see Slevin). Far from being passive recipients of a lecture from a professor on the field of Professional Writing and Rhetoric and the impact of organizational context on writing situations, and then blandly repeating these descriptions on an exam, the students themselves participated in generatively reconstructing and redefining the field, and recreating their own rhetorical, *praxical* subjectivities, as they engaged in complex and reflective writerly ways of being.

Conclusion

We now return, more directly, to the two central questions we proposed earlier and offer some preliminary responses, in the spirit of igniting further conversations about the role our pedagogical practices play in forming writers and the impact pedagogy can have on the formation of rhetorical subjects:

- "What defines a successful writer?" and
- "How can we best develop/teach such writers?"

As we also mentioned earlier, we are not claiming that PBL is the only or even the best pedagogy for creating active learning environments. We are, instead, proposing that by focusing our attention on designing PBL activities and then reflecting on the kinds of writerly behaviors in which they invited students to participate, we became more aware of how the very pedagogies we enacted in class created particular kinds of subjectivities for students to occupy. We found that PBL activities did indeed have the advantage of inviting students to behave more like "real" and what we have come to call "successful" writers, based on an interactionist model of writing. In this model, successful writers understand that writing is messy, iterative, and indeterminate; they know *how* to negotiate writing in such contexts;

and they *value* these messy processes as well. Unlike other engaged pedagogies, which rely on a model of presenting information to students first and then asking them to put that information into action second, PBL activities require students to immerse themselves in real-world problems and then generate the knowledge itself, as an act of heuristic invention. This difference seemed to lead to the creation, at least temporarily, of rhetorical, *praxical* student subjects who were confident relying on their own generative knowledge when finding themselves in novel situations that required them to decide how to respond appropriately. With other types of engaged pedagogies, when writerly ways of acting are "pre-packaged" and delivered outside of real writing situations, student writers routinely become flustered when these "pre-packaged" bits of information fail to respond adequately or fail to take into account the complexity of their writing situation. In contrast, students who engaged in generative problem-based learning as they experienced real writing situations and hurdles appear to be more rhetorically flexible and capable of taking responsive action. For example, when the students working on the "Adding to the Conversation about Organizational Context" project realized that one of their secondary, indirect audiences might be future employers, they decided to rethink entirely their project's organizational and navigational schemes. They decided that the academic resources they had been relying upon as examples, and with which they were most comfortable using themselves as students, were inadequate for this newly realized and yet very important audience. Instead of relying upon tried and true, and perhaps even dull, ways of organizing their content, they decided to engage in large-scale audience analysis to support their efforts to create a more audience-responsive organizational scheme.

While we want to be careful and refrain from arguing that PBL is the best pedagogy, we also think it is important to note that PBL does offer something special, and that is its quality of *initiating* instruction with, and then having all learning emerge out of, a well crafted problem. This feature helps to create a learning environment in which student writers/rhetorical subjects develop not only *rhetorical* subjectivities, but *praxical* subjectivities as well. It is worth noting again Sullivan and Porter's definition of praxis as "a kind of thinking that does not start with theoretical knowledge or abstract models, which are then applied to situations, but that begins with immersion in local situations, and then uses epistemic theory as heuristic rather than as explanatory or determining" (26). So in regard to the question of how we can best develop/teach such writers, we argue that one way is by using pedagogies that so intensely immerse students in local and real situations that engagement *itself* becomes part of being a successful writer. This ups the ante, so to speak, on our understanding of engaged learning: it is no longer just the means for transferring effectively writerly knowledge, but rather a way of "being" and acting. In other words, engaged learning becomes, in the interactionist model of writing, rhetorical praxis.

The two courses we use as illustrations here are not even the kind most readily adaptable to PBL, and yet that is in part why we chose to focus on them, both for our own pedagogical exploration and also for scholarly reflection. Courses that most readily spring to mind for adoption of PBL include what we might categorize as advanced practice or performance-based courses. These courses are typically populated by students who bring some advanced-level rhetorical/writing skills and experiences, to which they can turn when addressing complex, ill-structured, novel rhetorical/writing challenges. These practice- or performance-based courses common in RWS curricula (see The Committee on the Major in Writing and Rhetoric's "Writing Majors at a Glance")—"Writing for the Web," "Teaching Writing," "Tutoring Writing," "Environmental Writing," "Report and Grant Writing," "Technical Documentation," "Advanced Editing," "Publications Management," "Document Design," et cetera—also intuitively lend themselves to the creation of writing problems that can initiate and sustain highly engaged learning. For these reasons, advanced practice- and performance-based courses most readily lend themselves to PBL and would be excellent grounds, we say encouragingly, for broader exploration in RWS. However, what we observed happening in our first-year writing and introductory professional writing and rhetoric classes convinced us that even courses less readily adaptable to PBL can use this pedagogy effectively, as a way to immerse students in active learning environments and invite them to engage in rhetorical praxis.

Appendix

Critiquing Search Engines

Do you use different search engines for different purposes or when looking for different kinds of information? Or do you turn to the same search engine over and over again without really thinking about how the search engine functions or how it might affect the kinds of information you locate? Faculty who teach first-year writing at your university have noticed that a lot of first-year students seem to over rely on just one or two search engines for all of their research needs, which probably isn't the most efficient or productive research strategy. These faculty members have asked that you create some materials or a resource that will help first-year writing students understand how to decide which search engine to use when faced with a new research question or situation, or when looking for a particular kind of source.

Some of the complexities that make this problem unique are that different search engines may have different features (such as options for narrowing or filtering a search, or special Boolean terms), they may identify Web pages or Web sites differently (by their title, by their metadata), they may have user preferences that can be adjusted, or they may focus on particular kinds of sources (i.e., image, video, full-text, PDF file, etc.).

You can decide as a group what you think is the best way to address this problem.

Understanding & Using Databases

Have you ever felt like you were drowning in information, or conversely, that there was no existing research on the topic you wanted to study? Information that exists "out there" on the Internet or in databases, journals, or books is useless unless you know how to locate it. One way we can locate meaningful and useful information/sources is by using our library's academic databases. Your library has asked your class to create an online resource that will help other student-researchers conduct effective database research and avoid that "drowning in information" or "there's nothing on my topic" experience.

This activity asks you to determine how exactly different databases function and develop some strategies for deciding which ones to use for the different research situations. Some complexities that you might confront when examining databases and developing strategies for selecting among them include determining the sources searched by the databases, figuring out what kinds of advanced searching options or "filtering" options are offered, identifying what kinds of sources the databases return (i.e., journal article citations, and/or abstracts, and/or full-text, PDF, or HTML files), and determining whether certain databases serve particular audiences or disciplines.

How you create this online resource and what it will include is your decision.

Documenting Digital Sources

Your university has close ties with one of the local high schools; professors give guest lectures and the students visit our campus to attend summer classes and special talks. In an effort to help the senior class of high school students be better prepared for college, you've been asked to teach them to use one of the major documentation styles (MLA, APA, or Chicago). So the problem you're tasked with solving is identifying the values embodied in the different documentation features and explaining these values to an audience of high school students. You need to do much more than simply tell the students how to "fill in the blanks" of a Works Cited entry. Instead, you need to figure out a way to explain what the different components of an entry *mean*, and what kinds of *values* these different components convey about what that particular discourse community's values.

It's up to you how you decide to explain these documentation features/values to the high school students.

Defining the Field

It's the fall of your junior year, and you have decided that you want to get a summer professional writing internship before you go into your senior year. You figure that in the current slow economy, an internship would give you some much needed experience and possibly even open up a door to a full-time job at your internship site after you graduate.

To prepare, you've talked with your advisor and also a career counselor at the Career Center. Both have given you lots of good advice about narrowing down the kinds of internships you might want and how to go about finding them, but both have also strongly urged you to create a portfolio you can send as a follow-up to your initial application and resume, and then also use in any interviews you might get.

You get good advice about what should be in your portfolio, but one piece that surprised you was a definition of your field of study. When your advisor told you such a piece would be helpful, you only kind of believed her: "I mean she is only a professor. What would she know about job portfolios?" But when the career counselor told you the same thing, you started to think you'd better put some time into this piece.

When talking with the career counselor about this field definition piece, you ask, "Who would want to read that?" The counselor said, "Well, you'll have a person or group of people who may want to know in a quick glance sort of way what your expertise is and what you can bring to them. Then, there may be a second person or group who will want to read that portion of your portfolio to find out more than the quick and dirty. This other group will want to read something that illustrates your depth of knowledge, as well as something that showcases your writing abilities and abilities to reason."

Throughout your discussion with the career counselor, the issue about how professional writing and rhetoric are connected keeps coming up. She is really interested in hearing more about this connection, about how you define rhetoric, and what it means to connect the two. You've gotten the same sort of response from friends and family, most of whom simply leave out the term "rhetoric" when they talk with you about this topic. So far, you aren't able to respond very well to their questions, a situation you figure you shouldn't find yourself in when you're interviewing for internships. Maybe, you think, this is a key topic in your portfolio piece.

Adding to the Conversation about Organizational Context

Professional Writing and Rhetoric: Readings from the Field argues in the "Introduction" that the field of Professional Writing and Rhetoric can be defined as "organizationally situated authorship." But it also says that phrase requires a lot of "unpacking." In other words, you can't just say "organizationally situated authorship" and expect people will understand you, or even that *you* will know what the heck you're talking about.

PWR faculty have talked a long while about creating some sort of source that students in all PWR classes could turn to when trying to get a deeper understanding of professional writing and rhetoric as "organizationally situated authorship/action."

The following e-mail was sent by a PWR faculty member to all the other PWR faculty after a flurry of e-mail messages related to this issue:

> Hey, y'all –
>
> This "source" we've been talking about sounds like a great research project for a whole class. We've discovered again and again that none of us could handle this project alone, but a whole class could create something very helpful.
>
> In fact, this makes me think of a rhetoric resource site at Georgia Tech that was created by some students there. It's been a helpful and often used resource for people across the country for almost ten years. One of our classes could create something akin to that Tech site.
>
> Since the issue of "organizationally situated authorship" is so closely connected to *Professional Writing and Rhetoric: Readings from the Field*, which we know is being used in a number of places around the country now, the site would be a great resource for students and faculty outside of our university. That creates an effective and real audience for this work. Plus, our students would be able to point family, friends, internship and job interviewers, grad schools, etc to the site and say, "Hey, I did that!"
>
> What do ya think?

Notes

1. Further introductory information about PBL can be found in these valuable sources: James Rhem's "Problem-Based Learning: An Introduction" (1998); Barbara J. Duch, Susan E. Groh, and Deborah E. Allen's *The Power of Problem-Based Learning* (2001); Jose A. Amador, Libby Miles, and C. B. Peters's *The Practice of Problem-Based Learning: A Guide to Implementing PBL in the College Classroom* (2006); John R. Savery's "Overview of Problem-Based Learning: Definitions and Distinctions" (2006); and Michael Pennell and Libby Miles's "'It Actually Made Me Think': Problem-Based Learning in the Business Communications Classroom" (2009). Two excellent online sources for PBL schol-

arship are *The Interdisciplinary Journal of Problem-based Learning*, hosted by Purdue University, and *The PBL Clearinghouse*, hosted at the University of Delaware.

2. Elon University has made a long-term institutional commitment to engaged learning, a commitment which has become a hallmark of the school's reputation. This reputation is recognized externally by the National Survey of Student Engagement (NSSE), in which Elon consistently earns top scores. In 2009, NSSE surveyed 360,000 students from 617 four-year colleges and universities and is considered "one of the most comprehensive assessments of effective practices in higher education" (see http://www.elon.edu/e-web/news/nsse/). In the 2009 NSSE report, Elon students rated Elon highly on each of the five benchmarks of excellence: Level of Academic Challenge, Active and Collaborative Learning, Student-Faculty Interaction, Enriching Educational Experiences, and Supportive Campus Environment. For example, Elon's scores for a few of the Enriching Educational Experiences benchmark items were as follows:

	Elon First Year/Seniors	NSSE First Year/Seniors
Have done/plan to do an internship, field experience, co-op experience or clinical assignment	96%/92%	82%/76%
Have done/plan to do community/volunteer service	93%/92%	80%/75%
Have done/plan to study abroad	91%/76%	45%/24%
Have done/plan to do culminating senior experience (capstone project, thesis)	76%/93%	50%/64%

The university's internal commitment to engaged learning is evidenced by its focus on study abroad (71% of students study abroad at least once before graduating), undergraduate research, service-learning (supported by The Kernodle Center for Service Learning), internships, and civic engagement. The Center for the Advancement of Teaching and Learning (CATL) and the availability of numerous internal grants which aim to enhance pedagogy, active learning, and faculty-student interaction also speak to the university's commitment to engaged learning. Further, student and faculty participation in Student Undergraduate Research Forum (SURF) has steadily increased over the last 15 years. This forum gives students the opportunity to engage in large-scale research projects and present professionally their research at national and regional conferences.

3. Writing curricula objectives we collaboratively established over the years represent significant features of the context within which we studied PBL. Any decisions we would make or evaluations of possible pedagogies would undoubtedly be made with at least indirect reference to our curricula and the goals/objectives we had established for them.

Our first-year writing program goals reflect a significant connection to rhetoric, with special emphasis on process, strategies, reflection, and social context. In first-year writing, our goals state, all students will gain:

1. A more sophisticated writing process including invention, peer responding, revising and editing that result in a clear, effective well edited public piece.
2. A more sophisticated understanding of the relationship of purpose, audience, and voice, and an awareness that writing expectations and conventions vary within the academy and in professional and public discourse.
3. An appreciation for the capacity of writing to change oneself and the world.

As part of a mid-sized university with a core of Professional Writing and Rhetoric faculty, some of whom direct first-year composition and the university's writing center, and all of whom teach in the English department's Professional Writing and Rhetoric (PWR) concentration, we conceive of all of our writing classes as being intimately connected, not within a "major" curriculum but by the discipline of Rhetoric and Composition. Therefore, the goals and objectives of the professional writing and rhetoric curriculum reflect, in some significant ways, those of first-year writing. The assumptions or principles of PWR include the following:

1. We approach professional writing and rhetoric not simply as a functional art limited to *means* of production, but as a critical social practice that includes engaging in cultural production of social *ends*.
2. We approach professional writing and rhetoric as a way of *acting effectively and wisely* within complex situations, corporate, civic, and personal.
3. We understand professional writing and rhetoric to be a *situated art*.
4. We value the integration of theory and practice.
5. We see professional writing and rhetoric as one, integrated disciplinary field of study and practice.

From these principles, we have established the following set of student-focused objectives:

1. Students will understand that writing participates in socially constructing the worlds within which we live, work, play, et cetera.
2. Students will learn, often through working hands on with actual clients, how to analyze, reflect on, assess, and effectively act within complex contexts and rhetorical situations.
3. Students will study a wide variety of rhetorical *techne* or strategies and, by working within and reflecting on actual rhetorical contexts, learn to adapt and develop rhetorical strategies and heuristics appropriate to specific situations.
4. Students will show an ability to integrate theoretical knowledge and professional practice.
5. Students will adopt a disciplinary identity as a writer and see themselves as experts (i.e., professional writers/rhetors) who bring particular (e.g., rhetorical) ways of seeing and ways of acting in and on the world around them.

As we build curricula, develop new courses, conceive new assignments, assess programmatic effectiveness, et cetera, we actively reflect on and refer to these goals and objectives. Therefore, they have played a significant role in our inquiry about the place and value of PBL in writing instruction.

Works Cited

Amador, Jose A., Libby Miles, and C. B. Peters. *The Practice of Problem-Based Learning: A Guide to Implementing PBL in the College Classroom*. Bolton: Anker, 2006. Print.

Anson, Chris. "Writing in Support of Departmental Writing Goals and Learning Outcomes." Elon University Writing Across the Curriculum Program. Elon University. Elon, NC. 11 March 2010. Guest Speaker.

The Committee on the Major in Writing and Rhetoric. "Writing Majors at a Glance." NCTE/Conference on College Composition and Communication, 2010. Web. 14 July 2010.

Consortium for the Study of Writing in College. Indiana University, 2009. Web. 10 June 2010.

Couture, Barbara. "Modeling and Emulating: Rethinking Agency in the Writing Process." *Post-Process Theory: Beyond the Writing-Process Paradigm*. Ed. Thomas Kent. Carbondale and Edwardsville: Southern Illinois UP, 1999. 30-48. Print.

Dias, Patrick, Aviva Freedman, Peter Medway, and Anthony Paré. "Situating Writing." *Worlds Apart: Acting and Writing in Academic and Workplace Contexts*. Ed. Patrick Dias et al. Mahwah/London: Lawrence Erlbaum, 1999. 17-46. Print.

Driskill, Linda. "Understanding the Writing Context in Organizations." *Professional Writing and Rhetoric: Readings from the Field*. Ed. Tim Peeples. Longman: 2002. 105-21. Print.

Duch, Barbara J., Susan E. Groh, and Deborah E. Allen, eds. *The Power of Problem-Based Learning: A Practical "How To" for Teaching Undergraduate Courses in Any Discipline*. Sterling: Stylus, 2001. Print.

The Faculty Survey of Student Engagement (FSSE). Indiana University, 2010. Web. 12 June 2010.

Faigley, Lester. *Fragments of Rationality: Postmodernity and the Subject of Composition*. Pittsburgh: U of Pittsburgh P, 1992. Print.

Indiana University Center for Postsecondary Research (CPR). Indiana University, 2010. Web. 12 June 2010.

The Interdisciplinary Journal of Problem-based Learning. Purdue University, n.d. Web. 14 Oct. 2009.

Kuh, George D. *High-Impact Educational Practices: What They Are, Who Has Access to Them, and Why They Matter*. Washington: Association of American Colleges and Universities, 2008. Print.

Law School Survey of Student Engagement (LSSSE). Indiana University, 2009. Web. 12 June 2010.

National Survey of Student Engagement (NSSE). Indiana University, 2010. Web. 12 June 2010.

NSSE Institute for Effective Educational Practice. Indiana University, 2010. Web. 10 June 2010.

The PBL Clearinghouse. The University of Delaware, n.d. Web. 12 Oct. 2009.

Peeples, Tim, and Bill Hart-Davidson. "Grading the 'Subject': Questions of Expertise and Evaluation." *Grading in the Post-Process Classroom: From Theory to Practice*. Ed. Libby Allison, Lizbeth Bryant, and Maureen Hourigan. Portsmouth: Boynton/Cook-Heinemann, 1997. 94-113. Print.

Pennell, Michael, and Libby Miles. "'It Actually Made Me Think': Problem-Based Learning in the Business Communications Classroom." *Business Communication Quarterly* 72.4 (2009): 377-94. Print.

Rhem, James. "Problem-Based Learning: An Introduction." *The National Teaching & Learning Forum* 8.1 (1998): 4-7. Print.

Russell, David. "Activity Theory and Process Approaches: Writing (Power) in School and Society." *Post-Process Theory: Beyond the Writing-Process Paradigm*. Ed. Thomas Kent. Carbondale and Edwardsville: Southern Illinois UP, 1999. 80-95. Print.

Russell, David R. "Rethinking Genre and Society: An Activity Theory Analysis." *Written Communication* 14.4 (2002): 504-55. Print.

Ryan, Kathleen J. "Subjectivity Matters: Using Gerda Lerner's Writing and Rhetoric to Claim an Alternative Epistemology for the Feminist Writing Classroom." *Feminist Teacher: A Journal of the Practices, Theories, and Scholarship of Feminist Teaching* 17.1 (2006): 36-51. Print.

Savery, John R. "Overview of Problem-Based Learning: Definitions and Distinctions." *The Interdisciplinary Journal of Problem-based Learning* 1.1 (Spring 2006): n. pag. Web. 14 Oct. 2009.

Slevin, James. "Inventing and Reinventing the Discipline of Composition." *Introducing English: Essays in the Intellectual Work of Composition*. Pittsburg: U of Pittsburgh P, 2001. 37-56. Print.

Sullivan, Patricia A., and James E. Porter. *Opening Spaces: Writing Technologies and Critical Research Practices*. Greenwich: Ablex, 1997. Print.

Walker, Janice R., and Todd Taylor. *The Columbia Guide to Online Style 2/e*. New York: Columbia UP, 2007. Print.

Incendiary Discourse: Reconsidering Flaming, Authority, and Democratic Subjectivity in Computer-mediated Communication[1]

Timothy Oleksiak

> This article explores the relationship between teacher authority and flaming in asynchronous online communication. Teachers who rely on what I call stabilization and universal applicability—two concepts emerging from a liberal democratic theory—may actually be preventing a full and robust understanding of the complexities of 21st-century democracy. Iris Marion Young and Chantal Mouffe, two postmodern democratic theorists, provide a foundation for understanding a democratic subjectivity that counters the tendency toward stabilization and universal applicability. As an alternative to the rhetoric of liberal ideology, I suggest that teachers begin to understand flames not as deficient forms of communication that require remediation but as part of a discourse of challenge that requires nuanced, thoughtful community response.

"New technologies cannot automatically create new democracies. They can reify and reinforce already existing oppressions and inequalities."

–Juliet Eve and Tara Brabazon (58)

For more than two decades composition scholars as diverse as Gregory Clark, Kenneth Bruffee, Peter Elbow, and Patricia Bizzell have connected the work of the composition classroom with larger democratic concerns. As far back as Richard Ohmann's 1985 article "Literacy, Technology, and Monopoly Capital," the discipline has also critically reflected on how writing pedagogies might best deal with the challenges technological progress brings to the way democratic practices are understood and taught in our classrooms. Indeed, early edited collections—particularly Carolyn Handa's *Computers and Communities* and Cynthia Selfe and Susan Hilligoss's *Literacy and Computers*—reflect the critical relationship between the concerns of democratic sensitivity and advancing technology.

It is clear that the connection between technology, democracy, and composition pedagogy is and continues to be an area of scholarship that is important to our discipline. This paper examines the underlying assumption about democratic subjectivities that are reflected in teacher responses to the online phenomenon known as "flaming." I argue for a way to defuse authority outward from the teacher to the classroom community at large.

The consequences of this power sharing allow teachers and students alike to explore the complexities of contemporary democracy.

I take as a given the fact that the way instructors respond to flaming reveals assumptions about democratic subjectivity within a given classroom. Unlike some scholarly treatments of flames, however, I am not primarily concerned with the question of *why* students flame each other. The bulk of my attention is given to *how* writing instructors confront behaviors that cannot be ignored or responded to through rational modes of inquiry and the implications that follow. This paper's main contribution to pedagogical theory, therefore, is to articulate ways in which instructors and students might reconceptualize responses to flames. The goal here is to teach writing in ways that develop an understanding of the complexities of 21st-century civic engagement. This paper provides resources for understanding why current approaches to flames are limiting and how writing instructors might begin to overcome them. One of my aims here is to suggest how students and instructors alike might be able to make use of this incendiary behavior in ways that democratize communication among community members within and beyond the classroom.

In what follows, I discuss several responses to flaming and argue that such responses, though useful in many ways, are insufficient when it comes to contemporary democratic citizenship. By looking at teacher responses to flaming, it is possible to understand how liberal ideology plays out in the classroom. Second, I detail a critique of liberal subjectivity. This critique creates spaces for new ways writing instructors might confront flames. The last section makes the case for a theory of democratic subjectivity that does not rely on these liberal trappings.

Flames, Liberal Democratic Subjectivity, and Teacher Authority

Flaming, or what Alfred Rovai calls the "electronic equivalent of a prolonged tongue lashing" (229) is a form of communication that has been difficult to define usefully. However, Philip Thompsen's "social influence model of flaming" is an early and still useful conceptualization of flaming. According to Thompsen, the "social influence perspective holds that choices people make regarding technology use are neither entirely rational nor entirely subjective, but rather are 'subjectively rational'" (303). This model suggests that the choice to label a communicative act as "flaming" is highly contextual. A flame in one context is benign in another. Therefore, under the social influence model, flames can best be understood as a form of communication that disrupts a community to the extent that it is not productive to ignore it or respond in purely rational ways. Given my reliance on the social influence model, identifying a specific text as "flaming" is complicated because different discourse communities understand and respond to disruptions differently. With this difficulty in mind, I define flames within the context of computer-mediated communication as language that negatively impacts individuals within a community to the extent that ignoring such language is harmful to the community. My argument, therefore, centers on ways writing teachers respond to language choices students make that should not be ignored or treated exclusively through rational means of inquiry.

One way to respond to flames is through the rhetoric of liberal ideology. Focusing on such rhetoric and how expressions of authority are reliant upon it opens spaces for understanding why such expressions are problematic. However, as Wendy Brown notes, in the United States specifically, political theory is complicated by the slippery application of the term "liberal." In the United States, the concept of "liberal" is typically associated with Leftist political values most closely aligned with the Democratic Party. This distinction is both limiting and erroneous for democratic theorists. For Brown, "liberalism signifies an order in which the state exists to secure the freedom of individuals on a formally egalitarian basis" (39). Therefore, both conservatives (as in members of the Republican Party) and liberals (as in members of the Democratic Party) can exist under the same ideology of "liberty for all." In other words, the foundation of a liberal democratic theory relies on the deft negotiation between personal freedom of expression and a strong belief in equitable treatment for all community members.

Additionally, liberal democracy, for Brown and contemporary democratic theorists, has its roots in Enlightenment thinkers like Adam Smith and Jürgen Habermas, and more recently Amy Guttman and Denis Thompson. Under Enlightenment ideology, rational argument between equal members of a society will ultimately lead communities to the solutions to their problems. Thus, liberal democracy includes not only an ideal conceptualization of community members but it also includes a normative system for how those members should interact with each other.

Two elements of liberal democratic theory have special import for those concerned with flames and computer-mediated communication (CMC). First, the liberal notion assumes an identity that allows individuals to make sense of the world in ways that *stabilize* experiences. Presumably, then, the rhetoric of a stabilized liberal subject allows people to believe that they are engaging each other as *equals*. And if they do not see each other as equals then individuals are able to presume a necessary rationale for the inequality. If identity is stable or a thing that can be stabilized, individuals arguing and reasoning under a rational system of discourse can truly understand others in ways that are materially genuine. For example, the white heterosexual woman who thinks hard and listens long enough to the lesbian Latina's personal experiences with social injustice can eventually come to understand her suffering, and on the basis of that understanding, agree to remedies that are warranted and generated from a place of authenticity. In the classroom, the falsehood of stability most clearly plays out under the auspices of teacher authority. Yet, since Freire's devastating critique of the banking method, overt displays of teacher authority have become passé in critical pedagogical scholarship. More frequent displays of teacher authority in critical pedagogies rely on the assumption that students should have a limited role in shaping the classroom environment. Put differently, while students may be involved in choosing the texts that they read, and they may even have the chance to write in a variety of genres of their choosing, the chance to shape how they conduct themselves in the classroom or how they engage the material is still heavily directed by the instructor.

Second, liberal subjectivity assumes that social injustices can be dealt with through a fair system of distribution that has universal applicability. In *Justice and the Politics of Difference*, Iris Marion Young argues that liberal approaches to justice align themselves with a distributive model. The distributive model of justice assumes that rights are material in that they can be gained or lost and the amount of justice in the world is dependent on the amount of rights that are fairly distributed among those who have historically not had them. The lie of stability lends itself to the idea of equal distribution in part because it allows liberal democratic theorists to broadly conceptualize basic human needs around a *universal* understanding of humanity that presupposes a conversation about how we *should* understand humanity. In the classroom, universal application often plays out when teachers and students alike assume that there is a single proper way to deal with community problems and that these solutions should be based on a system of rationality accepted by everyone.

Recent approaches to the use of flaming reflect the pervasiveness of what I am calling the rhetoric of liberal ideology. The rhetoric of liberal ideology suggests that individuals understand deliberative discourses through the precepts of stabilization and universal applicability. These concepts are useful for writing instructors because they allow us to recognize the values embedded within contemporary responses to flaming. Separating these key terms—stabilization and universal applicability—is difficult since they are co-constitutive of liberal ideology. However, by focusing on these terms individually, it becomes clearer to see cracks in the foundations of liberalism.

In "'YOUR VIEWS SHOWED TRUE IGNORANCE!!!': (Mis)Communication in an Online Interracial Discussion Forum," Heidi McKee illustrates the tensions that often arise from a reliance on the rhetoric of liberal ideology and the willingness to understand flaming through a different perception. An important takeaway from McKee's work is that what writing instructors understand as flaming might not be flaming. Rather, disruptions to communication are understood through densely constructed social positionings. Her work, and the work I suggest we do as writing teachers, encourages us to avoid identifying flames until communities have worked out the consequences of statements that heighten negative emotional responses.

Nevertheless, beneath the surface of McKee's argument is a tension, not with what students have done, but with what I believe is a slow shaking off of the rhetoric of liberal ideology. When initially identifying flames in the Affirmative Action/Diversity/Multicultural forum on the Intercollegiate

E-Democracy Project, McKee was "*dismayed* because these statements seem characterized less by rational deliberation and more by impoliteness, charged outburst, and emotional venting intent, it seemed upon shouting down others rather than further dialogue" (413, emphasis added). What McKee's articulation of her feelings suggests is a response to the frustration instructors feel when students do not follow the dictates of a stabilized and universalized discourse for figuring out difficult social issues. Though McKee comes to understand the limits of her dismay, her narrative is illustrative of the deep entrenchment of the values I am suggesting that we interrogate and alter.

Mary Lenard's "Dealing with Online Selves: Ethos Issues in Computer-assisted Teaching and Learning," represents one way in which writing instructors stabilize minority students in ways that make realizing contemporary democratic agency more difficult. When students in Lenard's CMC course began to flame homosexuals, Lenard's concerns with what to do about it are revealing. She questions, "How can [teachers] prevent vulnerable students like homosexuals from being verbally abused in online environments?" (90). In such questions, "flaming" is considered something from which to shield students. Lenard's desire to protect the vulnerable casts the teacher in a dominant role of teacher as protector. She writes, "I responded to this episode by alerting the class to the ways that their communication was problematized by the networked classroom. I told them that since InterChange was a medium in which the lack of visual markers made misunderstandings even more likely, they (and I) needed to be particularly careful to avoid attacking other people unintentionally" (85).

Two things about an approach like Lenard's are worth mentioning. First, this response suggests a top-down approach to civic engagement where the teacher polices a concept of civility. This approach reveals that stability is closely akin to concepts of authority in the classroom and, therefore, implies that the teacher is the one who has the power to name, create, and regulate the stable subject. This is particularly interesting in an online environment that opens up the possibility for a *destabilized* subject.[2] Second, by casting homosexuals as a "vulnerable" group, the teacher makes particular assumptions about the impact of flames. As more and more students "come out of the closet," for example, it becomes more difficult for liberal educators to grasp how mundane some forms of homophobia become. Hearing the flame "you're so gay" is not always an experience that leaves homosexuals feeling disempowered. At times hearing such comments are understood as silly and ignorant. A more nuanced understanding of ignorant speech might allow us to pause on the contexts of its use in the moment and on particular individuals in the classroom. Simply put, liberal democratic subjects reject the use of words like "gay" because they assume that it is always-already hurtful to someone. It is important to reflect on this tendency toward stabilization and universal application. When we make assumptions about the stability of subjects and what hurts those subjects emotionally or intellectually, we speak for them. I can think of no greater affront to a fully realized democracy than taking away the voice of another.

After engaging many chat rooms and discussion boards with her students, Lenard created the following addition to her syllabus: "... Make your contributions *relevant* and *timely*, so that you are not posting on something that we covered many weeks ago or just repeating a comment that several other people have already made... Feel free to respond to your classmates' comments (politely, of course!)" (90, emphasis in original). And though Lenard acknowledges that the inclusion of "politely" is full of ambiguities and complications in a "culturally diverse world" (90), the tensions between cultural diversity's ability to question our values and the way in which students should engage each other is nevertheless symptomatic of a liberal notion of identity in that politeness, relevance, and timeliness are universal values necessary for communication. Universal applicability of any specific value system is fraught with foreclosures and dis-invitations. These foreclosures must be open to critique by our students. The point should not be to get students to express their feelings in order to create an emotional inventory with the larger goal of fostering empathy and mutual identification. Rather, students and teachers alike should be able to confront flames in ways that allow everyone to acknowledge how this disruption communicates in the *specific* online/classroom community. Therefore, a typical response to flames would not only require a statement of emotional response but also a reflexive question about *how* the flames complicate what the community was trying to do. Too frequently, as Lenard's pedagogy reveals, the majority of our attention is given to dealing with the emotional impacts of negative behavior. I want to be clear that there is nothing inherently wrong with the desire to protect students from physical, emotional, or rhetorical harm. However, we must enact this desire in ways that allow students to confront disruptions both individually and as members of a community.

The implicit notions about democratic citizenship undergirding arguments like Lenard's suggest that students must be protected from harmful language. More than that, whom she understands as vulnerable presupposes a particular democratic status. Though we must be cognizant of injustices and the material reality that there are groups of people who are inherently disadvantaged (ethnic, gender, religious, and sexual minorities), when instructors assume that students cannot find the voice to speak truth to injustice, it is time to re-evaluate the type of democratic citizenship we assume we are helping to foster.

In "Respond Now! E-mail, Acceleration, and a Pedagogy of Patience," Jeffrey Andrew Weinstock relies on the liberal tendencies I have articulated, but in ways that place the onus of responsibility for understanding proper modes of interaction onto students. This approach is different from Lenard's pedagogy because flames are confronted directly in a community and by students. The educational approach to flames that Weinstock advocates suggests that instructors should have students:

1. Consider a time when they sent an e-mail they regretted or when they received flames;
2. Write a flame and "not hold back";
3. Discuss the practiced flames as a class (379).

This rhetorically rich exercise requires the classroom community to explore a flame's impact on audiences. However, when instructors remove what they believe to be problematic speech from the contexts of its use, they implicitly advance a theory of communication that insists upon rational, logical public interaction. With flames taken out of contexts, students and teachers alike are able to disassociate from the emotional impacts of flames. Thus, an exercise such as this requires first that teachers rely on a theory of communication that brackets emotional responses as valid forms of community interaction.

Additionally, within Weinstock's "pedagogy of patience" we see flames as a communication failure. Understanding flames as failures brackets out challenges to hegemonic discourses. This failure centers on the subject's inability to deliberate properly rather than how communication breakdowns reveal fissures in the communicative system itself. Moreover, treating flames as a communication failure enacts a liberal notion of authority because it forces the teacher into the role of remediation or the assumption that the student who flames is somehow deficient or unable to appropriately respond to a system with which he is dissatisfied.[3] More to the point, however, the deficiency theory of communication suggests that students are in need of remediation. When instructors and like-minded students understand students who flame as deficient, it is difficult—though not necessarily inevitable—for flames to be understood as a strategic communicative act or as an act of de-legitimization.

Decontextualized flame exercises help students to understand mature forms of communication in democratic environments, but such pedagogical exercises are indicative of a traditional liberal ideology that reinforces ideals of democracy that are problematic. By removing the context of the flame from the actual moment of its use, teachers diminish students' abilities to find creative solutions to communicative barriers. Responses to flames that rely on the rhetoric of liberal ideology make it difficult for students to see flames as a part of communication systems that want to enforce certain social relations.

Finally, both Lenard's and Weinstock's approaches require writing instructors to struggle with the tension between learning outcomes that teach students appropriate academic roles and an openness to worldviews that differ from the instructor's own. Nevertheless, the idea undergirding Weinstock's teaching of flaming in classrooms originates from the ability to place oneself in the "shoes" of another, or what he calls "empathic identification" (379). This empathic identification is a rephrasing of Seyla Benhabib's concept of "egalitarian reciprocity" (30). The assumption is that we would not flame in CMC if we could empathize more fully with each other. Public interaction based on the principal of egalitarian reciprocity insists upon the notion that if we could only see the hurt flames cause individuals then we would seek better forms of communication. This conceptualization of flames ignores the fact that students who have not already bought into the established classroom community may feel very strong negative emotions when placed in such an environment. The democratically appropriate course of action is not to prohibit expression prior to or immediately after disruptions. Rather, if something happens within a community that impacts an individual directly, that person must be allowed the opportunity to engage the community as best they can at the moment.

Approaches for confronting difficult speech in online environments like Lenard's and Weinstock's solidify instructor authority in ways that should give instructors interested in democratic subjectivity pause. By functioning as gatekeeper—understood here as an authority that steps in "just in time" to protect students from feeling uncomfortable—instructors are unintentionally making deliberative discourse more difficult to realize. Contrasting with approaches like Lenard's and Weinstock's, I suggest that writing instructors can work with students to conceptualize approaches to flames so that classroom communities may begin to reconsider the hegemonic aspects of rational discourse that are pervasive in democratic systems of argument and the role of rhetoric in community formation. In what follows, I show how postmodern democratic theory opens spaces for new ways of conceptualizing flames.

Liberal Democratic Subjectivity and Systems of Social Relations

The rhetoric of liberal ideology articulated above does not exist in isolation; it carries with it particular forms of social interaction that must be understood before alternatives can be explored. In order to understand the forms of social interaction that liberal ideology suggests, I engage the work of Iris Marion Young and Chantal Mouffe. Pairing Young and Mouffe may seem odd, but I believe that Mouffe provides a critical insight into the negative consequences that a single hegemonic discourse has on democratic citizenship. In other words, Mouffe allows us to understand flames in a broadly realized conceptual context. Young, on the other hand, particularly her theories of distributive justice and asymmetrical reciprocity, allows us to envision a post-liberal theory of interpersonal communication. For the purposes of the argument I am advancing, Mouffe shows the failures of liberal ideology's articulation of stabilization, whereas Young's theories critique the concept of universal applicability.

For Mouffe, current liberal thinking prevents us from considering the ways societies are organized (9). In order to work through this problem, Mouffe takes pains to distinguish between *the political* and *politics*. The political is the antagonistic elements that comprise the structures of society. Politics, on the other hand, is the means by which the political is understood: the practices and institutions through which order is created. Politics organizes how individual bodies coexist around the forms of conflicts allowed or disallowed by the political. As Mouffe understands it, liberal theorists ignore the political. This, in turn, limits their ways of thinking about politics. In the liberal order, Mouffe maintains that the primary form of conflict is the friend/enemy distinction. This antagonistic structure focuses political thought and action on the ways in which rhetors can solve conflicts rather than paying attention to the way in which these conflicts are discussed. For Mouffe, the way liberals understand the political provides us with too narrow a set of predetermined rules for social behavior that make discussion of the structures that set the terms of the conflict unappealing and threatening for democratic action. Liberal theorists do not necessarily believe that there is only one solution, nor do they necessarily believe that that a plurality of voices should be minimized. Her concern with liberal theory is the system of social relations that limit the ways in which individuals can interact. Liberal ideology, Mouffe suggests, reduces all problems to a binary between those who are like-minded and those who are not: friend or enemy. Regardless of an individual's affiliation with the friend group or the enemy group, Mouffe argues, "consensus [with that group] is based on acts of exclusion" (11). The clash between friend and enemy creates factionalization that is finally in service of a single hegemonic order.

The civility organized by the liberal order demands consensus regarding the particular ways of engaging the world. When choices are limited to how to solve social problems, argument plays out along a binary, friend/enemy split comprised of two camps: those who agree with us and those who do not agree with us. The result can be a rupture in civility. It is Mouffe's notion of civility that brings us back to the concept of flames. Rather than a lack of understanding regarding how to comport himself, understood through the hegemonic logic of the friend/enemy binary, allow us to read the act of flaming as a radical disruption where the student who flames feels compelled to identify an "enemy" against which he can react. Under the political order of liberalism, flames are understood as a failure to engage the behaviors of a mature member of civil liberal society. Contrary to a liberal understanding of flames, a postmodern democratic order conceptualizes flames as a radical critique of the liberal political order. In this view, flames execute a new politics that calls on communities to understand the political in different ways.

Like Mouffe, Young suggests that liberal discourses often focus on outcomes and solutions to social problems. However, where Mouffe details how the political plays out, Young critiques liberal concepts of the political as socially unjust. It is this attention to justice that drives home the material consequences of a liberal theory of identity.

In *Justice and the Politics of Difference,* Young asserts that the major question for a liberal system of justice is how or even if the state should "mitigate the suffering of the poor" (19). Young calls this the distributive model of justice because the solutions found within this model are based on the allocation of resources according to whose needs are best met. The assumptions undergirding the model, however, center on a social atomism that does not allow individuals to see the relationships between people in a society (18). The distributive model of justice carries with it two problems. First, it "paradoxically affirms and ignores the institutional contexts that give rise to injustice." Second, when relating to nonmaterial goods, the "logic of distribution misrepresents them" (18). What we are left with in the distributive model is that the focus is on providing services to the individual rather than on how individual behaviors are "structured by institutionalized relations that constitute their positions" (25).

The connection between Mouffe and Young become clearer when we see that both critiques of liberalism focus on the limiting outcomes and procedures that liberal thinking insists upon. These critiques leave us with a question: If focusing on outcomes and procedures is problematic, how then should we consider injustice? To answer this, we can turn to Young's theory of asymmetrical reciprocity.

In "Asymmetrical Reciprocity: On Moral Respect, Wonder, and Enlarged Thought," Young developed the concept of asymmetrical reciprocity that begins not by trying to understand the position *from* another person's perspective, but by understanding the person's difference with respect to history and social positioning in a given cultural moment. Both the position from another and the position about another are aspects of a theory of moral respect, yet the asymmetrical approach incorporates differences in material ways that allow individuals to acknowledge the validity of these differences. The result is a new concept of interaction based on a more varied understanding of difference and identity.

One way composition studies professionals have thought about the tensions within what I have been calling the rhetoric of liberal ideology is through the relationship between rationality, emotion, and affect. This scholarship, moreover, provides a foundation on which to build a response to flames that does not reify the rhetoric of liberal ideology. In *Notes on the Heart*, Susan McLeod argues that writing instructors need to pay closer attention to affect. For McLeod, affect names the "noncognitive aspects of human behavior" of which emotion is part. However, for McLeod, though individuals "experience emotions physically" as when bodies tense up and stomach flutter at the sound of insult, individuals interpret and construct these emotions mentally (30). The result is a dialectic relationship between affect and rationality that cannot be separated. Similarly, Kristie Fleckenstein argues in "Once Again with Feeling: Empathy in Deliberative Discourse" that emotions are "tied up in a complex process of perceiving, valuing, and believing" (704). Here Fleckenstein helps us understand how the rhetoric of liberal ideology narrows the ways in which individuals come to understand affective responses students and teachers have regarding challenging moments in the classroom. Taking Fleckenstein's and McLeod's insights into consideration requires teachers of rhetoric and composition to explore with students these emotional-rational moments in class with our attention finely tuned to both aspects.

For students who are part of classroom environments where they feel that their modes of writing, arguing, thinking and feeling are not valued, anger at others may be an appropriate way to challenge authority. In "Multicultural Public Spheres and the Rhetorics of Democracy," Phyllis Mentzel Ryder argues that what makes "unsolicited oppositional discourse" so difficult to deal with is that it is used to "attack the benevolent self-image of those who are complicit in oppression" (521). For Ryder the consequences resulting from a dismissal of unsolicited oppositional discourse are profound. She argues that if an individual "cannot learn to hear anger as an act of good will—as a sign of possibility for a new kind of relationship" then the individual has foreclosed the possibilities of a relationship before that relationship has time to begin (522). Though Ryder has in mind the type of anger that is brought about through a material relationship with social injustice, I suggest that instructors who seek an alternative to the rhetoric of liberal ideology understand flames as a process of developing goodwill. I do not mean to imply that individuals who are the focus of incendiary attacks thank the student who flames. The concept of goodwill is more complex than that. Rather, I mean to suggest that when students flame, we should acknowledge the awareness that has arisen because of it.

As these composition scholars suggest, emotion does not make rationality irrational; rather, it allows us to understand and mobilize difference in ways that resist the rhetoric of stablization and universalization. It does this by helping us understand that one of the reactions people have when their differences are erased, when they feel that they are not or have not been heard, is frustration. The flame erupts, possibly, out of the feeling that the rules of civility and order are so contrary to an individual's understanding of them that they feel disempowered from participating in sanctioned ways. Thus, flames become a de-legitimization strategy for the entire process. The perceived anger of the student who flames is an invitation to understand new forms of social relations. These new relations forged are not necessarily to transform democratic interaction into a consequence-free environment where the default is to cause as much pain and suffering as possible. Rather, the scholarship on affect and emotion in rhetoric and composition is useful for understanding how to move beyond the rational response to flames and into a position that accounts more fully for the relationship between rationality and emotion.

I choose the phrase "you're so gay" as an example of the types of incendiary languages students often use. This phrase often exerts powerful influences in a contemporary moment that is characterized by the presumption of default heterosexuality.[4] When a student chooses, and I believe setting fingers to type is always on some level a conscience choice to write those words, to flame in this way, I believe that there are a number of responses that teachers might execute in ways that do not enact a universalized or stabilized discourse. Working against the rhetoric of liberal ideology suggests that we treat this flame as a de-legitimization strategy. Calling another student gay (whether or not the student is actually gay) is an attempt to protect a normative way of being that disallows contrary arguments from being suggested. However, by engaging the student who flames through a rational inquiry with a question like "What are you getting at by calling X 'gay'?" or "Can you help us understand how calling X 'gay' helps us understand your point?" opens the student to a response like "I said he's gay because he's a faggot" and very likely would increase the emotional tension because such questions do not take into account the rhetoricity of emotion. Alternatively, should the student who flames feel silenced by the rational line of questioning, the community is left with little choice but to ignore the incident and move on or to process the consequences of the flame without his input.

As an alternative to this, instructors might do well to develop responses that account for the rational and the emotional. In the illustration above, the instructor would do better to begin with something like the following, "When you said 'you're gay,' it sounds as if you might be frustrated with the way things are going. Help us understand what's going on here." Through the articulation and negotiation of the student's feelings, the teacher and student are in a better position to begin the work of understanding tensions arising from the way community members interact. The intention behind this emotional-rational approach to flaming is to guide the conversation in a way that helps the student who flames articulate frustrations as those frustrations relate to the structures of engagement. If the student evades or responds with silence, a teacher might offer an interpretation of what is going on and ask for clarification. Such interpretations might encourage the teacher to say the following, "To me, your frustrations seem to come from not being understood. If that's the case, take a moment to explain for us what was frustrating to you." Whatever the pattern of exchange between the student who flames and the teacher, the goal should be to engage each other in ways that push the student to develop his emotional vocabulary as it relates to the ways the community has been discussing a particular issue. Finally, the teacher should suggest ways in which the classroom community might change as a result of this experience.

Given the potential negative consequences for engaging flames through a predominantly rational mode of inquiry, writing instructors should develop a set of emotional-rational inquiries for students that invite the classroom community to reconsider the modes of civility that have been enacted prior to the flame. Developing such inquiries should be at the heart of our relationship to incendiary language.

Burning Down the Liberal Order: Toward a New Approach to Flaming

The consequences of flames as a reiteration of the we/they split, rather than as an immature display of student behavior, suggest that we may begin to value students' thoughts and opinions, allowing us new ways of opening discussions and community formations. Four considerations to flaming arise from a critique of liberal thought: One, flames must be treated in the contexts of their occurrence. Two, students can respond to flames both in the moment and how they see fit. Three, instructors must respond to flames in two ways: first, we should acknowledge that tensions occur as a result of flames, but before we act on them, we need to reflect about why students who flame decided to participate in that way; and second, we must explore the justification students have for their own behaviors and question them in ways that do not assume deficiency or a fixed identity. Four, the methods of exploration into incendiary discourses must serve emotional-rational modes of inquiry. Though these four considerations may also support the values I have been critiquing, how we've come to them is arguably more just. In this way, we can dislodge rationality from stability and universal applicability.

Liberal ideology understands these disruptions as part of the rhetoric of acknowledgement that assumes the injustices students perceive are based in a lack of recognition and that if these students found their voices within an established system, they would be acknowledged by the proper authorities and therefore able to lead more successful lives. The approach to flaming I advocate removes this assumption by suggesting that students are much more aware of the problems within the system than instructors may realize. This re-articulation of flaming allows us to also re-examine the teacher's role as authority figure.

We must never forget the power of the teacher, who, after all has presumably thought in systematic ways about her discipline and her pedagogy. It is important to not check out during these conversations where flaming occurs, but rather maintain a critical eye and show our students how we might read these moments. We can show our students to treat such languages as a much more complicated manifestation of rhetoric and language based on an implicit feeling that something might be horribly wrong with the procedural democratic and educational systems that have been in place for decades. The resultant conversations might allow students to shift their focus from the importance of rational critical debate and to a focus on the relational discourses between community members. By focusing too much on "what can be done" about students who flame, instructors minimize the time we can spend on how we can think about engaging with each other in ways that are courageous and mature. Ultimately, this approach reminds us that education begins by *listening* better and honoring the terrible things that get said not as appropriate choices, but as ways to further complicate ideas that are talked about and around.

Finally, I think that it is important to understand that classroom content can be the subject of rhetorical education. The unplanned happenings that occur in the classroom are ripe with opportunities for discussion and analysis. It makes sense that we would want to use these use these moments as a means for understanding reflexivity. The technology is advanced enough where students and teachers can keep record of what happens in chat rooms. In hybrid classes where students spend some time in virtual environments and sometime in F2F classrooms, we can analyze previous discussions in more fruitful ways than if the discussion happened only verbally.

Consequences for Democratic Citizenship

In his highly influential *Fragments of Rationality*, Lester Faigley argues that we teach based on the type of students we want to create. Faigley's assertion, however, does not take into account that we teach particular ways of being that we assume are desirable for *communities* beyond the classroom. The case I have made is that as online writing instruction becomes commonplace, writing teachers are in a unique position to be able to teach democratic subjectivity as a practice of writing. In other words, writing instructors are in the perfect position to write democracy in ways that traditional F2F classrooms cannot allow. In a sense, we are responsible for fostering the habits of democratic citizenship. And though this idea is nothing new for educators, the critiques of identity and values challenge existing modes of thought often in ways that make people uncomfortable. What I have shown is that the liberal notion of being is fraught with presuppositions about how students should engage their world that should not be taken as a given.

Flames do undermine the goals of democratic citizenship. It just so happens that some goals of democratic citizenship might become more democratic with a direct critique such as the ones that flames may implicitly make. But rather than focus solely on remedying a perceived failure of communication that liberal ideology suggests, the model that I have been advocating allows us to focus on the relationships between individuals. And though indelicate language complicates an "ideal classroom environment," to neglect such disruptions or to relegate them to a marginalized position enacts a liberal notion of teacher authority. Moreover, such "disruptions" to the classroom environment create opportunities for instructors to re-evaluate what they mean by ideal.

My argument relies on the treating of first-year students as adults worthy of receiving the full brunt of our mature communication. Not every student is going to be accepting of this form of communication. Students whose maturity levels do not recognize the love and attention it requires to treat students' concerns seriously might not understand why flames should receive the attention that I am advocating. This is where early training in *listening* behavior can help mitigate the responsibilities teachers often feel for the moral and critical development of their students. As Patricia Bizzell writes in a beautifully written response to Stanley Fish's polemic against teachers who want to save the world, it is okay for instructors to want to help students as members of our communities. It is okay to want to use the disciplinary knowledges we have worked hard to acquire to improve our communities. An initial place to turn could be Krista Ratcliffe's *Rhetorical Listening*. In her book, Ratcliffe makes important connections between writing studies and listening. If listening takes on valued critical purchase in our discipline, as I believe it should, then writing instructors would do well to extend listening to computer-mediated communication within our classrooms.[5] I suggest that we rely on our disciplinary knowledge not to bolster a liberal notion of superiority, but from a strong commitment to democracy of the type Young suggests.

I want to make clear that I am not advocating the idea that students should insult each other in a consequence free environment. Nor am I suggesting that we replace blame with praise. Flaming is disruptive. Yet how we understand disruptions speaks volumes about our values and our notions of democratic citizenship. It is this ability to challenge and unsettle values that are presumed to be free of baggage that is both beautiful and challenging about the democratic subjectivities I have been advancing. Decades of scholarship on the "basic" writer and thousands of pages written about first-year writing students demand that we carry the appropriate assumption that our students are capable of such challenges.

Notes

1. This paper would not have been possible without the generous support and guidance of Patrick Bruch and the two blind reviewers.
2. I am thinking here of the use of avatars and screen names that suggest a fluidity of identity that traditional face-to-face (F2F) classrooms cannot experience.
3. I have deliberately used the male pronoun, in part, because much of the scholarship on flaming suggests that males flame more frequently than females. Readers should not read this choice in pronoun use as an uncritical deployment of gender. For a reading of females' relationship to flames see Rhiannon Bury's *Cyberspaces of Their Own: Female Fandoms Online*.
4. Eve Sedgwick explains the heteronormative default position in her important and foundational book *The Epistemology of the Closet*.
5. A recent edited collection, *Silence and Listening as Rhetorical Arts* edited by Cheryl Glenn and Krista Ratcliffe, suggests that listening is gaining traction in our discipline. Though the collection includes many wonderful essays, Shari Stenberg and Wendy Wolters Hinshaw's contributions are particularly valuable given the lines of reasoning I have been developing.

Works Cited

Bizzell, Patricia. "Opinion: Composition Studies Saves the World." *College English* 72.2 (2009): 174-87. Print.

Benhabib, Seyla. *Situating the Self: Gender, Community and Postmodernism in Contemporary Ethics*. New York: Routledge, 1992. Print.

Brown, Wendy. *Edgework: Critical Essays on Knowledge and Politics*. Princeton: Princeton UP, 2005. Print.

Bury, Rhiannon. *Cyberspaces of Their Own: Female Fandoms Online*. New York: Peter Lang, 2005. Print.

Eve, Juliet, and Tara Brabazon. "Learning to Leisure? Failure, Flame, Blame, Shame, Homophobia and Other Everyday Practices in Online Education." *Journal of Literacy and Technology* 9.1 (2008): 36-62. Print.

Faigley, Lester. *Fragments of Rationality: Postmodernity and the Subject of Composition*. Pittsburgh: U of Pittsburg P, 1992. Print.

Fleckenstein, Kristie S. "Once Again with Feeling: Empathy in Deliberative Discourse." *JAC* 27.3/4 (2007): 701-16. Print.

Glenn, Cheryl, and Krista Ratcliffe, eds. *Silence and Listening as Rhetorical Arts*. Carbondale: Southern Illinois UP, 2011. Print.

Handa, Carolyn, ed. *Computers and Community: Teaching Composition in the Twenty-First Century*. Portsmouth: Boynton/Cook, 1990. Print.

Lenard, Mary. "Dealing with Online Selves: Ethos Issues in Computer-assisted Teaching and Learning." *Pedagogy: Critical Approaches to Teaching Literature, Language, Composition, and Culture* 5.1 (2005): 77-95. Print.

McKee, Heidi. "'YOUR VIEWS SHOWED TRUE IGNORANCE': (Mis)Communication in an Online Interracial Discussion Forum." *Computers and Composition* 19.4 (2002): 411-34. Print.

McLeod, Susan H. *Notes on the Heart: Affective Issues in the Writing Classroom*. Carbondale: Southern Illinois UP, 1997. Print.

Mouffe, Chantal. *On the Political: Thinking in Action*. London: Routledge, 2005. Print.

Ohmann, Richard. "Literacy, Technology, and Monopoly Capital." *College English* 47.7 (1985): 675-89. Print.

Ratcliffe, Krista. *Rhetorical Listening: Identification, Gender, Whiteness*. Carbondale: Southern Illinois UP, 2005. Print.

Rovai, Alfred P. "Building and Sustaining Community in Asynchronous Learning Networks." *Internet and Higher Education* 3.4 (2000): 285-97. Print.

Ryder, Phyllis Mentzel. "Multicultural Public Spheres and the Rhetorics of Democracy." *JAC* 27.3/4 (2007): 505-38. Print.

Sedgwick, Eve Kosofsky. *The Epistemology of the Closet*. Berkley: U of California P, 1991.Print.

Selfe, Cynthia L., and Susan Hilligoss, eds. *Literacy and Computers: The Complications of Teaching and Learning with Technology*. New York: MLA, 1994. Print.

Thompsen, Philip A. "What's Fueling the Flames in Cyberspace? A Social Influence Model." *Communication in Cyberspace: Social Interaction in an Electronic Environment*. Ed. Lance Strate, Ronald Jacobson, and Stephanie B. Gibson. Cresskill: Hampton, 1996. 297-315. Print.

Weinstock, Jeffrey Andrew. "Respond Now! E-mail, Acceleration, and a Pedagogy of Patience." *Pedagogy: Critical Approaches to Teaching Literature, Language, Composition, and Culture* 4.3 (2004): 365-83. Print.

Young, Iris Marion. "Asymmetrical Reciprocity: On Moral Respect, Wonder, and Enlarged Thought." *Constellations* 3.3 (1997): 340-63. Print.

---. *Justice and the Politics of Difference*. New Jersey: Princeton UP, 1990. Print.

Bodies of Knowledge: Definitions, Delineations, and Implications of Embodied Writing in the Academy

A. Abby Knoblauch

> This article differentiates three primary ways scholars in Composition and Rhetoric talk about embodiment as it relates to knowledge production and writing in the academy: embodied language, embodied knowledge, and embodied rhetoric. While these categories overlap and inform each other, clarifying the definitions themselves is important as there seems to be little agreement within the field about how one might define embodiment as it relates to writing. Additionally, this article illustrates how a strategic use of embodied rhetoric can disrupt the (faulty) assumption of a universalist discourse and provide concrete strategies for honoring difference and operationalizing a politics of location.

The link between bodies and language has a long history in Rhetoric, stretching back to Plato, Aristotle, and Montaigne. This tradition, of course, continues into the present: Carol Mattingly has drawn attention to women's bodies in *Appropriate[ing] Dress*; Cheryl Glenn has noted how women such as Anne Askew were able to use their positionalities as women, their female bodies, to subvert dominant ideas about authorship and power; Susan Kates has dubbed elocutionist Hallie Quinn Brown an embodied rhetor; Katie Conboy, Nadia Medina, and Sarah Stanbury brought together twenty-four pieces on female embodiment and feminist theory (also the title of their collection); and in 1999, Jack Selzer and Sharon Crowley published *Rhetorical Bodies*, a collection of sixteen essays on the intersections of rhetoric and the body. Even more recently, discussions of the body in Composition and Rhetoric have been highlighted in works concerning transgender rhetorics, such as Gayle Salamon's *Assuming A Body: Transgender and Rhetorics*; gay rhetorics (Alexander, Banks, and Gil-Gómez, for example); the burgeoning field of fat rhetorics (see, in particular, Kathleen LeBesco); works on disability and rhetoric, such as those collected in Wilson and Lewiecki-Wilson's *Embodied Rhetorics: Disability in Language and Culture*; and much work in feminist theories in general and in feminist compositions and rhetorics more specifically. And of course this is only a tiny sliver of the work done on rhetoric and the body, in part because it's difficult to imagine discussions of the rhetorical practices of members of marginalized groups *without* reference to lived bodily experiences.[1]

Yet what we might call "embodied terminology"—the use of terms such as *embodied, embodiment, bodily*, and references to *bodily acts* —also crosses disciplinary borders. Writing about the role of the body in science education, for example, Hui Niu Wilcox argues "embodied knowledges—central to our academic, artistic, and activist work—not only render science more accessible to women and underprivileged communities, but also help cultivate citizenry for action and change" (105). Here, embodied knowledges are those that are created and understood through "lived experiences, cultural performance, and bodily intelligence" (106). Wilcox draws attention to bodily performance such as dance as one form of embodied knowledge, noting, too, that such knowledge is not validated within the academy. Ecofeminist Carol P. Christ uses similar language when she defines "embodied embedded mysticism" as a "sensing through the body of connection to the larger whole or web of life of which we are a part" (166). And Dina A-Kassim, in her article "The Faded Bond: Calligraphesis and Kinship in Abdelwahab Meddeb's *Talismano*," argues that calligraphy, linked in some cultures directly to tattooing, can be considered a sort of "embodied writing" (124).

In just these three articles, embodiment is defined as physical motion and the knowledge that might stem from such motion, sensory or bodily response, and a metaphorical and physical connection between the body and writing. This obfuscation of terminology is also clear when Wilcox explains that she will "use the terms 'embodied ways of knowing,' 'embodied knowledges,' and 'embodied pedagogies' interchangeably to signal an epistemological and pedagogical shift that draws attention to bodies as agents of knowledge production" (105). This final conflation of terms illustrates that confusion surrounding definitions of embodiment are not limited to what might be seen as limit cases (dance, calligraphy), but are instead central to the ways in which we talk about knowledge production and classroom practice. Here, Wilcox conflates *ways* of knowing, *forms* of knowledge, and *practices* of teaching, all linked to that term "embodied." For Wilcox, all three are related to knowledge production, but I would argue that, while related, a physical motion like dance differs (or at least can differ) from an understanding of the world through lived experience in a particular body (a body that is transgendered, differently abled, or elderly, for example).[2] It is for this reason that I believe it important to differentiate the ways in which we talk about embodiment, particularly within English studies broadly, and Composition and Rhetoric more specifically. If critics conflate terms in the way that Wilcox does, it becomes too easy to further marginalize any form of embodied writing or ways of knowing within the academy.

I see three major categories of embodiment within the scholarship of our field: embodied language, embodied knowledge, and embodied rhetoric. This is not to say that these three categories are (a) mutually exclusive, or (b) the only ways in which one could categorize embodiment within Composition and Rhetoric. As is true in other disciplines, within English studies, too, these categories overlap, inform each other, even bleed into each other. And scholars interested in embodiment rarely consider or utilize just one category. And yet such delineation is important, in part because there seems to be little agreement within our field about how, exactly, we might define embodiment as it relates to writing. Not understanding the differences between such concepts can also serve to hide the distinct contributions each form of embodiment can bring to Composition Studies. In this article, then, I will first clarify the terms and categories, exploring the benefits and drawbacks of each. I will then focus more specifically on *embodied rhetoric*, to illustrate how a strategic use of this rhetorical approach can provide concrete strategies for enacting Adrienne Rich's call for a politics of location in scholarly writing.

In brief, I define embodied language as the use of terms, metaphors, and analogies that reference, intentionally or not, the body itself. Embodied knowledge is that sense of knowing something *through* the body and is often sparked by what we might call a "gut reaction." Finally, embodied rhetoric is a purposeful decision to include embodied knowledge and social positionalities as forms of meaning making within a text itself. I will now flesh out these terms more fully, beginning with embodied language.

Embodied Language

As Debra Hawhee points out, connections between language and the body were common in Greek culture. In fact, there was substantial slippage between terminology used to describe rhetoric and that used to describe athletics. Hawhee argues that the famous *agon*, as a place of both athletic and rhetorical engagement, was "a point of cultural connection between athletics and rhetoric," and therefore between the body and language (15). Hawhee also notes the connections between sports and the body in the term "stasis," explaining that stasis was used not only as a reference to one's rhetorical positioning or one's stance on an issue, but also one's position, stance, or posture in boxing (33). In this example, terminology, the very language itself, is embodied in that it echoes bodily functions and bodily motions.

In a more contemporary sense, I see embodied language in my introduction as I note that embodied categories "bleed into each other," and that I will "flesh out" my terms—phrasing that calls forth an image of the workings of the body. Such embodied language is common in English studies. As scholars, we "wrestle" with texts and ideas, we "embrace" arguments, we try to "wrap our minds around" complex concepts. Such language use might not immediately seem troubling, yet because it references the body itself, it is hardly uncomplicated. For one, *any* mention of the body in academic work can garner skeptical responses. While terms and phrases such as "grappling" with an idea have become normal parlance in academic writing, sustained use of bodily references still tends to provoke attention, as we will see in a moment. Perhaps more importantly, because embodied language speaks to and from bodies, it can carry multiple meanings, acting as a catalyst for both identification and disidentification. The work of Peter Elbow serves as one such example.

As Kate Ronald and Hephzibah Roskelly show, Elbow's work is rife with what I am calling embodied language. They note that Elbow makes space for "the role of the body—in all his writing" (210). In brief, the authors "argue that Elbow's voice is embodied—physical and present—in ways that bring an audience close both to Elbow's persona and to his ideas about writing and in ways that few academic writers attempt" (210). For example, Elbow uses images of eating, embracing (wrestling, holding, exercising), and seeing. Such references and metaphors, according to Ronald and Roskelly, situate the reader in Elbow's argument; they "become his way to make meaning and his way to connect" (214). In other words, because readers can relate to such bodily experiences as eating and embracing, and find satisfaction in many of these experiences, Elbow's use of such terminology may help readers identify with the author. It may help readers feel closer to the work and, in turn, closer to the act of writing itself.

But just as the embodied language that Elbow employs can serve to pull readers closer, it can also marginalize. Will Banks explains how Elbow's metaphor of the "marriage" between literature and composition leaves him (Banks) feeling "left out" because he, as a gay man, cannot marry.[3] He wonders, "while Elbow *embodies* his understanding of English department rifts through the heteronormative trope of marriage, how would I embody it? And why do I feel so left out of his metaphor?" (29, emphasis in original). Banks illustrates how such language can actually keep some readers at bay, pushing them outside of the sense of inclusiveness that Ronald and Roskelly imagine, as Elbow's marriage metaphor does for Banks.

Perhaps even more troubling is when embodied language feels threatening and violent. In "Feminism and Composition: A Case for Conflict," Susan Jarratt famously draws attention to Elbow's embodied language in his discussion of the Doubting and Believing Game. In this well-known piece, Elbow suggests that the doubting game "tends to reinforce those personal styles which the culture also defines as male: aggressive, thrusting, combative, competitive, and initiatory" (180). He goes on to say that the doubting game is marked by "trying to remain *open*," says Elbow, or "a kind of trying-to-not-try" (181, emphasis in original). According to Elbow, to ask intellectuals to act or think in such ways often makes them feel as though all they can do "is just go soft and limp" (181). Furthermore:

> The believing game asks us, as it were, to sleep with any idea that comes down the road. To be promiscuous. We will turn into the girl who just can't say no. A yes-man. A flunky. A slave. Someone who can be made to believe anything. A large opening that anything can be poured into. Force-fed. Raped. (185)

For Jarratt, Elbow's discussion raises two problems. The first is that Elbow's believing game reinforces for female students a passivity in which they must accept everything offered to them. Secondly, Jarratt gestures to the possible responses to Elbow's embodied language, including her own response, when she writes "only read Elbow's rhetoric of surrender as female subject, which I must do, and that positioning becomes frighteningly clear" (274). Such a positioning, according to Jarratt, "puts a woman [...] in a dangerous stance" (274). Her use of the term "dangerous" here is telling: Not only is the passivity that Elbow advocates potentially dangerous for women as it asks that women remain silent, but that term also references the physical danger associated with some of Elbow's language: promiscuity, force-feeding, and rape.[4]

Like Jarratt, I am disturbed by this sexualized language, especially what seems like a rather casual use of the term "raped." Perhaps similarly, as a woman reading these passages, I bristle at the phrase "a girl who just can't say no" in a way that I don't bristle at "yes-man," in part, I believe, because of the sexual(ized), gendered, and sometimes violent connotations that swirl around the girl who "just can't say no." I imagine many men reading these sections might respond differently than I do to the assertion that intellectuals might just "go soft and limp." I do not mean to imply here that Elbow *intended* to make readers feel uncomfortable or, at times, even threatened but, as Krista Ratcliffe has reminded us, sometimes the intent and the effects of language are strikingly different (89). Regardless of intent, the effect of these passages is, at least for me, bodily. And the effects of particular embodied language use might be different for any given reader based in part on that reader's sexuality, gender, race, class, able-bodiedness, or size, for example. The multiplicity of potential response is one of the things that makes embodied language so tricky. Yes, it can serve to hail the reader, to connect with the reader, to bring a reader closer to the writer, but it can also push readers away, threaten them, disturb them, alienate and exclude them.

Embodied Knowledge

The above discussion of the effects of embodied language leads us into the realm of what I am calling embodied knowledge: knowledge that is very clearly connected to the body. Embodied knowledge often begins with bodily response—or what we might call "gut reactions." As a trigger for meaning making that is rooted so completely in the body, embodied response is rarely legitimated in academia. Even so, I would argue that such response is a driving force behind much scholarly activity. For example, Betty Smith Franklin notes that her body, like all of ours, reacts when she encounters something exciting or boring, explaining, "As I listen to someone's powerful story, the hair on my arms stands up. When I am held captive in a meeting listening to the droning of endless cover stories, I feel a deadening tension in my lower back" (18). Sara Ahmed further reflects this concept when she writes that "knowledge cannot be separated from the bodily world of feeling and sensation; knowledge is bound up with what makes us sweat, shudder, tremble, all those feelings that are crucially felt on the bodily surface, the skin surface where we touch and are touched by the world" (171).

What does this mean for us as academics and scholars? We, too, make sense of our worlds through our bodies and although such connections may not always be valued or sanctioned in the academy, some scholars are talking about the role that emotion *does* play in our academic work. Joy Ritchie, for example, explored the generative power of anger in a 2006 CCCC talk, and bell hooks has explained that rage can be a strong motivating factor for people who are oppressed, sparking an examination of the means of oppression in their lives and a determination to act (Crawford 683). I would imagine the marginalia of most scholars' books and articles would reveal strong emotional responses to these texts. And my hunch is that these reactions often prompted scholars to some form of academic action: a change in pedagogy, the writing of a response article, the launching of a new research project.

Banks draws attention to how his bodily responses inform his understanding of one of his courses. Writing about his reaction to a teacher who reminds him of his bullying older brother, Banks explains that the professor's booming voice made him "uncomfortable," and left him "feeling insecure and meek" (25). Because the professor's demeanor in class reminds Banks of his older brother, with whom he had never won an argument, Banks wonders if he was projecting, or "mapping one body onto another and responding through my body" (26). Banks further contends that the text of that class is now wrapped up in his bodily reaction to that teacher. He cannot separate the two (26). He has made sense of that class, and his experience of that class, in part through his embodied response to it. He has made sense of the world through his body.

Similarly, Jane E. Hindman, in her article "Writing an Important Body of Scholarship: A Proposal for an Embodied Rhetoric of Professional Practice," comments on her physical reaction to her graduate students' response to assigned readings, in particular those surrounding the foundationalist/anti-foundationalist debate in Composition and Rhetoric.[5] Hindman reveals that in a frustrating classroom moment her "visceral responses were many," including an elevated heart rate and flushed skin (113). Yet, because the classroom is often imagined as a place of mind, of intellect, and not emotion, Hindman tried to keep such reactions hidden. Her dissatisfaction with her students' responses to this discussion, and with her own unwillingness to reveal her emotional reaction to her students, "produced and organized [her] professional process of producing knowledge," leading Hindman to develop her theories about embodied writing (112). Hindman's emotional and embodied response not only sparked a research project, it informed her construction of theories of embodiment and embodied rhetoric, theories that draw attention to the role of emotion and the body in academic work. This was knowledge that began, in very real ways, in Hindman's visceral reaction, a bodily knowledge that there was something worth exploring.

More broadly, Smith Franklin argues that "we know each other and ourselves through our bodies" (18). Our bodily responses become a form of embodied knowledge—a way of making knowledge through the body.

As Madeline Grumet points out, "whatever we have noticed, touched, and grabbed probably becomes part of our intuitive sense of the world" (252). Expanding on this notion, Grumet contends that "we see what we look for, and what we look for is constituted not only by what my body can do, but also what it cannot do" (253-54). In some ways, our bodies constitute our noetic fields—what can and cannot be known. While I can conceive of flight even though I cannot fly, I can only conceive of flight because I, in my body, have both felt close to flight (jumping off of picnic tables, running very fast, bouncing on a trampoline) and very far from flight. It is through my body, our bodies, that we know the world.[6]

Sometimes this knowing is even more concrete and physical. In her 2004 article "Words Made Flesh: Fusing Imagery and Language in a Polymorphic Literacy," Kristie Fleckenstein relates the story her five-year-old daughter, Anna, learning how to draw a star. Her hand over her daughter's, Fleckenstein guides Anna through the motions, whispering "up down up over down" as the two of them make stars on the page. Fleckenstein gradually lets go of Anna's hand and the young girl continues to draw rough stars on her own. Eagerly watching, Anna's four-year-old sister asks Anna to teach her how to make stars, too. "No, Baby, I can't," Anna replies, "I don't know how. Only my hand knows" (612).

Of course, the mind/body distinction here is not only problematic, it's also overly simplified. But we cannot, I think, dismiss Anna's experience. At that moment, only her hand "knew" how to make a star, or at least that's the way it felt to her. Her mind doesn't seem to have processed the information in a way that would allow Anna to explain it to her sister. I imagine the delight in this new skill, the making of stars, but also the fear that if the hand stops, the skill will be lost. I have certainly had similar experiences, relying primarily on muscle memory, and confident that if I think about something too much (a PIN number or online passcode, for example), I won't be able to accomplish my task. My hand, at those points, appears to know better than my mind. Such knowledge, it often seems, is of the body.

It is one thing, however, to draw on embodied knowledge as a generative force; it is another to include such aspects of embodiment in the writing itself. Such inclusion has often been met with resistance (although that resistance itself has not been without challenge). I posit that such reticence is due to a conflation of the forms of embodiment in writing discussed this far as well as the inclusion of what we might call bodily urges.

Perhaps the most famous example of the inclusion of the body in academic writing is Jane Tompkins's 1987 article "Me and My Shadow," in which Tompkins highlights the intersections between her personal life and her professional life, arguing that her desire to separate the two is quite simply a matter of academic conditioning (169). Tompkins comments on what she feels is an academic need to address a mistake in a colleague's article. Such an approach should, in a traditional model, be calculated, rational, professional, *intellectual,* and would leave the body at the proverbial door. Yet Tompkins breaks the academic mold by admitting that she doesn't know how to enter this debate (or conversation) with a colleague without leaving her personal life behind. "The criticism I would like to write," she explains "would always take off from personal experience, would always be a chronicle of my hours and days, would speak in a voice which can talk about everything" (173).

In a moment, I will turn to Tompkins' *rhetorical* use of the body in her article, shifting the discussion from embodied knowledge to embodied rhetoric. First, however, it is useful to draw attention to the moments in Tompkins's landmark article that can make it too easy to dismiss references to the body. I do not mean to dismiss Tompkins—over twenty years after its initial publication, I return to this article because I am still struck by the power of what Tompkins calls her "interruption" of academic conventions, her inclusion of the personal—but there are moments that are more productive than others.

Tompkins's belief that she would like to write criticism that would "be a chronicle of my hours and days" undercuts the radical potential of embodied rhetoric. While Tompkins argues that there are connections between her personal and professional lives, that her marriage, her childhood, her reactions to a summer teach-in, her emotions, and her scholarship are all intertwined, productive scholarship must also move beyond a chronicle of hours and days. There might, in fact, be a connection between Tompkins's father's illness, the grief she has over a friend who had committed suicide, her bodily urge to go to the bathroom, and her response to Messer-Davidow. There might be a connection, but these connections aren't clear to me as a reader. Tompkins's inclusion of the fact that she needs to pee does little to forward the conversation, and provides fodder for those critics who feel that the body has no role in academic writing. When she uses her own embodied response to critique the lack of bodily recognition in scholarship, however, the article moves toward productive embodied *rhetoric* and not simply the inclusion of bodily urges.

Embodied Rhetoric

Embodied rhetoric, like all rhetoric, is *purposeful* and therefore moves beyond "simply" including bodily urges in academic writing. I return now to the work of Hindman and Banks to construct and hone a definition of embodied rhetoric and illustrate the benefits and potential drawbacks of embodied rhetoric. Finally, I argue that clarifying the ways in which we incorporate aspects of embodiment in academic writing can encourage this form of productive *rhetorical* uses of the body.

While embodied language draws attention to the body itself and embodied knowledge recognizes the generative force of the body, Hindman argues that embodied rhetoric "requires gestures to the material practices of the professional group and to the quotidian circumstances of the individual writer" ("Writing an Important Body" 103). More specifically, she believes we, as scholars, must "gesture to our bodies, our lives" in our work "by calling to the surface at least some of the associations that [our] thinking passes through, associations evoked by [our] gender, race, class, sexual orientation, politics, and so on" ("Writing an Important Body" 104). Importantly, this "gesturing" must be included *in the text itself*. Hindman's work on embodied rhetoric is invaluable, but linking it more clearly with these further modes of embodiment both refines and operationalizes the definition. Embodied rhetoric, then, becomes more clearly the purposeful effort by an author to represent aspects of embodiment within the text he or she is shaping. Furthermore, when practicing embodied rhetoric, the author attempts to decipher how these "material circumstances" (Royster 228) affect how he or she understands the world.

Why would one choose to practice an embodied rhetoric? What purpose does it or might it serve? Perhaps most importantly, as Jacqueline Jones Royster argues:

> knowledge is produced by someone and [. . .] its producers are not formless and invisible. They are embodied and in effect have passionate attachments by means of their embodiments. They are vested with vision, values, and habits; with ways of being and ways of doing. These ways of being and doing shape the question of what counts as knowledge, what knowing and doing mean, and what the consequences of knowledge and action entail. It is important therefore, to specify attachments, to recognize who has produced the knowledge, what the bases of it are, what the material circumstances of its production entail. (228)

Banks echoes Royster when he remarks that it is "quite simply impossible (and irresponsible) to separate the producer of the text from the text itself. Our belief that we could make such a separation has allowed masculinist rhetorics to become 'universal' in modernist discourses because the bodies producing the discourse have been effectively erased, allowing them to become metonymies of experience and knowledge" (Banks 33). The belief, at least in professional circles, that we could erase the body in favor of the mind (as if the two were separable), imagines what Susan Bordo has called "a dis-embodied view from nowhere" (4).[7] Such a view assumes a sort of normed intellectualism, a seemingly utopian belief that place and body do not matter. That the academic, the intellectual, can transcend such material matters. But as all of these scholars draw attention to, there is no such disembodied place of nowhere. We are all situated beings, bodies situated in culture and language.

The disembodied view from nowhere further assumes that, because bodies do not matter, "any *body* can stand in for another" (Banks 38). In some ways, this is a comforting thought. As members of minority groups struggle for recognition within the academy, the lack of embodiment in prose might lead one to believe that we're all on a level playing field. To be able to erase or ignore markers of difference, at least in written texts, might imply a sort of race/gender/sexuality blindness. I am sometimes seduced by the thought of erasing the body, my body, in my texts because some of the markers of my identity are less valued than others.

Yet I am persuaded by Banks's argument that to ignore the body privileges the white masculinist discourse as universal. Such ignoring, in effect, erases difference, subsuming all into a discourse that has traditionally been white, male, and privileged. This imagined view from nowhere then functions like essentialism in a whole new fashion. A view from nowhere, a belief that bodies don't matter, seems much easier to imagine if one lives in a body that is not always already marked as other. It seems to imagine that others can forget their bodies, too. As bell hooks points out, "the person who is most powerful has the privilege of denying their body" (137). Who is asked to deny the body and who is asked to reveal is a question I believe we must continually ask ourselves.

The view from nowhere assumes, then, that each body is equally constructed, equally accepted, and equally provided for in this society. Of course this is not the case. The way my body moves through this world is often different than the way that your body moves through this world. And it's different than the way my brother's does, my grandmother's does, my niece Elenor's does, my friend Mei's does. To ignore the body in scholarship might, in some ways, aid those from minority groups, but only by asking them (us) to pass, to act as if our bodies, our experiences don't matter, to act as if we are white, heterosexual, able-bodied, privileged men. And that just doesn't sit right with me.

Instead, an attention to the body as reflected in an embodied rhetoric speaks to the concerns of Royster and Banks, as well as to Adrienne Rich's call for a politics of location in our scholarship. By locating a text in the body (understanding the importance of embodied knowledge) and by locating the body in the text, writers utilizing an embodied rhetoric work against what might be seen as the potential hegemony of (some) academic discourse, thereby beginning to enact Rich's politics of location. But, as Gesa Kirsch and Joy Ritchie have noted, a politics of location in composition scholarship is remarkably complicated.[8] Kirsch and Ritchie caution scholars that "it is not enough to claim the personal and locate ourselves in our scholarship and research" (140). Furthermore, drawing on Rich, the authors explain that we need to do more than "make the facile statements that often occur at the beginning of research articles, to say, 'I am a white, middle-class woman from a Midwestern university doing research.'" (142). Instead, a politics of location must "challenge our conception of *who* we are in our work," and must be "accompanied by a rigorously reflexive examination of ourselves as researchers" (142). As researchers, as scholars, as teachers, and, I would argue, as human beings.

Rich urges us to begin this process of location "not with a continent or a country or a house, but with the geography closest in—the body" (64). Rich believes that doing so helps us "reclaim" our bodies, "to reconnect our thinking and speaking with the body of this particular living human individual" (65). This is what embodied rhetoric asks of the rhetor, to reconnect our thinking with our particular bodies, understanding that knowledge comes from the body. But, lest we forget, these are bodies both shaping and shaped by culture. And these bodies, and the cultures they inhabit, are complex entities, not to be reduced to singular essential tags such as "woman" or "Chinese." These terms signify differently in different contexts, and the terms themselves are socially constructed. By locating our thinking in our particular bodies, scholars in Composition and Rhetoric—perhaps any field—need to keep in mind the cautions of postmodern theorists, as well as the cautions of scholars such as Kirsch and Ritchie. Those cautions are (at least) two-fold.

The first caution comes from postmodern scholars who might argue that an embodied rhetoric, drawing from a politics of location that begins in the body, assumes a stable and unified body from which to speak. Scholars such as Foucault and Butler would of course remind me that bodies are constructed, that social positionalities are performed, and that there is no unified body that needs to or could stand in for another.[9] Bodies are texts and are therefore unstable and subject to shifting positionalities, transformation, and continually revised and reconstructed histories. To write *from* the body, as asked by an embodied rhetoric, one must *have* a body, and in a postmodern world there is no unified body from which to write.

This critique reminds scholars such as myself that positionalities shift in different contexts. The work of postmodern scholars forces me to keep in mind that my body is in some ways always already constructed by culture, written on by discourse. But that writing, I think, can take many different forms and can be read in a variety of ways. Bodies may be imagined as texts, as cyborgs, as discourse itself.[10] But that does not dismiss the very real lived experiences of that flesh, of *people*, not metaphors. Because whether or not I imagine myself to be a unified Cartesian subject or a shifting, slippery postmodern amalgamation of discourses, someone walks the dog in morning. Someone looks back at me in the mirror. This body, my body, has been cut into, has had violence inflicted upon it, has inflicted violence upon others, has been ignored and silenced, has been touched and celebrated. This body, my body, moves through this particular world visually marked as white, overweight, and female. In less obvious ways it is marked by class and assumed heterosexuality. This is how I am often read and, in turn, this is how I often read. So I turn to embodied rhetoric because one body cannot stand in for another, constructed or not, as lived experiences in a specific body help shape the ways in which that body, that person, makes sense of the world.

This assertion leads to the second caution concerning academic references to the body: that well-worn charge of essentialism, a critique often leveled at embodied rhetoric, and with good reason. Drawing attention to one's body as a locus for meaning making can, if not carefully practiced, cause either thinker or reader to imagine that this particular body stands in for all bodies of a certain gender, race, class, or sexual orientation. In other words, if I say that my experiences in a female body lead me to such-and-such a claim, the statement may be read (and could be intended to be read) as if I were saying that "as a woman, I think like this," as if all women think as I do because of our shared biology.[11] Drawing on the work of Sandra Harding, Kirsch and Ritchie caution that "claiming our experience, then, may be as inadequate for making claims to knowledge as traditional claims from objectivity are. Harding points out that 'our experience may lie to us' just as it has lied to male researchers who believed their positions were value-free or universal" (144). In other words, in speaking from our own experience we must always keep in mind that that experience is local and specific, not universal.

In response to this essentialist critique, Kirsch and Ritchie ask that scholars "be unrelentingly self-reflective" (Kirsch and Ritchie 143), always keeping in mind how our own positionalities can not only help us make meaning of the world, but also keep hidden meanings not revealed by our positionalities. Hindman calls it "unflinching self-reflection" ("Making Writing Matter" 101). In other words, we must recognize that we cannot speak for others, and that our own viewpoints are always limited by our experiences, standpoints, positionalities, and bodies (and the ways in which they receive and are received in the world). We must constantly, unrelentingly, unflinchingly reflect on our own terministic screens and what these screens both obscure and draw into focus.

This reflexivity can refer not only to a reflection on our bodily experience and standpoints, but on our *professional* positionalities as well. Hindman extends her call for self-reflection by asking that academic writers practicing an embodied rhetoric make "gestures to the existing discursive conventions of the discipline," drawing attention in the text to these conventions ("Making Writing Matter" 101). According to Hindman, this is necessary because in order to be heard in the academy, in order to construct the proper ethos, a writer must first prove that she understands the conventions, yet, in order to embody the rhetoric, the writer must also call attention to the fact that these *are* conventions, and that she is both working within them and intentionally challenging them. Hindman calls this an "interruption" that can unsettle the supposed mastery of an author who can work within these conventions. Those practicing embodied rhetoric can disrupt this mastery in order to reflect the writer's positionality within the academy.

The writer's positionality within the academy and her social positionality are not necessarily mutually exclusive. In fact, social positionality often affects standing within the academy, and standing within the academy often affects the ways in which one is "allowed" or sanctioned to write, as Tompkins illustrates. She explicitly outlines the conventions of academic writing—what she is supposed to do in a critical response article—but then undercuts these expectations by including aspects of embodiment. As I note above, not all such inclusions are productive, but her rhetorical strategy of gesturing to her lived experiences and positionalities allows her to highlight academic and professional conventions while simultaneously subverting those same conventions. Doing so illustrates for a reader that she can write in the ways she has been taught that she is not allowed to write and can still contribute to professional knowledge. In this case, part of that knowledge is an expanding of genre conventions. The form of the article itself helps to create and/or legitimate new professional practice. The self-reflection that Tompkins practices, itself a form of embodied rhetoric, further illustrates the potential of such a rhetoric. It moves the personal beyond the private and places it squarely in the realm of the social and professional, ultimately critiquing the exclusion of the body in professional practice. Tompkins makes clear that her knowledge comes from somewhere, from a particular body. Highlighting the personal source of embodied knowledge gives specificity and voice to the bodies behind the words on the page, helping enact that politics of location in a way that is more than a mere biographical blurb. In this way, an embodied rhetoric born from embodied knowledge can disrupt what is often assumed to be an academic or professional mastery (by gesturing to conventions as conventions), and can rattle loose the privileged white masculinist discourse to which Banks draws attention.

This is, for me, the benefit of an embodied rhetoric in professional practice. While not appropriate for all purposes, an embodied rhetoric that draws attention to embodied knowledge—specific material conditions, lived experiences, positionalities, and/or standpoints—can highlight difference instead of erasing it in favor of an assumed privileged discourse. Furthermore, a scholar employing an embodied rhetoric to illustrate self-reflexivity in terms of bodily or academic positionalities can open up a space for new professional practices and discourses, practices that consciously position knowledge as of the body. In order to fully enact this rhetorical practice, however, we need to be clearer about embodied terminology so as not to confuse embodied knowledge with embodied rhetoric (or embodied response or even references to bodily urges). Such specificity will also make clearer for both writers and critics that such writing is social, not solipsistic, personal but also professional. Embodied rhetoric, when functioning *as* rhetoric, connects the personal to the larger social realm, and makes more visible the sources of *all* of our knowledge.

Notes

1. Especially as much of this rhetorical practice was in response to marginalization that was based on human difference, or perceived human difference.
2. While a bodily motion like dance might lead to embodied knowledge, embodied knowledge is not only born of bodily motion. As someone who has never been a dancer, I can imagine that dance, itself, might be a form of embodied knowledge, but I am hesitant to say that one always knows about the world through motions like dance.
3. At the writing of this article, same-sex marriage or unions are legal in only a handful of states across the nation.

4. Because female students are often already socially conditioned to be passive receptors of information, such a reading is indeed gendered. But assuming that only females can be positioned as "opening[s]," that only females can be asked to "swallow," or be "force-fed," or raped illustrates the assumed heteronormativity of this discussion.
5. Students read a number of scholars, including Stephen North and Patricia Bizzell, who make a case for anti-foundationalism. When students then read a counter-argument by Stanley Fish, they were "outraged," wondering why scholars kept making a case for anti-foundationalism when Fish had already "proved—and that was several years ago—that practice has nothing to do with theory" (Hindman, "Writing an Important Body" 110).
6. Of course, in the most basic sense, *all* of our senses are embodied; our very cognitive processes, too, are embodied.
7. Bordo credits Thomas Nagel with the phrase "view from nowhere" (217).
8. Kirsch and Ritchie focus primarily on issues of feminist research methodology in their article "Beyond the Personal: Theorizing a Politics of Location in Composition Research," but their discussion of a politics of location is relevant to embodied rhetorics as well.
9. Lynn Worsham, too, would remind me that emotion is also socially constructed (397).
10. Donna Haraway cautions that "feminist embodiment, then, is not about fixed location in a reified body, female or otherwise, but about nodes in field, inflections in orientations, and responsibility for difference in material-semiotic fields of meaning" (195). Her point is well taken: I am, in some ways, imagining a sort of reified body in that I imagine a body that is bound to itself, that is bounded by flesh and therefore contained. But all bodies shift and change, sometimes naturally, sometimes violently. And the positionality of any body is constantly shifting within varied power structures and social situations.
11. Such thinking also privileges a gender and sex binary, juxtaposing men and women as if these were the only two biological categories of sex.

Works Cited

A-Kassim, Dina. "The Faded Bond: Calligraphesis and Kinship in Abdelwahab Meddeb's *Talismano*." *Public Culture* 13.1 (2001): 113-38. Print.

Ahmed, Sara. *The Cultural Politics of Emotion*. New York: Routledge, 2004. Print.

Alexander, Jonathan. "Transgendered Rhetorics: (Re)Composition Narratives of the Gendered Body." *CCC* 57 (2005): 45-82. Print.

Banks, William. "Written through the Body: Disruptions and 'Personal' Writing." *College English* 66 (2003): 21-40. Print.

Bordo, Susan. *Unbearable Weight: Feminism, Western Culture, and the Body*. Berkeley: U of California P, 1993. Print.

Christ, Carol P. "Embodied Embedded Mysticism: Affirming the Self and Others in a Radically Interdependent World." *Journal of Feminist Studies in Religion* 24.2 (2008): 159-67. Web. 20 August 2009.

Conboy, Katie, Nadia Medina, and Sarah Stanbury. *Writing on the Body: Female Embodiment and Feminist Theory*. New York: Columbia UP, 1997. Print.

Crawford, Ilene. "Building a Theory of Affect in Cultural Studies Composition Pedagogy." *JAC* 22 (2002): 678-84. Print.

Elbow, Peter. "Appendix Essay: The Doubting Game and the Believing Game—An Analysis of the Intellectual Enterprise." *Writing Without Teachers*. 1973. 25th anniversary ed. New York: Oxford UP, 1988. Print.

Fleckenstein, Kristie. "Words Made Flesh: Fusing Imagery and Language in a Polymorphic Literacy." *College English* 66 (2004): 612-31. Web. 20 January 2007.

Franklin, Betty Smith. "The Teacher's Body." Freedman and Holmes 15-22.

Freedman, Diane P., and Martha Stoddard Holmes, eds. *The Teacher's Body: Embodiment, Authority, and Identity in the Academy*. Albany: SUNY P, 2003. Print.

Glenn, Cheryl. *Rhetoric Retold: Regendering the Tradition from Antiquity Through the Rennaissance*. Carbondale: Southern Illinois UP, 1997. Print.

Gil-Gómez, Ellen M. *Performing La Mestiza: Textual Representations of Lesbians of Color and the Negotiation of Identities*. New York: Routledge, 2000. Print.

Grumet, Madeleine. Afterword. "My Teacher's Body." Freedman and Holmes 249-58.

Haraway, Donna J. *Simians, Cyborgs, and Women: The Reinvention of Nature*. New York: Routledge, 1991. Print.

Harding, Sandra. *Whose Science? Whose Knowledge? Thinking from Women's Lives*. Ithaca: Cornell UP, 1991. Print.

Hawhee, Debra. *Bodily Arts: Rhetoric and Athletics in Ancient Greece*. Austin: U of Texas P, 2004. Print.

Hindman, Jane E. "Making Writing Matter: Using 'The Personal' to Recover[y] an Essential[ist] Tension in Academic Discourse." *College English* 64 (2001): 88-108. Web. 27 July 2006.

---. "Writing an Important Body of Scholarship: A Proposal for an Embodied Rhetoric of Professional Practice." *JAC* 22 (2002): 93-118. Print.

hooks, bell. *Teaching to Transgress: Education as the Practice of Freedom*. New York: Routledge, 1994. Print.

Jarratt, Susan C. "Feminism and Composition: The Case for Conflict." Kirsch, Spencer Maor, Massey, Nickoson-Massey, and Sheridan-Rabideau 263-80.

Kates, Susan. "The Embodied Rhetoric of Hallie Quinn Brown." *College English* 59 (1997): 59-71. Print.

Kirsch, Gesa E., Fay Spencer Maor, Lance Massey, Lee Nickoson-Massey, and Mary P. Sheridan-Rabideau, eds. *Feminism and Composition: A Critical Sourcebook*. Boston: Bedford/St. Martin's, 2003. Print.

Kirsch, Gesa E., and Joy S. Ritchie. "Beyond the Personal: Theorizing a Politics of Location in Composition Research." Kirsch, Spencer Maor, Massey, Nickoson-Massey, and Sheridan-Rabideau 140-59.

LeBesco, Kathleen. *Revolting Bodies?: The Struggle to Redefine Fat Identity*. Amherst: U of Massachusetts P, 2004. Print.

Mattingly, Carol. *Appropriate[ing] Dress: Women's Rhetorical Style in Nineteenth-Century America*. Carbondale: Southern Illinois UP, 2002. Print.

Ratcliffe, Krista. *Rhetorical Listening: Identification, Gender, Whiteness*. Carbondale: Southern Illinois UP, 2005.

Rich, Adrienne. *Arts of the Possible: Essays and Conversations*. New York: W.W. Norton, 2001. Print.

Ritchie, Joy. "Cross-Cultural Transference: Reciprocal Learning Relationships." Conference on College Composition and Communication. Palmer House Hilton, Chicago, IL. 26 March 2006.

Ronald, Kate, and Hephzibah Roskelly. "Embodied Voices: Peter Elbow's Physical Rhetoric." *Writing with Elbow*. Ed. Pat Belanoff, Marcia Dickson, and Sheryl Fontaine. Logan: Utah State UP, 2002. 210-22. Print.

Royster, Jacqueline Jones. "A View from a Bridge: Afrafeminist Ideologies and Rhetorical Studies." Kirsch, Spencer Maor, Massey, Nickoson-Massey, and Sheridan-Rabideau 206-33.

Salamon, Gayle. *Assuming a Body: Transgender and Rhetorics of Masculinity*. New York: Columbia UP, 2010. Print.

Selzer, Jack, and Sharon Crowley. *Rhetorical Bodies*. Madison: Wisconsin UP, 1999. Print.

Tompkins, Jane. "Me and My Shadow." *New Literary History* 19.1 (1987): 169-87. Web. 20 August 2009.

Wilcox, Hui Niu. "Embodied Ways of Knowing, Pedagogies, and Social Justice: Inclusive Science and Beyond." *Feminist Formations* 21.2 (2009): 104-20. Web. 20 August 2009.

Wilson, James C., and Cynthia Lewiecki-Wilson. *Embodied Rhetorics: Disability in Language and Culture*. Carbondale: Southern Illinois UP, 2001. Print.

Worsham, Lynn. "On the Rhetoric of Theory in the Discipline of Writing: A Comment and a Proposal." *JAC* 19 (1999): 389-409. Print.

Reclaiming "Old" Literacies in the New Literacy Information Age: The Functional Literacies of the Mediated Workstation

Ryan Shepherd and Peter Goggin

For many writing faculty, electronic or digital literacies may not play an overtly significant role in their course designs and teaching practices, but these literacies still play a significant role in how students write. Whether or not writing teachers want to accept it, functional computer literacies are an important aspect of teaching writing. In order to test how well acquainted writing instructors were with these literacies, two informal surveys were conducted on writing instructors knowledge of computer peripherals and security. These surveys found that writing instructors may need to reconsider the role of functional literacies in their classrooms.

As Peter Vandenberg notes, the evolving definition of *literacy* is always accompanied by a deep-seated belief in its ameliorative guarantee. "We tend to see a less benevolent disciplinary face only in the rearview mirror" (547). Perhaps no aspect of Writing Studies illustrates this idea more than education in digital literacies. As newer and "better" technologies come along, they enhance brave new possibilities for teaching, learning, and theorizing the study of writing. Not surprisingly, scholars quickly turn their attention to these new technologies and the potential they promise. After all, academia rewards innovation, and scholarly publishers are always on the lookout for the newest creative finding for literacy research and teaching. But the emphasis on technological innovation which has so powerfully influenced the study of digital literacy has accelerated the decline in the perceived disciplinary significance of technologies and literacies that are not on the "cutting edge" of innovation. The result is that older, still vital, technologies and their related still-existing issues that generated so much scholarly investment not so long ago are no longer viable in contemporary discourses other than as remnants of a previous era. At the same time, the shift to the innovative runs the risk of Writing Studies losing sight of the very aspects of those older discussions of digital literacies that have given shape to newer discussions. As David Kaufer and Kathleen Carley have pointed out:

> There is an unfortunate "futurist" bias that impels many to assume qualitative differences between older and newer communication technologies before exploring whether their differences might lie on common quantitative continua. The result of this tendency is to think of new technologies

as a rupture from the past and to cluster the technology immediately superseded closer to the technologies it itself superseded. (17)

For many writing faculty who teach in traditional classrooms, electronic or digital literacies may not play an overtly significant role in their course designs and teaching practices, but these literacies still play a significant role in how students write. All writing faculty, even those in unmediated classrooms, are assumed to have (and care about) the functional skills that enable them to sustain their computing systems, administer their courses, and communicate with students via their office (and home) computer workstation. As Ilana Snyder points out, "preparing the current generation of students to become literate is difficult, not only because it is uncertain what the literacies of the future will be, but because the task falls to educators who are not fully literate themselves in the use of these new technologies" (3-4).

Whether we view the proliferation of system security peripherals (such as virus protection programs, product and system updates, backup systems, and firewalls) as undesirable background clutter or desirable computer-mediated composition (CMC) technologies, the demands for increased knowledge and use of these peripherals adds to the already complex multiple literate, pedagogical, and administrative practices that comprise writing instruction. These functional literacies are significant elements in the ecology of technological literacy that Cynthia Selfe (*Technology*) exhorts us to pay attention to but, as Staurt Selber notes, have, for the most part, been left out of our conversations on new information literacies.

In recent years, much scholarship has been written in the field of computers and writing on the subject of technological literacy. The idea of "technical literacy" in writing as the basic abilities to operate keyboards, computer systems, and various hardware and software applications has morphed into the idea of a more critically reflexive "information literacy" that strives to account for the multiple dynamics of social/ideological contexts that are overtly and tacitly embedded in the technologies that shape and mediate every facet of written communication. Notable scholars such as Faigley, Selfe and Hawisher, LeBlanc, Wysocki and Johnson-Eilola, and Sullivan and Porter, to name a few, have helped to promote reflexive questioning about what it means to be digitally literate.

The technologies and scholarly investment in digital literacies associated with bulletin boards, Web site design, HTML, online writing labs, and even e-mail have, for the most part, been superseded by wikis, blogs, texting, gaming, and social networking sites. But even those earlier technologies superseded scholarly prior interest in word processing, hypertext, and electronic textbooks. To oversimplify for the sake of perspective, Writing Studies as a field has generally shifted from emphasis in the functional/how-to literacies to an emphasis in social and critical literacies. But in the ecology of writing and Writing Studies, the functional is still there. This goes right down to the mechanical how-to knowledge, the basic nuts and bolts of digital communication, from the act of tapping on a QWERTY keyboard and clicking a mouse to running virus protection and other security protocols. This essay makes the case that we need to reclaim some of the interest in the essential basic functional literacies of the digital media we use, not necessarily for instructive purposes, but rather as consumers and managers of those technologies. For this we focus on just one basic key function—system security peripherals—to make the argument for why Writing Studies needs to include a literacy of mundane functionality to re-establish an important element in our discussions of digital literacies.

Crisis to Commonplace

A little over a decade ago the nation faced a "technological literacy crisis," as it was termed by the Clinton administration, when the heady rush to mediate America's classrooms and thrust college writing into the digital age gave widespread credence to the already well-established scholarship, research, and teaching of writing and digital technologies. This "crisis" also signaled an end to the days of the techie gurus in writing programs—the few who understood, or at least enjoyed dabbling in, the mechanics of hardware, software, and the rapidly evolving technologies and interfaces of the Internet. Their emphasis was very much on "how to" approaches that emphasized functionalist literacies, that is, the mechanics of text production through the new media, or personal growth literacies that validated traditional approaches to writing education via the new technologies that validated them (see Goggin). Now, just about anyone who teaches in higher education in the U.S. has come to use computer technology for a variety of teaching, administrative, and research purposes. With this now widespread and commonplace dependence on digital technologies has also come the sort of general disciplinary disconnect from digital writing instruction that was already being attributed to traditional writing instruction (see Connors; Graff; Vandenberg).

CMC scholarship and pedagogy asks us and our students to critically examine the sociopolitical agendas that are embedded in writing technologies and to consider the multiplicities of cultural perspectives and contexts. But as digital writing studies has moved further into the realm of social criticism, it has also divorced itself from the emphasis on functional technical skills that so marked its early years. Sheridan-Rabideau, McLaughlin, and Novak studied some of the resulting confusion that such a departure has caused. They note that in university writing courses, instructors typically teach students from a range of disciplinary backgrounds. The disciplinary values, methods, and expectations that students bring into the writing class become evident in Web authoring courses as the students and their instructors struggle with competing ideologies, definitions, and assumptions of what it means to be technologically literate (348-9). For many instructors, the growing preference for social/ideological theories of literacy, and post-process theories of composition have redefined what we mean when we speak about literacy.

Technological literacy as an ideological model of critical/social theory, it seems, cannot readily coexist with what are now understood as autonomous literacy approaches (see Street, *Literacy in Theory and Practice*; Street, *Social Literacies*) that view computer-based literacy merely as a set of mechanically acquired skills. This is understandable. As Selber notes:

> Functional literacy has been reduced to a simple nuts-and-bolts matter, to a fairly basic skill based on mastery of technique [...] This view understands functional literacy in much the same manner that current-traditional rhetoric understood written texts: not as socially or rhetorically embedded but as expressions of grammar, style, and form, all of which could be learned in prescriptive and decontextualized ways. (32)

Functional literacy skills have, for many teachers, become an invisible part of the writing process.

The tendency has been to ignore the important aspects of necessary functional knowledge and awareness of the increasing options in writing for digital technologies. Function itself has come to be recast as a mere afterthought (if thought of at all) of the more scholarly relevant subject of a social/critical technological literacy model. Selber argues that students need to be exposed to multiple ways of conceiving literacy, both functional and critical literacies as well as other types of literacies like rhetorical and visual literacies involved in Web site design and production (35). Selber, however, does not propose that we approach functional literacy from a functionalist perspective. He is not suggesting that we return to a narrow focus on text production, grammar drills, or spelling and punctuation exercises. Rather, he is arguing for a postcritical stance, that is, a contextual reckoning through which we view functional literacy in computer-based writing as an integral and necessary aspect of the broader social problems and concerns that are addressed as technological literacy.

From such a postcritical perspective, we would further argue that we not only pay attention to functional literacy for the sake of our students, but that we also need to recognize that our own functional literacies in the technologies we use for teaching, for instance, system and workstation security, are integral and necessary aspects of the work we do. With few exceptions[1] we have paid little attention to the impact that system peripherals and institutional expectations for technological know-how have on our own day-to-day communication and teaching practices. Composition's role in transdisciplinary discourse on technological innovation and design futures in the academy is that of passive recipient unless we can demonstrate functional/mechanical know-how to accompany our theoretical arguments.

Because the field of Composition seems reticent when it comes to acquiring the literacies of what Gunther Kress terms the New Media Age, the field risks squandering the gains in scholarly and pedagogical value it has made in the academy as what we do with technology becomes merely the new "business as usual." One symptom of this has been the pendulum swinging too far away from emphasis on the "how to" aspects of writing with technologies. Understandably, in view of the general shift in recent years to critical and social theories of literacy, there is a general tendency to ignore the ecological role of functional literacies associated with the day-to-day technologies that inform the study and teaching of written communication.

In its narrowest sense, literacy may be seen merely as the basic ability to read and write certain forms of scripted text. This view stands in contrast to other ideological constructs of literacy such as those based on activism, criticism, personal growth, or cultural gatekeeping. Yet the key common feature across literacy ideologies is that literacy always involves making and doing and, therefore, requires some degree of functional knowledge and ability within the making and doing.[2] Selber argues that rather than the sort of functional approaches to writing instruction often equated basic skills learning and teaching methods fostered by current-traditional rhetoric, "functional literacy need not be disempowering and that functional and critical literacies need not be mutually exclusive" (497-98).

For writing instruction professionals, as basic educational computing has become increasingly mainstream, non-techie friendly, and highly automated, the technologies and the infrastructures that sponsor them have become increasingly commonplace and rhetorically invisible. Just as Selfe and Hilligoss predicted more than a decade ago:

> It is possible to imagine that computers (or some related word like hypermedia) may become a linguistically "unmarked" term for devices of reading and writing, even for text, as paper, pen, and type have been....What we have here named as knowledge will evaporate into the tacit practices of any number of fields, with both losses and gains for us and, more important, for those who come after us. (340)

An example of the crucial day-to-day technologies that we pay little attention to are computer security peripherals. System security hardware and software have become increasingly necessary for supporting digital writing practices for students and instructors alike. In terms of access and success, these technologies have become increasingly, and some might say insidiously, invisible gatekeepers of technology-based writing instruction and new-media composing. They serve as barriers, only visible on breakdown, for students and instructors who do not fully understand how they function. So, why haven't we paid more attention to them? Research and teaching in composition is already demanding enough. Do we now have to be the technicians also? Well, if we want to be players in the transdisciplinary conversations that are shaping the directions of higher education, then yes. And we need to focus with some awareness of the infrastructural frameworks that we operate in and how those infrastructures both shape and are informed by the basic functions of our own workspaces and the systems we depend on (DeVoss, Cushman, and Grabill 16). Even for writing instructors who already have, or wish to, move into the realm of new-media composing that has students reinvent the possibilities for writing (such as video editing, podcasting, and other forms of multimedia presentations), functional technological literacy is a crucial element for inclusion in institutional design. DeVoss, Cushman, and Grabill state:

> To understand the contexts that make possible and limit, shape and constrain, and facilitate and prevent new-media composing, new-media teachers and students need to be able to account for the complex interrelationships of material, technical, discursive, institutional, and cultural systems....Our claim is that in order to teach and understand new media composing, some understanding of new-media infrastructure is necessary. Without such an understanding, writing teachers and students will fail to anticipate and actively participate in the emergence of such infrastructures, thereby limiting—rhetorically, technically, and institutionally— what is possible for our students to write and learn. (37)

DeVoss, Cushman, and Grabill contend that without a means to recognize, comprehend, and account for the infrastructural contexts of new-media composing, students (and instructors) can never fully come to grips—both critically and functionally—with the social, political, cultural, and material aspects of technological literacies that composition has the potential to explore.

This essay takes DeVoss, Cushman, and Grabill's argument for an infrastructural framework in Composition Studies to a micro level by looking at one aspect of the composition instructor's mediated environment—workspace system security. It is one aspect of the day-to-day "clutter" that is integral to the institutional/pedagogical infrastructure, yet seemingly invisible—until the system is compromised. It is our contention that implementing a successful infrastructural framework for mediated composition studies will require greater disciplinary appreciation for the value of such mechanical micro-knowledge of the "mundane" systems that inform every aspect of the teaching we do. An assessment of such current functional micro-knowledge literacy practices suggests that we may have some ways to go.

A case-study survey and a short online follow-up survey (described here in the following pages) were conducted on awareness of computer security peripherals by writing program faculty at a large state university. These surveys illustrate just how far outside of the loop we already are when it comes to mechanical know-how of the very technologies that inform our teaching and scholarship. The purpose here is not to offer yet another account of "problems" that composition instructors have with technology. Mediated composition for the most part is pretty old hat now. Technical skills and pedagogical applications and outcomes are accessible and simple to acquire for anyone who wants to and has the support (and/or mandate) from their institution. Rather, this essay underscores Selber's view that theoretical awareness on its own in Composition Studies is no longer sufficient. Mechanical awareness, if not expertise, about the most basic computer functions is also crucial to awareness of the social and cultural impacts of the shift in meaning making from page to screen. Technological literacy in all aspects of electronic discourse will determine our discipline's ability to reinvent writing in the New Media Age and ensure that we are active participants in a multimodal future.

"Protect your chicken from Dokken"

This slogan is one in a series of ads produced by Norton Internet Security. Other slogans include "Protect your caterpillar from Kimbo Slice," "Protect your unicorn from Dolph Lundgren," and "Protect your oscillating fan from David Hasselhoff." While these ads present the information in a rather absurd and humorous way, the commercials effectively communicate that your computer is weak and vulnerable, and viruses and other malware are strong and dangerous. These ads feed into the public's growing concern for online security, as do other ads by companies such as K7 TotalSecurity, Trend Micro, and McAfee. All of these companies are effectively communicating the same message: you are vulnerable to attack, our company can protect you, update now. The ads are stating that you are already in danger: your finances, your credit, your records, and even your very identity may be compromised, hacked into, stolen, or destroyed. If it hasn't happened to you already, it's only a matter of time until it does.

Scare tactics to sell product aside, computer system security is clearly an important issue as more and more institutions and individuals go digital. A 2004 cover report on security products in *Consumer Reports* titled "Protect yourself online," warns, "Shielding your computer from online hazards is no longer an option. It's a necessity. What were once annoyances—viruses and spam—have become major concerns" (12). Just a year later, *Consumer Reports* issued a second exclusive feature rating security products, this time titled "Net Threat Rising," stating, "Use the Internet at home and you have a 1-in-3 chance of suffering computer damage, financial loss, or both because of a computer virus or spyware that sneaks onto your computer" (12). Recent events with online hackers such as the collective known as Anonymous or the group Lulzsec have shown that even groups such as Fox News, Public Broadcasting, Bank of America, and even governmental agencies are not safe. Anonymous and Lulzsec have exploited gaps in the Internet security of these groups to embarrass them and bring attention to these vulnerabilities. Their lax security has resulted in serious leaks, such as company emails and other documents and private information about individuals within these groups.[3]

This is not to say that it is only people in these high-profile positions that need to be aware of internet security and the functions of their computers. System and online security may be the most pervasive yet least visible aspects of mediated writing instruction. Advertised security and virus protection services and *Consumer Reports* cover stories are strong indicators that personal system security has become a mainstream issue as more and more of the public rely on online services and are potential victims of phishing, pharming, spying, spamming, adware, and so forth. Of course, personal workstation/system security is something most writing scholars and teachers have long had to cope with, particularly as more and more of our academic institutions require online and networked correspondence. As education professionals, the separation of workplace between home and office is blurred, perhaps more than most professions. Cross-contamination between workplace and home systems, corrupted student files, and increased visibility via institutional Web sites increase the potential for risk for security problems. Further, even in the "official" workplace, proficiency in installing, operating, and maintaining the hardware and software peripherals that are necessary for security at the user end of academic information technology systems is often the responsibility of faculty, even for systems that are owned, managed, and serviced by the institution. At the same time, we suspect it is unlikely in many academic institutions that non-technical faculty are actually consulted in the computing infrastructure policies and designs that office workstations are dependent on. Selber suggests that, "If universities are not quick to consult humanists on technical issues, then teachers of writing and communication must look for ways to enter the conversations that shape technical infrastructures on their campuses" (195).

Selber is quite right about the need for faculty to be aware and involved of computing technologies as they concern institutional policy, but for day-to-day routine instructional and administrative purposes functioning, the divide between computing specialist and writing faculty may already be too great. Selfe even goes so far as to say that "technology is either boring or frightening to most humanists" ("Technology and Literacy" 1164), and Chris Anson, in an interview with Coley and Erickson, states that humanists often feel that learning about technology "take[s] time from their work." While some in Writing Studies may actually welcome opportunities to serve as system watchdogs for their institution and take the time to stay current with security updates, backup systems, spam filters, ad-buster software, and the like, we suspect they are relatively few. "Computer maintenance technician" is not posted in most writing instructor job descriptions, and it is fair to say that the majority of our profession would be uncomfortable (perhaps fearful) with the suggestion that they accept such a role. Our top academic journals value scholarly theoretical knowledge over practical, applied knowledge so there is little disciplinary incentive, in terms of promotion and tenure, to sacrifice commitment to the former to devote publishing effort to the latter.

An interesting thing about computer technology is the tacit assumption that faculty teaching on behalf of an academic institution will take on the functional skills necessary for protecting the security of the institution's data network. There is no other high-end technology for literacy education that requires such a commitment. Copiers, telephones, projectors, and all those other technologies that are essential for teaching require minimal operating skills, and less responsibility for maintenance. Sure, instructors may handle minor maintenance problems like removing a feeder-tray paper jam or changing a burned out projector bulb, but in terms of actual servicing, it's "hands-off instructors, bring in the mechanic." Yet, when it comes to computers, there is an assumed level of technical ability for instructors, not merely as users and work station administrators, but as front-line protectors against hackers, spammers, crackers, phreakers, cyberpunks and malware writers. Somehow, the "personal" in personal computing, even in institutional settings, implies that if the machine sits on your desk, it is nominally yours, but the photocopier in the workroom belongs to the department/university. So, why isn't this issue something we talk about more? While most writing instruction still takes place primarily in traditional classrooms the technologies on our office desks are no less pedagogically relevant for writing instruction than the technologies of the mediated classroom or the digital contexts of the Web.

Even DeVoss, Cushman, and Grabill while arguing for an infrastructural lens for composition instruction focus primarily on the student/classroom perspective on infrastructure. The instructor workspace setting receives only scant attention. Obviously workplace situations and conditions are determined by their local contexts, but personal and anecdotal experience suggests that most writing programs do not have *carte blanche* for all their technological needs and desires. Much of what determines workspace setups has less to do with individual instructors or program directors than with departmental administrators and the decision-making on macro and micro levels that go on behind the scenes. Budgetary concerns, office administration politics, personal and technological favoritism, seniority, unforeseen crises, upper administrative directives, to name a few are a constant fact of life in university departments. Multiple decisions, directly and indirectly, are made involving workspace technologies that are part of the infrastructural framework that is the underlying context for pedagogical practices. Yet these day-to-day workplace realities (and functional workplace literacies) are generally ignored in our literature because they are so localized and seemingly separate from the teaching part of what we do.

A Case of Basic Functional Know-How

We wanted to find out just how much time, effort, and responsibility writing instructors were putting into their office workstation security peripherals in order to ensure the technologies would support their teaching. The motive behind the two surveys was to see just how functionally tech-savvy full-time composition instructors were with basic workstation security. It seemed to us that if Selber's call for a postcritical stance on composing and DeVoss, Cushman, and Grabill's call for an activist approach to infrastructure are to be implemented in programmatic and individual levels in the new information literacy age, we need to see just where we stand to know where to begin. As system security is an underlying factor affecting all aspects of innovation, policy, and practice in institutional computing, an assessment of basic functional awareness of end-users would illustrate how prepared composition professionals to effectively respond to those calls.

The initial informal survey (see Appendix 1) was a small-scale case-study survey conducted in 2008. This survey was conducted by Peter through face-to-face interviews in the subjects' offices. Each participant had a computer in the office issued by the university's English department. The survey began with a few general questions to establish frequency of use of computer technologies for teaching and then went on to ask specific questions relating to basic critical security functions such as scanning for update of the operating system, virus protection, and firewall. The next group of questions related to e-mail and Internet security settings, the use of backup systems, and estimates of overall time spent on securing and updating the computer workstation. The last questions related to technical assistance and any changes to course design or teaching practices mandated by institutional policies or changes affecting instructional software. For comparative purposes, in addition to questions about office computer security, Peter also asked the participants about their attention to security on their home computers.

The follow-up survey was conducted by Ryan anonymously online in 2011 (see Appendix 2). The purpose was to both update information and add additional insights toward our central claim. The survey followed a very similar pattern to the initial survey, starting with general questions about computer use and maintenance and then moving into more specific questions about operating system updates, virus protection, firewalls, and additional security measures.

Both surveys drew their participants from full-time instructors, lecturers, and professors teaching in the writing programs at a large state university. Twenty-eight instructors participated in the initial survey, and 18 participated in the follow up. Because the second survey was conducted anonymously, it is unclear how many of the respondents participated in both surveys. However, it is safe to assume that there is some overlap. All of the participants in both surveys had university-issued computers. The faculty taught a range of writing courses including general university requirements, first-year writing, upper-division writing, and a number of writing program electives at the undergraduate level.

For the initial survey, Peter interviewed each of the 28 instructors in their offices rather than having them respond to a questionnaire on their own. He found that for questions concerning awareness of individual computer workstation security settings, this approach helped to prevent the participants from checking their office machines and self-correcting. The result was a lot of ambiguous and inaccurate responses about system security from a group of writing instructors who are otherwise very proficient in operating computers, particularly for teaching purposes. Many of the participants apologized in advance for not knowing settings or attempted to check the accuracy of their responses during the interview despite assurances that the survey was not a test and that findings would be confidential. The unease many expressed about lacking expertise and due care of their computer security peripherals suggest that on some level there is an expectation that they should be more technically savvy and devote more time to operational maintenance of their office machines—this despite the fact that they all already teach full time.

It is important to note this unease, inaccuracy, and ambiguity when reflecting upon answers given for the anonymous and more general second survey. There was no way to verify the answers that the respondents gave, as Peter was able to in the first survey, but the anonymity provided by the second survey does offer some protection and ease that the initial survey did not.

Almost all of the instructors who participated in the initial survey reported a high use of multiple computer functions for teaching, including word-processing, e-mail, online instruction, discussion boards, document preparation, Web site development, file transfer, electronic editing, assessment, and so forth. Most of the full-time instructors at the university who teach for the writing program teach in computer labs, teach online, or teach hybrid courses for at least part of their workload. Only 2 of the 28 instructors said they did not teach any designated CMC courses and used their computers mostly for e-mail and document preparation. All of the instructors said they used computers daily for teaching functions.

In both surveys, all of the security and privacy settings about which we asked the instructors were, from our perspective, fairly basic. They included such subjects as virus scans, firewalls, browser security, and back-up systems. When we say that the settings were "fairly basic" we realize that the term is relative. We are not talking about the sort of system management that requires specialized technical knowledge, but basic, low-tech user awareness of the off/on switches and settings for essential security applications. To use an automotive analogy, it is the equivalent of checking the tire pressure; to put it in terms of cooking, it is the equivalent of following instructions for microwaving a prepared frozen dinner. Technical expertise with computers in the initial group Peter surveyed ranged from participants who saw their computers as little more than turbo-charged typewriters and expected to use them for teaching support with minimal user maintenance (to continue the automotive and cooking analogies think passive seatbelt restraints or pizza delivery), to instructors who built their own computers and spent a great deal of time keeping peripherals maintained and updated. Most, however, fell into a mid-range of writing professionals who were proficient in using their hardware and software in multiple ways for a variety teaching purposes and were at the very least aware of such things as virus scans, firewalls, and e-mail filters.

In the follow-up survey, the range was equally broad. Exactly 50% of respondents said that they had a "strong" or "good" sense of Internet security, with the other 50% saying they had "some," "a weak," or no sense of Internet security. Only 33% of respondents said that they were in charge of the security on their university-issued computer, despite 50% admitting that they were the ones who should be responsible for this. This is an even more surprising finding when considering the fact that 83.3% of instructors stated that Internet security was "a subject about which English/writing instructors should be knowledgeable" and not a single respondent responded that they should not be knowledgeable in this subject (the remaining 16.7% stated they were unsure). This finding reiterates Peter's previous finding: the instructors felt a sense that this was a subject about which they should know, but they were not entirely comfortable with their current knowledge on the subject.

All of the instructors that Peter met with face to face had self-purchased computers at home which they used extensively for teaching purposes. Almost all of the home computers were PCs. Only two instructors had purchased Macintosh computers for their home use. Both of these instructors stated that they understood PCs were more vulnerable to virus attacks and had purchased Macs primarily because of security concerns for their personal investments in their home computer systems. A number of the instructors, even those with university-issued wireless laptops, mentioned that they used their own home computers more than the office computers. This was especially the case for instructors who taught online or hybrid courses. Overall, the instructors spent far more time maintaining their home systems and were far more aware of security needs and settings on their home computers than on their office computers. Results of the second survey reflected this: 72.2% of the instructors stated that they were in charge of the security for their home computers or personal laptops, while only 33.3% stated that they were in charge of the security on their university-issued computers.

Fourteen of the participants in the initial survey said that they ran a firewall application on their home computers, while only 4 said they ran a firewall on their office computer, and when Peter checked actual settings on office computers, one instructor unknowingly had the firewall turned off. Eighteen instructors said they did not know if they were running a firewall on their office computer. Out of those, 10 actually were but did not know it. This carried over into the second survey where 27.8% of respondents were also unsure of whether or not they were running a firewall.

Only 6 participants said they ran spyware and adware blockers on their office computer (only 2 actually did), while 14 said they ran blockers on their home computer. Peter was able to assume that this information was accurate because they were able to identify the software application they ran at home. In most cases they cited Spybot and/or AdAware. In the follow-up survey, 83.3% said that they ran pop-up blockers, 33.3% said that they ran adware blockers, and only 22.2% said that they ran script blockers. Pop-ups seemed to be a greater concern than more pressing Internet security issues. Only 2 of the 18 respondents to the second survey could name additional software that they had outside of those mentioned above to protect their computers.

Only 1 participant in the initial survey had a full backup system for the office computer, while 7 said they had one at home. (2 participants thought the office system was automatically backed up by the department—it isn't). This response differed greatly in the online survey where 75% of respondents said that they backed up files onto an external USB drive and an additional 8.3% of respondents said that they backed up files onto a Web-based hosting service.

On the whole, office systems did not fare well in terms of user awareness and maintenance. Seventeen of the participants in the initial survey were running Microsoft XP as their operating system, 3 had Windows 2000, and 5 had Windows 98. Because the XP operating system provides many automated features with Service Pack 2 that had been set up by computing administrators before issuing them to instructors, many of the office computers were set to automatically scan and install critical security updates. Those with older operating systems were less likely to manually access Windows Update and run a scan (only 11.1% of respondents in the second survey ran manual system updates; this is likely due to a larger prevalence of automatic system updates in newer operating systems, but it is unclear whether or not users were actually taking advantage of the automatic updates).

Non-automated tasks further highlighted the discrepancy. While all the office computers ran virus protection at start up, 19 subjects in the initial survey said they had never run a full virus scan of the hard drive and 31.3% of the subjects in the second survey were unsure when the last anti-virus scan took place. When it came to virus protection updates, 7 of the participants in the initial survey did not know if their virus protection was updated, while 9 said they never updated their virus protection. It turned out that 8 of the "nevers" and "don't knows" were automatically updated. The interesting thing about this was that while the participants were more attentive to security needs on their home computers, actual virus infections were pretty much equal at both home and office. Thirteen instructors said their office computers had been infected at some point, and 14 experienced this on their home computer. These similar numbers may suggest that ownership still might not result in better maintenance. A number described infections serious enough to slow down or crash their systems requiring hard drive reformatting, and in at least two cases causing irreparable damage. One participant described a relatively "benign" virus that infected his workplace computer though an e-mail attachment. A soft drink manufacturer logo would pop up, along with music, and the CD drawer would open. "The virus also attached itself to most of my computer's sub-directories. I called tech support, and they came over and cleaned it out. But by then I had already sent it out to a whole lot of other people on a national listserv. Whoops!"

Only 2 out of all the instructors in the initial survey were aware of what their Internet security and privacy settings were on their office computer. This number was far higher in the second survey (only 16.7% stated that they were unsure of their settings), but follow-up questions revealed that as high as 50% of the respondents were unsure of settings for running scripts, blocking ads, and real-time spyware/virus scanning.

Another discrepancy turned up in the amount of time participants spent on peripheral matters. When participants were asked how many unsolicited (i.e., spam) messages they received on a daily basis, results averaged at around 33 messages per day in the initial survey and only about 4 per day in the second survey. When Peter asked participants in the initial survey if they had a spam filter installed, 16 said they did, 6 said they did not, and 6 didn't know. Out of the 16 who said they did filter spam, 7 did not actually have a spam filter set up. In the second survey, however, nearly everyone (93.8%) stated that they had a spam filter. This, most likely, reflects a change in e-mail providers between the first and second surveys.

When Peter asked the participants in the first survey how much time they spent with e-mail they felt was "a waste of their time," that is scanning, opening, reading, and deleting mail that they deemed irrelevant or unnecessary, the average came out to 98 minutes per week (but only 11 minutes per week in the second survey), while the amount of time they spent maintaining and securing their computer systems averaged 27 minutes per week (about 22 minutes in the second survey). Aside from the obvious difference in how this non-teaching time is prioritized, the grand total for peripheral time usage on a weekly basis for 28 instructors is 3403 minutes, almost 57 hours. That is an average of 2 hours a week per instructor—almost 2 full class sessions. This is not insignificant considering that the time spent maintaining security, both at home and in the office, is not recognized as work time, like grading and course preparation, even though it is necessary to ensure effective conditions for teaching. There is a tacit understanding that devoting such time to securing and maintaining the technologies for teaching is institutionally required and is just an unquestioned part of the job—merely the price one pays for the benefit of working with computers. As one survey participant suggested, the demands of computer technologies for educators was like going back to the days where the teacher of the one-room schoolhouse had to chop wood, mend furniture, and do many other chores simply to keep the schoolhouse in functioning condition in order to do their job.

On a related note, Peter also asked the participants if they had ever had to change or compromise their writing course design or teaching practices due to institutional policies or changes in instructional software or hardware. Eighteen in the initial survey responded that they did, and cited online discussion and teaching systems that get dropped in favor of another, security policies that require learning new Web editing programs, and desktop publishing and word-processing programs that get dropped. Three in the second survey also stated that they did, all 3 citing Blackboard constraints. Generally, instructors were not happy about having to give up practices they had become comfortable and proficient with and forced to learn new ones on their own time in order to do their jobs. They were particularly frustrated in having to discard lesson plans and projects they had spent a lot of time developing because they were incompatible with the new programs. One described having to restructure his dissertation in progress because of his university's new IT constraints, and another stated, "I don't want any more mid-term surprises. I don't believe it when they say the system will run forever. We should have more input in tech support for the work we do."

Following the initial survey, Peter conducted an interview with the Humanities Computing Facility (HCF) Technology Support Analyst Coordinator who supervised technical support for a number of departments in the College of Arts and Sciences, including the English department. HCF maintains about 600 machines and works with about 500 faculty and teaching assistants. HCF for the college consists of two full-time staff and one part-time student worker. The coordinator explained that a big part of the problem with security issues was that with so many departments, programs, and individuals in the college, there was no accurate inventory on who was operating what machines. The HCF coordinator did report, however, that there was a good deal of ongoing discussion among university administrators and information technology specialists about security, and a number of ideas for future policies were being considered. One possibility was to require all university system subscribers to use complex passwords (combinations of upper and lower case letters, numbers, and punctuation) that would automatically expire after a certain time and require updating to continue access (this requirement has since been implemented). Another possibility being considered was to remove administrative permissions on personal workstations so that faculty and staff would only function as users. This would mean that any time someone wanted to download a program they would have to call HCF to approve and install the new software. Although highly restrictive, the effect would be to prevent backdoor intrusions. Although this seems rather drastic and likely unworkable given current technology support conditions, in theory it would effectively absolve individual instructors from the responsibility of securing their workstations. Whether this would actually be true in practice or not is debatable. The obvious impact would be on the sense of personal identity that instructors imbue their computers with and the teaching they do with those computers.

In the meantime, the HCF coordinator explained that the university considered users responsible for the security of their workstations, even though there is no unified security concept in place. He reckoned it would probably require 1 hour per person to train and explain security settings and maintenance—that's for 500 people just in humanities. He estimated that up to 50% of the work that HCF did was related to security prevention and cure. The coordinator's observation on the cause for the security problem was that when it comes to the functional side of computer technology in the university, people on all levels make decisions about computers and usage in a vacuum. "As people learn more about technology," he stated, "they implement it without being aware of the consequences." The coordinator's view of the future was that of more policies on computer use to be handed down to instructors that would require even more attention to peripherals and more user responsibility for maintaining security.

Paying Attention to Technology

A review of articles over the past decade in Writing Studies journals reveals little to no scholarly attention or interest in technologies related to computer security. If discussed at all, system security is only obliquely mentioned in the context of providing secure password-protected environments for students to write in, but for the most part the subject is neglected. In Garza and Hern's *Kairos* article on the use of wikis as tools for collaborative writing, the authors address the pedagogical potential for students to function differently in the "open environments" of wikis from the "closed environments" of other learning formats. They also acknowledge resulting institutional reaction and concern for student protection. The originally open wikis the authors present as examples of their collaborative venture are now password protected. However, there is no overt discussion in the article about just exactly what the concerns of their institution are and how these may have impacted on teaching practices. In the same *Kairos* issue, Hewett and Powers address principles and processes for training online writing instructors. While training methods, both functional and theoretical, are discussed in detail, the focus is on the pedagogical issues of instructor training. There is no discussion of instructors' work setting functions and the realities of the workstation administration and system security aspects of maintaining and sustaining online instruction. The sense one gets in reviewing the literature on mediated composition studies is that the mechanics of computing and computing systems, the security protocols, and support technologies are not worthy of intellectual consideration—that somehow these things are not relevant to pedagogy.

By comparison, Selber points to a computer competency test offered by the computer science department at Florida State University that has substantial components of its study guide devoted to important security issues including, "Computer Virus, Macro Virus, Worm, Denial of Service attacks, Antivirus Software, Virus Hoaxes" (16-17). This is not to suggest that every article in writing journals should include functional aspects of computer mediated education, or that writing instructors should necessarily take on the role of computing specialist. But the absence of any emphasis on protection and system security highlights that these very issues that are considered significant and basic elements of digital literacy are not recognized as significant elements, both for our students and ourselves. Requirements for security software and hardware both limit and necessarily validate continued use of computer-mediated writing studies, yet these functional elements of the workplace appear to have received little validation in the discipline.

While it is in the best interests of the individual academic institutions to provide security and backup peripheral services for all subscribers to its system, writing and technology scholars Charles Moran ("Emerging") and Mark Werner have pointed out that funding to support peripheral technologies and upgrades may come at the cost of additional faculty lines, internal grants, student support services, and learning materials that are not compatible with the technologies. Further, because in-house tech support is often sparse or stretched to the limit, institutions often require that faculty themselves keep their workstations' security systems upgraded, often with little or no training. For example, at the large state university where we conducted our surveys on knowledge of workstation security, faculty and students were warned during a virus attack that they would be "kicked off" the university system if it was determined that their computers were infected or vulnerable to infection. The university's writing program offers around 400 sections per semester. Roughly 20% of those are designated CMC courses, although all of the instructors we surveyed utilized computer support. Shortly after the virus attack, new security protocols were put in place that required faculty to install new software and reconfigure access procedures to online accounts. In another move, WebBoard, an online discussion board subscribed to by the English department and used by many writing instructors teaching hybrid and online courses, was cancelled in favor of the university supported Blackboard system. Access to, and use of, the new discussion board is controlled not by individual programs or departments, but by the university's Information Technology office which disabled many of the "manager" options and features that had previously been available to instructors.

It would seem that Selber's call for a postcritical approach to computer literacy not only creates a space for bringing awareness and questions of technology and education design into the writing classroom, but can also be implemented for examining the multiliteracy (critical, functional, social, rhetorical) aspects of the workspace. It is the functional literacies that seem to get the least amount of attention. DeVoss, Cushman, and Grabill effectively illustrate this point in their account of a breakdown in security policies and technological needs between the institution and multimedia composition instruction on the subject of memory storage in mediated classroom workstations. The authors and their students bring an analysis of preexisting institutional policies and infrastructures to negotiate change and introduce a new structure for new-media composing. The authors' skill, experience, and technical know-how in mediated instruction and system management, along with their commitment to multimedia composition, provide a functional as well as scholarly/pedagogical basis from which to transform a rupture (their term) in institutional policies into a teachable opportunity for themselves and their students. But for most writing instructors who use computers for their teaching and administrative duties, technology needs (predominantly e-mail, word-processing, and Internet-based research) are relatively more discrete than those invested in new-media composing. However, the necessary peripherals for such needs are no less than those for more high-tech end users in other disciplines such as engineering, the sciences, and business. Increasingly, writing instructors (including full time, adjunct and teaching assistants), who are often among the lowest paid university faculty, are having to learn to be end-user technicians or lose their required access "privileges," pay out of pocket for necessary home computer work stations, personal back-up systems and other peripherals, and redesign, reconstruct, or abandon teaching materials that are rendered obsolete by mandated university computing policies.

Conclusions

Evolving technological infrastructures and the challenges for composition professionals to play a role in determining the future of mediated education highlight the necessity for functional technological literacy. For instance, as this survey shows, with the increasing threats to system security, identity theft, and institutional expectations for end-user/employee technical skills, it seems likely that the technologies we use to teach writing will require even greater attention to the functional aspects of digital literacy than we already do. A postcritical perspective may provide the theoretical space in which Writing Studies may play a role in new information literacy designs, but at the same time, we should not privilege only the deeper philosophical questions at the expense of awareness and discussion of the basic functional knowledges and literacies. Despite the fact that most of us get along just fine with our workstation "black boxes" and are happy to let tech support and our lurking software agents keep the systems running, it is clear from the survey that in practical terms, many writing instructors who are already devoting a great deal of time to non-teaching related peripherals may lack sufficient knowledge and awareness about even basic security operations on their workstations. Perhaps this will come as no great surprise to those who read this essay, and therein lies the crux of the problem. The lack of know-how of basic computing maintenance in the survey results reveals a blind spot in the perspective that many writing professionals have in their relationship with technology: it appears as though many of those involved in the survey did not have a personal relationship with what have essentially become the tools of our trade, computers. The results of the survey should come as a shock—that so few of the participants were aware of and actively maintained their computer workstations while simultaneously considering maintenance a significant and necessary part of their jobs as Writing Studies professionals. But we suspect that this is the case for writing instructors in most institutions. Selfe states, "if teachers pay attention to technology and literacy problems on a local level, they can collectively work to construct a large vision of these issues on a professional level" (*Technology* 147). But this can only work if the problems are first recognized as problems. We first have to know that there are blind spots and then we can pay attention to them and come up with strategies to address them.

But the pragmatic question that still remains for many Writing Studies professionals is *how*? How do they find the time and motivation to do this? Computer technology provides wonderful opportunities for instructors to teach and for students to learn in exciting and innovative ways, but should writing instructors have to devote substantial amounts of personal time and personal resources to maintain the systems that are essential to do their job? Should they have to assume increased personal responsibility for risks of security breaches in an institution that requires instructors to use computers for correspondence, administration, grade reporting, self-evaluations, and so forth, but does not provide adequate technical support? Most of the writing instructors we surveyed indicated that they felt they could be more functionally literate and vigilant when it came to security peripherals, but were concerned about the extra time this would take beyond the time they were already devoting to security and maintenance. They all recognized the importance and value of computer security, but there was no consensus on just how much they were responsible for the university's property. It is unlikely that problems such as these will be solved universally, but if, as Selfe suggests (above), specific problems can be tackled creatively on a local level (and we would add here that it is the responsibility of those already technologically savvy to lead the way in this), then we can claim more disciplinary space that includes functional literacy. For instance, in the very act of conducting an interview survey on workstation security, many of the participants came face to face with their own levels of awareness and proficiency of this functional aspect of their professional work. As a result, many of the participants not only acquired new knowledge of their security software and hardware peripherals and ways to maintain and update them, but expressed desire to learn more and to keep up with ongoing and future developments in system management. In this case, the key to recognizing and dealing with a technical blind spot was simply to talk to people and see firsthand what their actual awareness was. It is a good place to start.

Here's the thing. If, as writing professionals, we are to have a place at the table when it comes to infrastructural awareness and transdisciplinary discourse on new information and multimedia designs in teaching and scholarship, then we are responsible for making that space. We need to be proficient in the functional literacies that allow for critical analysis of the infrastructures that sponsor and implement institutional policies and electronic technologies. We need, as one survey participant observed, to be willing to reacquire the role of the teacher of the one-room school house. We need to be active participants in all the literacies of digital writing, from the functional knowledges of the material workspace (both office and classroom) to the institutional infrastructures that the workspaces are embedded in, to the disciplinary and transdisciplinary theories and questions that inform scholarly discourse in digital composition and new media studies. If we are going to work with computers, if these technologies enable us to reinvent writing and envision the myriad potentials that technological innovations can offer for practical, social, and critical pedagogies, then we need to know how and why they do what they do. In his review of the twentieth anniversary of the journal, *Computers and Composition*, Moran observes that scholarship on mediated writing studies has generally moved from emphasis on eliminating the "drudgery" of writing, improving student writing, and improving the marginal status of writing instruction to a more recent emphasis on looking "less at and more through technology" (345). Perhaps the pendulum has swung too far away from the "looking at" of technology and writing. Perhaps it is time to apply the critical lens of looking through to reclaim a new emphasis on the functional aspects of mediated writing studies.

It is certainly a dilemma, and one, which more and more writing professionals and the field will be forced to face, whether they want to or not as computer peripherals become an increasingly overt aspect of writing instruction. Selfe's (*Technology*) call that we pay more attention to the social and political agendas that construct and drive the connections between technology and literacy is important and necessary. As Writing Studies professionals, we do need to make sure we are active participants in shaping what it means to be technologically literate. Likewise, Selber's call for a postcritical stance by writing instructors underscores the need for Composition Studies to have a voice and an investment in computer literacies and educational technology designs. Additionally, we also need to address the institutionally functional literacies and technical skills that are inherently and integrally bound to the technologies themselves and to question how those functions are relevant to social context. Functional knowledge of security peripherals and other system maintenance software and hardware is increasingly relevant for a field that relies so much on computer technologies for teaching and research. We need to bridge the disconnect between the privileged pedagogical literacies of the mediated classroom that warrant significant space in our scholarly journals, and the day-to-day, mostly invisible, functional literacies of our office workspaces. It is important and necessary that when it comes to digital literacies our scholarship also pays attention to the whole ecology of writing—and that includes the functional.

Appendix 1 – Initial Survey Questions

Name

Date

1. How do you use your office and/or home computer for any aspect of teaching writing, including e-mail, online instruction, document preparation, assessment, information retrieval, and so forth?

2. How often, per day/per week, do you use the computer for these functions?

3. Do you scan your office computer for critical updates? **Yes No**

If yes, how often?
How about your home computer?
Do you scan? **Yes No**

If yes, How often?

4. Do you have a virus protection application on your computer? **Yes No** *(If no, go to 4a)*
If yes, What kind/version?
Do you have it set to run on access (when you turn the computer on)? **Yes No**
How often do you run a full system scan?
How often do you update your virus protection?

4a. Have you ever had a computer virus on your office computer? **Yes No**
What kind?
What happened?
How did you solve the problem?
How do these questions apply to your home computer?

5. Do you have a firewall application on your computer? **Yes No**
If yes, what kind/version?
Do you have it set to run on access (i.e., when you turn the computer on)? **Yes No**
What level of protection/security are your firewall filters set at? **High Medium Low**
How often do you update your firewall software?
How do these questions apply to your home computer?

6. How often do you correspond with students or colleagues by e-mail?
Do you have a SPAM filter your e-mail? **Yes No**
About how many unsolicited e-mail messages do you get on a daily basis?
How often do you check the filter and delete suspected SPAM?
Have you ever opened a message that turned out to be SPAM? **Yes No**
About how often does this happen?
About how much time per day/per week do you spend on e-mail messages you consider to be a waste of your time? At the office? At home?

7. Do you access the Internet? **Yes No**
What are your Internet options for security and privacy set at? **High Medium Low**
Do you ever discover unwanted spyware on your computer? **Yes No**
If yes, what kind?
How often do you delete cookies, your temporary Internet files, your history folder?
How do these questions apply to your home computer?

8. Do you have backup system for your office computer? **Yes No**
Home computer? **Yes No**
If yes, what kind? How often do you back up your system at home or at work?

9. How much time overall, at the office, at home, do you spend securing and updating your system?
How often do you seek out technical assistance from humanities computing, information technology, instructional support? **Yes No**
If yes, how effective has technical assistance been from these sources? Please explain.

10. Have you ever had to compromise or change your writing course design or teaching practices due to institutional policies or institutional changes to instructional software?
Please explain.

Computer Checklist

Hardware
Operating System
Firewall Software
Security Level
Version/Update
Virus Protection
Software Version/Update
Last Scanned
Scheduled Scan
Spam Filter Version - On or Off
Spyware Filter Version/Update
Internet Settings
Browser
Security Level
Privacy Level
Pop Up Blocker
Backup System
Version Scheduled/Last run

Appendix 2 – Follow-Up Survey Questions

1. How do you feel about your knowledge of Internet security?
2. Do you feel that Internet security is a subject about which English/Writing instructors should be knowledgeable?
3. Primarily, who is in charge of Internet security on your home computer or personal laptop?
4. Primarily, who is in charge of Internet security on your office computer or university-issued laptop?
5. Who do you think holds the responsibility for the security of your office computer or university-issued laptop?
6. Is your office computer or university-issued laptop password protected?
7. Do you scan your office computer or university-issued laptop for critical operating system updates?
8. If you answered yes (either manually or automatically) to question number 7, how often are these scans performed?
9. Does your office computer or university-issued laptop have anti-virus software installed?
10. If you answered yes to question 9, who provided this software?
11. Please provide the type of anti-virus software installed on your office computer or university-issued laptop.
12. Approximately how often is this anti-virus software run?
13. Do you have a firewall on your computer?

14. Have you ever had a virus on your office computer or university-issued laptop?
15. If you answered yes to question 15, please explain the type of virus, what it did to your system, and how the issues were resolved to the best of your ability.
16. Do you regularly use wifi on your personal or university-issued laptop?
17. If so, do you adjust security settings when connecting to a public network?
18. Do you store sensitive student information (grades and/or personal information) on your office computer or university-issued laptop?
19. If you answered yes to question 18, what type of service do you use to do so?
20. Do you back up these files elsewhere?
21. Which Internet browser do you use on your office computer or university-issued laptop?
22. What are your browser security settings set to?
23. When using your browser on your office computer or university-issued laptop, do you use a pop-up blocker?
24. When using your browser on your office computer or university-issued laptop, do you use a script blocker (such as No-Script)?
25. When using your browser on your office computer or university-issued laptop, do you use an ad blocker (such as Adblock)?
26. When using your browser on your office computer or university-issued laptop, do you use a real-time virus scanner, often part of your virus protection suite?
27. When using your browser on your office computer or university-issued laptop, do you use a Web site advisor that lets you know if sites have been reported as dangerous (such as McAfee SiteAdvisor)?
28. Do you generally adjust the privacy settings on Web sites that contain your personal information (such a social networking sites, dating sites, or any other sites that contain a profile)?
29. Do you browse Facebook or other sites with your personal information in secure mode when given the option (https:// at the beginning of the address instead of simply http://)?
30. Do you use an e-mail system that filters spam messages?
31. On average, how many spam e-mails do you think that you receive per week that are not caught by your filter?
32. On average, how much time do you think you spend per week deleting or dealing with these spam e-mails?
33. How often do you open spam messages thinking that they are legitimate e-mail messages?
34. How often do legitimate e-mail messages accidentally get routed into your spam folder?
35. Have you ever accidentally downloaded a file attached to a spam message?
36. Have you ever accidentally opened a link in a spam message?
37. How often do you seek assistance for your office computer or university-issued laptop from humanities computing, information technology, or instructional support?
38. How effective has this assistance been?
39. How much total time per week do you spend securing and updating your office computer or university-issued laptop?

40. Have you ever had to compromise or change your writing course or teaching practices due to institutional policies or changes to instructional software? Please explain.
41. Have you ever had problems with a class you were teaching due to computer problems or computer security issues? Please explain.
42. Do you think that the security on your office computer or university-issued laptop is related to Internet security for your students? Please explain.

Notes

1. For instance, Moberly's article examining spam in the context of often conflated concepts of public speech and commercial speech offers an interesting perspective on filtering technologies for integrating functional and technological literacies into a teachable moment.
2. In *Professing Literacy in Composition Studies*, Goggin differentiates between functionalist literacy, "that views the acquisition of certain reading and writing skills as the way to learning and as the solution to learning 'problems,'" and functional literacy, "as a component of a multiliteracy view in which the acquisition of discrete learning skills can contribute to various forms of learning" (71-3).
3. Our own institution knows these breeches too well. On June 29, 2011, our university sent out a campus-wide e-mail reminding instructors of the importance of security in light of recent Lulzsec attacks. The e-mail stated, "The recent attacks on computer systems across the country, including here in [this state], by the LulzSec group highlights the need to take appropriate steps to safeguard our own systems from intrusion and theft of sensitive information," and went on to remind instructors that "each member of the faculty and staff have the responsibility to secure their own servers, desktop, and laptop machines" (Wishon). The online university login system was hacked less than 6 months later on January 18, 2012. Many users' passwords were downloaded, forcing every user on campus to reset his or her password. The extra traffic from this brought down the login system for several days. Classes that depended on online course materials were disrupted, and online instruction was effectively cut off until the system was restored some days later.

Works Cited

Anson, Chris. Interview by Toby Coley and Joe Erickson. "New Media and Multimodality in Compositions Students: An Interview with Chris Anson." *Computers and Composition Online*, 2009. Web. 14 Jun. 2011.

Connors, Robert J. "Crisis and Panacea in Composition Studies." *Composition in Context: Essays in Honor of Donald C. Stewart*. Ed. Ross Winterowd and Vincent Gillespie. Carbondale: Southern Illinois UP, 1994. 86-105. Print.

DeVoss, Danielle N., Ellen Cushman, and Jeffrey T. Grabill. "Infrastructure and Composing: The When of New-Media Writing." *CCC* 57.1 (2005): 14-44. Print.

Faigley, Lester. "Literacy After the Revolution." *CCC* 48.1 (1997): 30-43. Print.

Garza, Susan Loudermilk, and Tommy Hern. "Using Wikis as Collaborative Writing Tools: Something Wiki This Way Comes—or Not!" *Kairos* 10.1 (2005): n. pag. Web. 15 Dec. 2005.

Goggin, Peter N. *Professing Literacy in Composition Studies*. Cresskill: Hampton, 2008. Print.

Graff, Harvey J. *The Legacies of Literacy*. Bloomington: Indiana UP, 1987. Print.
Hewett, Beth L., and Christa Ehmann Powers. "How Do You Ground Your Training? Sharing the Principles and Processes of Preparing Educators for Online Editing Instruction." *Kairos* 10.1 (2005): n. pag. Web. 15 Dec. 2005.
Kaufer, David S., and Kathleen M. Carley. *Communication at a Distance: The Influence of Print on Sociocultural Organization and Change*. Hillsdale, NJ: Erlbaum, 1993. Print.
Kress, Gunther. *Literacy in the New Media Age*. London: Routledge, 2003. Print.
LeBlanc, Paul. "The Politics of Literacy and Technology in Secondary School Classrooms." *Literacy and Computers: The Complications of Teaching and Learning with Technology*. Ed. Cynthia L. Selfe and Susan Hilligoss. New York: MLA, 1994. 22-36. Print.
Moberly, Kevin. "Spam Wars: The Sooper Sekrit Rhetoric of Frea Speech." *Kairos* 9.2 (2005): n. pag. Web. 20 Apr. 2005.
Moran, Charles. "*Computers and Composition* 1983-2002: What We Have Hoped For." *Computers and Composition* 20.4 (2003): 343-58. Print.
- - -. "Emerging Technologies: Some Implications for Writing, Learning, and Teaching in the Disciplines." Conference on College Composition and Communication. Denver. March 2001. Presented paper.
"Net Threat Rising: Crime Abounds But You Can Fight Back." *Consumer Reports* 70 Sept. 2007: 12-18. Print.
"Protect Yourself Online." *Consumer Reports* 69 Sept. 2004: 12-19. Print.
Selber, Stuart A. *Multiliteracies for a Digital Age*. Carbondale: Southern Illinois UP, 2004. Print.
Selfe, Cynthia L. "Technology and Literacy: A Story about the Perils of Not Paying Attention." *The Norton Book of Composition Studies*. Ed. Susan Miller. New York: W. W. Norton, 2009. 1163-85. Print.
- - -. *Technology and Literacy in the Twenty-First Century: The Importance of Paying Attention*. Carbondale: Southern Illinois UP, 1999. Print.
Selfe, Cynthia L., and Gail E. Hawisher. *Literate Lives in the Information Age: Narratives of Literacy from the United States*. Mahwah: Lawrence Earlbaum, 2004. Print.
Selfe, Cynthia L., and Susan Hilligoss. *Literacy and Computers: The Complications of Teaching and Learning with Technology*. New York: MLA, 1994. Print.
Sheridan-Rabideau, Mary P., Rachel McLaughlin, and Jennifer Novak. "Contested Knowledge: Technological Literacies and the Power of Unacknowledged Disciplinary Investments." *Computers and Composition* 19.3 (2002): 347-59. Print.
Snyder, Ilana. *Silicon Literacies: Communication, Innovation and Education in the Electronic Age*. New York: Routledge, 2002. Print.
Street, Brian V. *Literacy in Theory and Practice*. Cambridge: Cambridge UP, 1984. Print.
- - -, ed. *Social Literacies: Critical Approaches to Literacy in Development, Ethnography, and Education*. London: Longman, 1995. Print.
Sullivan, Patricia, and James Porter. *Opening Spaces: Writing Technologies and Critical Research Practices*. Greenwich: Ablex, 1997. Print.
Vandenberg, Peter. "Taming Multiculturalism: The Will to Literacy in Composition Studies." *JAC* 19.4 (1999): 547-68. Print.
Werner, Mark. "Challenges in Supporting Faculty Who Use Technologies in Composing Communities." Conference on College Composition and Communication. Denver. March 2001. Presented paper.

Wishon, Gordon. "Information Security Update." Message to Peter Goggin. 29 June 2011. E-mail.

Wysocki, Anne F., and Johndan Johnson-Eilola. "Blinded by the Letter: Why are We Using Literacy as a Metaphor for Everything Else?" *Passions, Pedagogies, and 21st Century Technologies*. Ed. Gail E. Hawisher and Cynthia L. Selfe. Logan: Utah State UP, 1999. 349-68. Print.

Course Design

Writing 302: Writing Culture

Jamie White-Farnham

WRT 302: Writing Culture is an upper-level elective in the Department of Writing and Rhetoric at the University of Rhode Island (URI). As part of a group of four 300-level courses, Writing 302 draws many junior and senior majors in Writing and Rhetoric, English, and other majors who are looking to add creativity and experience with design to their skill sets. Writing 302 and its counterparts (Public Writing, Writing for Community Service, and Travel Writing) are a cluster of courses that can fulfill any student's general education requirement in the category of English Communication/Writing. The course's unique approach offers students the chance to write a range of genres not immediately associated with culture *qua* text, art, or artifact; that is, students in Writing 302 study and create the kinds of writing that surround a cultural milieu and support it as an institution, such as descriptive art museum placards. The production of these types of documents, what I refer to in the course as "unsung" or "overlooked" genres, is the main focus of the students' writing after a process of (1) library and field research into a cultural milieu (which range from the large and well documented to the local and obscure); (2) scouting of real-life models of documents that are necessary or important to sustaining the milieu; and (3) application of rhetorical concepts and principles in both the analysis and production of documents of the students' choosing. The aim is action through writing.

Alongside turning their attention to "culture" through collections of objects up for interpretation as one might expect in an English or Cultural Studies class in which students write analytic essays about culture, students in Writing 302 also examine the materiality of culture in its capacity to emerge as institutions—places, events, performances, and rituals. The course poses this scenario: you've got an interest in, understanding of, and perhaps a role in some cultural milieu with rich and interesting histories and points of view. In order to propagate this interest in the world at large, what might you need to write? Who is your audience? How will you deliver it? As students immerse themselves in four cultural milieus throughout the semester and face these questions, they create projects not easily listable or categorizable, but which I will exemplify and explain further throughout this course description. The course catalog description attempts to summarize the course products as: "noncanonical writings that sustain or reshape culture."

Institutional Context

With a combined undergraduate and graduate population of about 16,000, URI's main campus is located in the rural town of Kingston, Rhode Island.

The creation of a freestanding Department of Writing and Rhetoric, a major institutional change at the university, occasioned a boom in writing course offerings and influenced the design of upper-level writing courses including Writing 302 nearly a decade ago. Departing physically, financially, and curricularly from the English department, Writing and Rhetoric built major and minor programs of study inspired by foundational arguments for writing's worthiness as a field of study for undergraduates. Such arguments sprouted where they live, documented by URI faculty members Robert A. Schwegler's and Linda K. Shamoon's contributions to the 2000 volume *Coming of Age: The Advanced Writing Curriculum*.

In "Curriculum Development in Composition," Schwegler calls for the righting of a "curricular imbalance" perpetuated by the simultaneous devaluation of writing/production and valuation of literature/analysis (25). Explaining that writing's role in curricula has ridden (some unpleasant) waves over time, Schwegler forecasts writing's next role in a wave of "the growing sense that the things that should be studied and practiced in writing courses—the processes of composing; discourse genres; contexts; readers; media; links among texts, knowledge, power, and action—form clusters distinct enough to deserve courses of their own, yet related enough to constitute a discipline and a curriculum" (29). Additionally, Shamoon considers the practical results of such a discipline and curriculum, articulating what students need to become professional writers of all sorts: "the best education for the profession must include [...] active knowledge of the historical foundations of the profession along with an array of critical approaches with which to encounter the always-changing economic and technical conditions of production [and] guided practice in the public and social roles of the writer as an agent for good in society" (50).

Why the emphasis on career, on professionalization? Alongside the disciplinary movement toward independence, the growth of the Writing and Rhetoric major at URI is also a practical reaction to the role higher education currently plays in the economically troubled U.S. and Rhode Island in particular, where the unemployment rate in August 2011 was 10.6% (Rhode Island Department of Labor and Training). A survey study posted on The Chronicle of Higher Education's Web site reports that 77.6% of undergraduates indicate that the most important reason to attend college is to train for a specific career (University of California at Los Angeles). Likewise, URI's Office of Institutional Research Fall 2010 report lists university's top eight majors, none of which are in the humanities and all of which constitute professionally focused fields: Nursing, Communication Studies, Psychology, Kinesiology, Human Development and Family Studies, Textiles, Fashion Merchandising and Design, Biology, and Accounting.

Attendant to students' expectations that their educations will lead them toward reliable career paths is the encouraging rise in the number of Writing and Rhetoric majors since the first graduating class of three students to almost eighty majors in only a handful of years. Both the department and the College of Arts and Sciences promote the usefulness of the major in students' pursuits of "careers for the digital age." Therefore, Writing & Rhetoric offers writing courses from the first year to a Senior Capstone informed by rhetorical theory and composition research with an emphasis on rhetorical knowledge and the production of writing. This "vertical curriculum" builds on rhetorical and writing process knowledge introduced in the 100- and 200- levels and reinforced throughout a student's education up to the 300- and 400- levels. Such a curriculum offers opportunities for students to practice a range of genres in many different rhetorical situations and with various writing technologies, as Jeremiah Dyehouse, Micheal Pennell, and Linda Shamoon have recently described in "Writing In Electronic Environments: A Concept and A Course for the Writing & Rhetoric Major." It also emphasizes revision and reflection in a portfolio-based assessment model drawn on the work of Nedra Reynolds and Rich Rice. Like the other electives for the major and Gen. Ed. courses, Writing 302 supports the following Learning Outcomes (specific criteria of which can be found online):

- Rhetorical Knowledge
- Composing, Revising, and Editing Processes
- Collaborative Production and Evaluation of Texts
- Reflective Learning
- Conventions and Craft

The major itself requires 30 credit hours grounded by five required courses (15 credits) and a minimum of 15 elective credits, five credits of which are drawn from the 300+ levels (Writing 302 and its counterparts as previously listed comprise the elective choices.) The required courses include:

- WRT 201: Writing Argumentative & Persuasive Texts
- WRT 235: Writing in Electronic Environments
- WRT 360: Composing Processes and Canons of Rhetoric
- WRT 490: Writing and Rhetoric
- WRT 495: Capstone in Electronic Portfolios

Graduating seniors demonstrate their knowledge of *and* practice in writing via an electronic portfolio suitable for such audiences as potential employers or writing agents. The variety of courses in the curriculum doesn't ask what students should write *about*, but *what* students should write, to whom, and for what purpose (i.e., rhetorically).

This is a key point in support of a vertical curriculum. Students in URI's Gen. Ed. and major writing courses write *in* the arenas around which the course is focused (such as community service, culture, electronic environments) and not only *about* them. The opening lines of the Writing 302 syllabus help to distinguish between these two prepositions: "Rather than writing about culture (like in an essay), you will write to help shape, create, sustain, or alter the direction of a cultural institution, activity, performance, or event." As a three-credit elective, the course holds a relatively low-stakes position in the curriculum and on students' schedules. This has allowed for the course's design and near-constant revision by each instructor to whom it is assigned to approach it quite differently. Though each section of the course follows a roughly similar four- or five-project structure, with each project following a two to three week writing process, the end product of each unit can differ significantly.

For instance, another instructor with whom I have collaborated in plans for Writing 302 has, based on his own interest in and love of punk rock, assigned his class to produce a collaboratively written 'zine, or low-budget, small-circulation magazine written by fans. His students write their 'zine on a topic of interest on campus (the music scene, for instance). However, having no personal interest in or experience with 'zines, my ideas for what students can produce are drawn from other cultural topics also worthy of exploration such as cuisine or couture. For example, last fall, students in my class wrote publishable recipe articles modeled on the trial-and-error style write-ups of recipes in publications like *Vegetarian Times* or *Cooks Illustrated*. In other units, students made use of free and user-friendly floor-planning software (such as Google's SketchUp 8 or floorplanner.com) to conceive of and design museum galleries dedicated to the work of, in one instance, the designer Alexander McQueen.

Without belaboring the distinction, to those of us teaching the course, writing *in/for* is a matter of institutional history and differentiation from curricula whose primary focus is analysis. I feel it's necessary to emphasize the course designers' strength of conviction that Writing 302 and its counterparts be necessarily distinct from writing-heavy literature courses at the university in which students read about a topic (cultural or otherwise) and respond to it—critically, persuasively, expressively, what have you—in an essay. David Beard has recently described the expansion of rhetorical purposes for students' writing in a similar way: "Further, because we are interested in a broader array of writing and reading activities, we can focus on a greater variety of sociocultural effects of writing. We can be interested in the ways *that a variety of writing forms sustain institutions*, generate communities, and enable (or domesticate) individual and social cognition" (par. 2, emphasis added). In the philosophical move away from English/analysis as a basis of the curriculum at the University, Writing 302 was designed to focus more on teaching types of contextual writing that the participants in various cultural milieus actually use (like 'zines in punk rock culture or recipes in foodie circles) than on content for acontextual/for-teachers'-eyes-only essays.

This perspective is shared by others in the field whose major programs take similar shapes for similar purposes. Contributors to the 2010 volume *What We Are Becoming: Developments in Undergraduate Writing Majors* by Greg Giberson and Thomas Moriarty present an array of examples. Although sometimes a bumpy road, writing major programs are working within many an institution for reasons similar to those at URI. For one example, Rebecca de Wind Mattingly and Patricia Harkin suggest that "what a rhetoric and composition major can do is introduce students to a broad range of situations that call for what Bill Hart-Davidson characterizes as 'solving problems by writing.' These situations require conscious attention to audience and context in ways technology-sphere natives may not otherwise encounter" (16). Rodney F. Dick suggests similar opportunities for the students in his institution to gain rhetorical knowledge and writing practice: "Students are exposed to a wider variety of rhetorical situations for analyzing and producing texts; students can professionalize as writers and gain more practical and varied experiential knowledge than studying literature alone can afford" (125).

Dick's mention of the study of literature in comparison to the study and practice of writing invokes the continuous tension between the work of analysis and the work of production. Schwegler historicizes the division:

> From the end of the nineteenth century through most of the twentieth, the definition of literary study as a subject matter acted as an expansive ideology, encouraging division and development and enabling literary study to occupy considerable curricular space [in budgets, catalogs, and physical space in institutions]. In contrast, the definition of writing as a skill that is largely impervious to scholarly analysis led to the restriction of its curricular development. (26)

While we know the attitude toward writing as a skill has become far more nuanced and the subjugation of writing as an inferior field of study has abated (in lots of places, though certainly not everywhere), the problem of analysis versus production is still a chief subject of concern within the conversation regarding the development of undergraduate writing curriculum.

For instance, the approach to first-year writing referred to as Writing About Writing (WAW) offered by Douglas Downs and Elizabeth Wardle in their 2007 article, "Teaching About Writing, Righting Misconceptions: (Re)Envisioning 'First-Year Composition' as 'Introduction to Writing Studies,'" has gained traction and drawn criticism. Contending that "our own research and theory about the nature of writing has done little to influence public conceptions of writing," Downs and Wardle draw on the considerable body of research and knowledge in the field to "[teach] students what we as a field have learned *about* writing as an object of study. Thus, the course acquires an attainable goal and a clear content while continuing to help students understand how writing works in the academy so that they can succeed there" (578). Todd Ruecker's account of a successful attempt at this model was published in this journal last spring. Echoing Barbara Bird's defense of students' ability to participate in disciplinary discourse, Ruecker recounts Libby Miles et al.'s critique of Downs and Wardle's placement of sophisticated disciplinary texts in the first year (Ruecker 90). Miles et al.'s main problem with WAW is its focus on FYW as the appropriate place to impart writing theories; that is, Miles et al. believe it serves the field more appropriately to use writing theories to build a full curriculum rather than deliver writing theories as course material in a readings model of a composition course (Miles et al. 508).

This debate persists: On the one hand, including disciplinary work as course content, as texts up for analysis, provides students with an introduction to a field, practice in academic discourse, and opportunities to practice writing-as-learning with reflective writing. On the other hand, this model gives rhetorical concepts short shrift with its emphasis on essay writing. However, to serve undergraduate students whose chief concern is preparing themselves for the job market, upper-level writing electives such as Writing for Community Service or Travel Writing tip the balance between academic writing and practical writing, of analysis and production. Writing Culture stands, then, as a sort of extreme experiment in completely prioritizing production.

Theoretical Rationale

While the previous section presented a local rationale for upper-level writing curricula in the institution, this section explains the theoretical rationale for Writing 302 as a writing course generally speaking. The theoretical rationale exemplifies the idea that the rhetorical theories and composition research developed and articulated in Writing Studies should inform writing curricula, not only be presented as course content. Therefore, Writing 302 is inspired by theories of language in general and writing in particular that account for connections between institutions, discourse, and people, or what is sometimes termed "material" or "materialist" rhetoric. The scholarly conversations concerning writing that intervenes into unfair systems or changes material conditions frame the course products and serve as a point of departure for the students' research and writing processes.

The introduction of Foucault's *Discipline and Punish* serves as both a powerful example of the link between institutions, discourse, and people, as well as an eye-opening first reading for the course. With Leon Foucher's timetable of a Parisian prison as an example of the post-Enlightenment move on reliance from brute force to rhetorical force, Foucault suggests that discipline is enacted through "tactics," or "the art of constructing, with located bodies, coded activities" (167). As the "highest form" of disciplinary practice, coded activities such as a timetable to manage a daily routine elevate the material and interpretive aims of the code-maker (writer); that is, in this case, the timetable increases efficiency of the punitive system and attends to the former lack of humanity and dignity (of torture, a gory description of which mostly comprises the piece). Given codes-makers' attention to "located bodies" (167), or the audience to whom the code is directed and the situation in which it is expected to work, such tactics are rhetorical in nature. Excise the punitive aims of the prison timetable, and the theory—that rhetorical forms can be deployed to direct the behavior of people within institutions—is extendable to and productive within contemporary cultural institutions.

Many examples of Writing Studies scholarship demonstrate this. The well-known work of Ellen Cushman exemplifies personal intervention into the documentary bureaucracy on behalf of her neighbors who are less literate than she is. This iteration of rhetorical intervention changes the material conditions of peoples' everyday lives (13). Similarly, Carl Herndl, in his "Tactics and the Quotidian," looks to the subversive rhetorical moves a biologist makes on the job to combat the institutional discursive limits of report writing, which reduce complicated and sensitive environmental issues to quantifiable data and thus allows his employer to ignore them (par. 21). Herndl uses Foucault's word, "tactics," to describe the moves the biologist makes such as "sneaking" clauses into documents that open up the interpretation of regulations (such as the phrase "the letter and the spirit of the law") and suggests that the writer's "action takes advantage of the institution's procedures to increase the amount of information available and to force it into wider circulation, effectively resisting the institution's attempt to silently extend its control of information" (par. 27).

Tactics, perhaps a little ironically, are effectively constructed only within an institution. That is, when code-makers write, they are resisting through measures of compliance—changes in or additions to existing codes that will sustain the institution, making it more habitable for its members. The change, in other words, doesn't throw the baby out with the bathwater. The writers in the particular examples above rely on writing tactics that undermine, but that also work within the structures of their institutions: writing on someone's behalf, revising policy, and generally making the best use of resources at hand. Working within the system this way is less risky, according to Herndl, though perhaps no less effective than working against it: "highly charged action makes resistance such a dangerous and costly project that it becomes practically impossible" (par. 6). The "double logic" that Kristie Fleckenstein articulates of discursively constructed institutions constitutes, on a basic level, trading a measure of freedom for a measure of justice (762). In such a system, a freedom one loses includes expediency, as the discursive road to institutional improvement is neither easy nor exciting. As Herndl describes, "resistance can be understood as a social agent's conscious attempt to put her expanded discursive knowledge of structural properties [of an institutions] into action, thus attempting to make incremental social change" (par. 12).

Admittedly, this theoretical framework asks for a bit of a leap from serious considerations of implementing social change within material circumstances to creating art and fashion shows.

However, this pedagogical extrapolation of rhetorical theories constitutes an appropriate level of reading, understanding, and application for Gen. Ed. undergrads and contrives to make accessible to majors and non-majors in the classroom the possibility of rhetoric described in the work of James Porter et al.: if institutions (of all stripes) are rhetorically constructed and rhetorically alterable, students themselves can be the types of writers prepared to face them (631). To do that, students in Writing 302 embark on a process of learning about and using rhetoric that begins with becoming aware of connections between institutions, discourse, and people. Stefanie, a student in an online section, makes some early connections based on her understanding of the timetable as a controlling force:

> Foucault uses the timetable as an example of a new form of power that the newly instituted penal code was now enforcing. Instead of compelling the body to endure physical torture as a form of punishment, these codes seek to control the body and conform it to the desired "discipline" of the institution.

This kind of recognition of the power of a simple document (in juxtaposition to the power of violence, which had previously done the job of punishment) is important to encouraging students to analyze the interpretive, not just the functional or formal, aspects of institutional documents. Another reading selection, "Civil Disobedience: A Case Study in Factors of Effectiveness" by Courtney Dillard in the journal *Society and Animals*, takes the students to this next step of acknowledging the values and agendas of institutions who create such documents.

In her piece, Dillard describes a failed protest by the animal rights group Fund For Animals during a traditional pigeon shoot in Hegins, Pennsylvania. After some protestors display violent behavior towards participants in the pigeon shoot, the organization reflects on its values and agenda and is moved to dictate appropriate behaviors for protestors at the next rally through a circulated list of rules. Emphasizing the group's leaders' reflection on the group's values in order for their writing to direct bodies in the way the group wishes, Dillard writes: "They wanted to demonstrate their sympathy more accurately for the birds and encourage others to adopt their position concerning the shoot [...] in doing so, they tried to better understand their audience and more clearly represent themselves" (53). Consequently, the next rally is far more successful, non-violent, and gains positive attention from the media. The piece exemplifies well that "coded activities" sustain the group itself and the larger institution of animal activism by preempting damage to its image generally, and it also manifests the articulation of values that is critical to using rhetoric, but not always apparent. This works to help students balance their eagerness to design a cool Web site with the challenge of determining the values of the community they are imaginarily serving and the audiences to whom their writing is directed. Another student in an online section, Justin, posts his realization about the articulation of values in this way:

> Because the activists changed to a nonviolent and peaceful approach, rather than involving themselves in unproductive and hostile behavior, their cause became much more transparent and well-understood. In this manner, people could identify with what their aim was and the essence of civil disobedience was in itself a constructive means.

This particular piece, as a relatable case study, bridges the more esoteric and extreme Foucault piece to students' own possible contexts for writing; it also, incidentally, provides a model of the types of projects students might consider creating. The class, with burgeoning rhetorical and design knowledge, moves on to produce documents that work within institutions such as museums, events, performance spaces, and publications.

To prompt the writing process, the course assignments provide a general scenario and lists of possible documents, demonstrated by the below unit centered around "Parks, Monuments, and Memorials" (see Syllabus below). Such prompts have kick-started a range of research endeavors and unusual-for-the-classroom genres: posted rules and information for a state park hiking trail; plans for an Oktoberfest event with a descriptive beer menu; revised placards for a fishermans' memorial in a coastal town park; an informational Web site on loose-leaf teas with brewing instructions and tips; a proposal and the specifications for arranging a flash mob on campus—to name a few examples of students' recent work. With these types of projects, students discover and contribute to the discursive construction of institutions recognizable and enjoyable to them in one semester. However comfortable scholars are claiming that cultural institutions are "constructed," students often believe in a definition of culture absent of their own local knowledge and personal involvement. Here, students practice the idea that cultural institutions are constructed and changed by code-makers—real people like them—who have been prepared during their rhetorical educations to recognize, understand, and respond to the needs or interests of a niche audience within a specific cultural milieu, and by extension, other institutions to which they belong, through writing and rhetoric.

Critical Reflection

In considering the successes and failures of teaching Writing 302, some logistical problems persist alongside the pipedream-ish quality of the hope of linking material rhetoric into writing curricula.

Logistical Problems

The idea of leaving campus to conduct field research makes students nervous at the outset of the course. In the first semester I taught Writing 302, the number of panicky e-mails from students concerned about traveling off-campus was alarmingly high. Therefore, I lightened the expectations of the students' field research by limiting the number of off-site visits required to two visits among four projects on the syllabus. I also tried to make the field research a more collaborative portion of the course by providing a space on our Sakai site for students and me to share interesting and potentially useful events, activities, links, and locations with each other. Finally, to prepare the students to seek out real-world models of such things like art museum placards, show posters, and menus on their own later in the semester, I've worked in mini-field trips around campus to visit outdoor monuments and memorials and our small but lovely Fine Arts Gallery early in the semester. One spring semester, the trajectory of a project corresponded with students' Spring Break plans, which allowed some students to visit an array of cultural institutions in our own and neighboring states, finding a number of useful and inspiring milieus and models.

Another logistical problem arises in the non-standard assignments of the course. While fun and liberating for instructors and some students, they cause other students anxiety, especially in regards to experience with design. Comments in student evaluations suggested some helpful way that these early concerns might be dispelled:

- "If you introduced the class with a sample prompt and a sample that answered the prompt featuring very different documents, it might help make your expectations clearer."
- "The only problems I initially struggled with were understanding (generally) what the documents were—I was nervous in my first assignment that I wasn't fulfilling the expectations. But after the first go-around I definitely felt more comfortable with the material."
- "At first I was a little confused by the whole concept, and the idea that we had such a wide range of documents we could create. In other classes we usually have certain guidelines to follow. When describing what the assignment is, it might be helpful to provide an example of what a document may look like. I think it would help better explain what you are looking for."

Models are, of course, necessary in writing classes to help students understand rhetorical patterns and then produce their own responses using appropriate conventions, tone, and the like to address a particular audience. While the syllabus offers lists of possibilities for each project, students seem to want something more concrete (see Syllabus for examples). Considering the students' feedback in light of the theoretical foundation of the course, the power of documents to model behavior as "coded activities" is especially robust in an educational context. I believe that, in this case, the code has the potential to limit students' imaginations, perhaps tamping down their curiosity to try out a genre new to them or preventing individual understandings of how mundane, easily overlooked documents really can play a part in sustaining cultural institutions. The final, polished semester's worth of work of another class may also be too impressive in an inventional sense. For instance, consider the project of another student, Grace: after researching and visiting her hometown beach, she determined the need for and created mock-ups of historical markers that memorialize the infamous Hurricane of '38. This project is so interesting and well executed that it would have induced a number of replications (all potentially great, I'm sure, but still not inspired by students' own interests and processes). I am therefore hesitant to share previous classes' work. My response to the panicked has been to listen to their worries with kindness and patience. I have seen some success, despite the lack of models, with the emphasis on finding models through field research together early in the semester, exemplified by this end-of-the-semester comment: "I do believe the course description sounds much scarier than it truly is. I loved this class and loved the opportunity to write different documents, not just boring old essays."

Two more logistical problems go unsolved: peer review remains a largely chaotic show-and-tell session with lots of impromptu opening of files and on-the-spot revision that sometimes distracts peer review groups' attention from each person in the group. While it is exciting to work amid twenty-odd students who really are workshopping—discussing the merits of their choices, listening to advice, and making new rhetorical and design choices right there in class, by the third and fourth projects, the class's comfort with the routine can railroad any specific instructions or prompt I might provide.

Grading is also a challenge. To overcome any tendency to downgrade students without a natural aesthetic sense or over reward students with design software experience (since experience is not required to enroll in the course), grades are determined mostly by students' participation in the writing process through drafts and peer review, as well as the quality of students' research on each topic around which they produce documents. To that end, I use a four-part research heuristic to shape students' research efforts, blending their own interest in and knowledge about the topic, library research, and field research: "What You Know," "Read More," "Ask Somebody," and "Go There." Alongside the documents the students produce for each assignment (four altogether, themed around a broad topic such as "Parks, Monuments, and Memorials"), they also write a Field Analysis Report, an accounting of the research they conduct on each topic. These reports are simply arranged by the four headings that make up the heuristic. Additionally, this is the appropriate space for students to cite their research sources, since the genres the students write such as art museum placards or brochures often preclude conventions of typical researched writing assignments.

Pipedreams

To exemplify the support that a production-focused upper-level curriculum could lend to students' efforts in becoming professional writers, I share a happy instance in which the imaginary scenarios in Writing 302 led to "real" writing for a real audience. This instance highlights the fruitful interaction of the main elements of the course—the production of unsung genres in the writing class, a multi-method research heuristic, and a constructed, contextualized understanding of "culture." Imagine the excitement of reading the following e-mail from Aly, a senior Writing and Rhetoric major, in late Fall 2010:

Hi,

I wrote in my post-write that Nancy Martini was going to post the profile I wrote on her blog. She posted it today so I thought I would send you the link to her blog so you could see it there, too (in addition to the paragraph I wrote about myself as a guest blogger on her page)! http://nancymartini.blogspot.com/

—Aly (D'Amato)

As part of their research for a collaborative project on green art, Aly and her groupmates interviewed a Florida-based artist known for using reclaimed materials in her sculptures, Nancy Martini. Their project resulted in an informational Web site for budding green artists that included do/don't lists, how-to instructions, and, at my suggestion, a profile on the artist herself. The group had been unusually proactive in seeking out research sources, and I encouraged them to make the most of their interview experience by writing the profile, responding to Ms. Martini to say "thank you," and offering to share the project with her. Aly, having taken ownership of this portion of the project, was thrilled when Ms. Martini replied with a request: would Aly mind featuring the profile she wrote on the artist's professional blog? As an aspiring freelance art and music writer, Aly was thrilled to add to her credentials a project written for a real site with a real audience. (Note: the link is live; you can search for Aly's piece by its posting date: 19 November 2010.)

However, since Aly's writing is the sole instance such as this in three years of teaching Writing 302, it is clear that other pedagogies in our field such as service learning are better platforms for creating a variety of documents that actually contribute to institutions or organizations. David Coogan, in "Service Learning and Social Change: The Cast for Materialist Rhetoric," describes such an arrangement, a course focused on learning the rhetorical history of a real-life organization, analyzing its needs and audience, and providing pieces of professional writing for public use. Coogan argues for a materialistic rhetoric to create service-learning programs that don't rely on the standard approaches of teaching students to be good citizens and try to enact social change (such as critical consciousness, community literacy, or community-based organizations). He writes: "[it is] not just a case for rhetorical activism in service learning but a case for rhetorical scholarship in the public sphere: a challenge to test the limits of rhetorical theory in the laboratory of community-based writing projects in order to generate new questions for rhetorical theory, rhetorical practice, and rhetorical education" (670). Coogan's pedagogical heuristic—Discover, Analyze, Produce, Assess—under the term "Materialist Rhetoric" attends nearly perfectly to the question at hand: how does rhetoric lead students to produce documents that make a material impact on its audience or constituents? The ideal circumstance—an arrangement with willing constituents from whom the students can learn and for whom they can write—frames Writing 302's counterpart, Writing for Community Service. Those types of experiences are invaluable for students and make an excellent rhetorical fit given the civic roots of the discipline, as Coogan points out.

The connection to culture is yet another, distinct way to consider what "institutions" can be and how writers/rhetoricians can participate discursively in them; yet, perhaps it seems less important without the connection to civic or community action. Since clients for such projects are in demand, students must gain practice in this materialist rhetoric model of Writing 302 by learning to conduct field research and analyzing the contexts of imagined audiences to whom their writing is directed.

As long as preparing students for their civic and professional futures has been the goal of public higher education, writing teachers, with their ability to impact so many college students each semester, have been interested in how best they can contribute to this preparation. Writing 302, and the vertical writing curriculum generally, contributes to career goals of writers in a unique way. The course asks students to take a gamble when they enroll in the course, but the risk has paid off in some cases when students have stretched out of their writing comfort zones, learned to incorporate design elements and principles into their work, used software useful to them in other courses and extracurricular interests, and delivered documents from Writing 302 projects to real audiences. Aly's "real" writing, albeit an unusually exciting result of a writing assignment, speaks not only to the ways teachers see writing as potentially useful to students, but, perhaps more importantly, it also speaks to the ways students see our writing courses: useful to them as writers.

Works Cited

Beard, David. "The Case for a Writing Major: University of Minnesota Duluth." *Composition Forum* 21 (Spring 2010): n. pag. Web. 10 Jan. 2012.

Cushman, Ellen. "Rhetoricians as Agents of Social Change." *CCC* 47.1 (Feb. 1996): 7-28. Print.

Coogan, David. "Service Learning and Social Change: The Case for Materialist Rhetoric." *CCC* 57.4 (2006): 667-93. Print.

D'Amato, Alyson. Message to the author. 19 Nov. 2010. E-mail.

Dick, Rodney F. "The Writing Major as Shared Commitment." Giberson and Moriarty 98-129.

Dillard, Courtney L. "Civil Disobedience: A Case Study of Factors in Effectiveness." *Society and Animals* 10.1 (2002): 47-62. Print.

Downs, Douglas, and Elizabeth Wardle. "Teaching About Writing, Righting Misconceptions: (Re-)Envisioning 'First-Year Composition' as 'Introduction to Writing Studies.'" *CCC* 58.4 (June 2007): 552-84. Print.

Dyehouse, Jeremiah, Michael Pennell, and Linda Shamoon. "Writing in Electronic Environments: A Concept and a Course for the Writing & Rhetoric Major." *CCC* 61.2 (Dec. 2009): W330-350. Web. 21 Nov. 2011.

Fleckenstein, Kristie S. "Bodysigns: A Biorhetoric for Change." *JAC* 21.4 (2001): 761-90. Print.

Foucault, Michel. *Discipline and Punish: The Birth of the Prison*. New York: Pantheon, 1977. Print.

Giberson, Greg A., and Thomas A. Moriarty, eds. *What We Are Becoming: Developments in Undergraduate Writing Majors*. Logan: Utah State UP, 2010. Web. 10 Jan. 2012.

Herndl, Carl G. "Tactics and the Quotidian." *JAC* 16.3 (1996): n. pag. Web. 26 Mar. 2011.

Mattingly, Rebecca de Wind, and Patricia Harkin. "A Major in Flexibility." Giberson and Moriarty 13-31.

Miles, Libby, Michael Pennell, Kim Hensley Owens, Jeremiah Dyehouse, Helen O'Grady, Nedra Reynolds, Robert Schwegler, and Linda Shamoon. "Thinking Vertically: A Response to Downs and Wardle's 'Teaching about Writing, Righting Misconceptions.'" *CCC* 59.3 (2008): 503-11. Print.

Porter, James E., Patricia Sullivan, Stuart Blythe, Jeffrey T. Grabill, and Libby Miles. "Institutional Critique: A Rhetorical Methodology for Change." *CCC* 51.4 (2000): 610-42. Print.

Reynolds, Nedra, and Rich Rice. *Portfolio Teaching*. Boston: Bedford, 2006. Print.

Ruecker, Todd. "Reimagining English 1311: 'Expository English Composition' as 'Introduction to Rhetoric and Writing Studies.'" *Composition Studies* 39.1 (Spring 2011): 87-111. Print.

Schwegler, Robert A. "Curriculum Development in Composition." Shamoon, Moore Howard, Jamieson, and Schwegler 25-31. Print.

Shamoon, Linda K. "The Academic Effacement of a Career: 'Writer.'" Shamoon, Moore Howard, Jamieson, and Schwegler 42-51. Print.

Shamoon, Linda K., Rebecca Moore Howard, Sandra Jamieson, and Robert A. Schwegler, eds. *Coming of Age: The Advanced Writing Curriculum*. Portsmouth: Boynton/Cook, 2000. Print.

Rhode Island Department of Labor and Training. "Key Stats." *State Department of Labor and Training*. n.d. Web. 10 October 2011.

University of California at Los Angeles Higher Education Research Institute. "The American Freshman: National Norms for 2010." *The Chronicle of Higher Education*. 27 Jan. 2011. Web. 26 Mar. 2011.

University of Rhode Island Office of Institutional Research. "Just the Facts Fall 2010 Campus Highlights." *Northeastern Land Grant University*. 6 Dec. 2010. Web. 26 Mar. 2011.

Department of Writing & Rhetoric. Home page., Dept. of Writing & Rhetoric, U of Rhode Island, 2011. Web. 29 Nov. 2011. <http://www.uri.edu/artsci/writing/>

Syllabus

WRT 302: Writing Culture

Welcome to WRT 302! The first thing to know about this course is that it is unique among writing courses at our university or anywhere for that matter. Rather than writing about culture (like in an essay), you will write to help shape, create, sustain, or alter the direction of a cultural institution, activity, performance, or event. The aim is action through writing. I think you will enjoy the creativity, energy, and collaboration that this class requires.

This course fulfills a Gen. Ed. requirement for English Communication (ECw). Upon its completion, you will have:

- conducted both textual and field research
- read and discussed critical and popular sources
- found, studied, and rhetorically analyzed documents that shape, create, sustain, and alter culture
- created a host of practical documents
- engaged in all steps of the writing process
- sought feedback from classmates and instructor to revise, edit, and polish writing
- reflected on your learning and writing

Course Texts

Note: not all books and readings are required to be purchased; some are available as PDFs posted on Sakai.

Dillard, Courtney L. "Civil Disobedience: A Case Study of Factors in Effectiveness." *Society and Animals* 10.1 (2002): 47-62. Print.
Foucault, Michel. *Discipline and Punish: The Birth of the Prison*. New York: Pantheon, 1977. Print.
Marback, Richard. "Detroit and the Closed Fist: Toward a Theory of Material Rhetoric." *Rhetoric Review* 17.1 (1998): 74-92. Print.
Palmquist, Mike. *Designing Writing*. Boston: Bedford, 2005. Print.
Schilb, John, ed. *College English*. Spec. issue of *College English* 70.4 (Mar. 2008). Print.

Other readings drawn from various popular publications.

Course Technology

Computers for writing
Our classroom is equipped with laptops for use with writing. You may bring your own if you'd like. Please save files in formats compatible across old and new Mac and PCs (such as .doc, .rtf, or .pdf).

Sakai
Our course documents, including the syllabus and assignments, are housed on Sakai. In addition, responses to readings in the Forums section on our Sakai site are a main element of the class. Please check into Sakai regularly.

Design Software and Production Technology
Writing 302 benefits from the technology available in the Writing & Rhetoric Production Lab in Roosevelt 320. As this class might require the use of computer software that may be new to you such as Web site-building software, MS Publisher, Photoshop, and floor-planning software, we will rely mainly on free online software or those available in the Lab. You may also print your documents in black and white and in color there, as well as laminate and bind your work.

Technology for Field Research
You might spend a bit of money on your field research this semester, for such things as gas, bus fare, or other costs associated with travel; however, you can borrow equipment such as digital cameras, voice recorders, and tablet PCs from the Production Lab to conduct your field research. A lab monitor is available to help you when you're there.

Requirements:
1. Completion of all assignments on due dates (including readings, on-time submission of drafts, thoughtful revision between drafts, workshop, and postwrites).
2. Completion of a Final Portfolio including a Reflective Essay and three revised, edited, and polished documents.
3. Active and consistent participation in individual and collaborative work.
4. Responsible communication with instructor.

Grading
- Four Unit Projects, for process and potential: 40 pts (10 each) (An acceptable project includes all drafts, workshop responses, genuine revision between drafts, and a postwrite)
- Good citizenship, class participation, and careful feedback: 10
- Research (showing a variety of sources and high level of energy): 10
- Final portfolio (showing evidence of significant revision on three chosen pieces): 40
- Total: 100 points available

University Grade Chart

A	93	C	73
A-	90	C-	70
B+	88	D+	68

B	83	D	63
B-	80	F	59
C+	78		

Writing Projects and Workload

Projects

Each project is a collection of documents that you submit at the end of a unit. I don't assign a paper; you produce a group of four documents.

The contents of your project will differ from the contents of others'. You will decide what kinds of documents you write according your topic, research, audience, technologies, and the feedback from me and others in the class.

The projects are judged on five components at two points each:

- the writer's participation in the writing process and workshop
- the documents as a response to the readings and discussions in each unit they represent
- the documents as a performance; that is, an aesthetically appealing rhetorical delivery
- a properly formatted and cited Field Analysis Report
- a thoughtful and detailed postwrite

A note on delivery: present your documents as a mini-presentation on the day it is due by including in the presentation any interesting visuals, props, or other artifacts that illuminate your topic.

Field Analysis Report

In order to produce documents, you will spend much of the three units conducting field analysis by researching your topic in the four ways described below. Then, as part of your project, you will write a Field Analysis Report. These reports will describe your research efforts in four activities for knowledge-making:

What You Know: Jumpstart your invention by recording recollections, personal experience, examples in popular culture, common knowledge, folklore, stories you've heard, etc.

Read More: Reading comprises much of a writer's process. Readings should include a wide variety of sources, including personal/popular, professional, academic, and functional texts. This effort will be complemented by class readings as they are listed on the syllabus, but you must also read other articles and sources on your own to fit your topic for each unit. Proper MLA citation is required in Field Analysis Reports.

Ask Somebody: Having conversations with people is integral to field analysis. Like a reporter, you've got to be curious and confident. This can mean formally requested interviews or on-the-street fact-finding.

Go There: To enhance your invention and drafting, as well as jar your memory about your field when you're writing, you'll go to places that are relevant to your topic, take photos, collect artifacts, draw sketches, and record all pertinent details for your inquiry. At least two "Go Theres" are required in WRT 302.

A 3-4 page Field Analysis Report is due alongside each bundle. Remember, it's a report, not an essay; consult *Designing Writing* for genre conventions. Include photographs and artifacts where relevant.

Forum Posts
According to our class schedule, you will read course materials and write responses or "Forum Posts" on Sakai by class time that day. These responses should be thoughtful and well crafted, questioning, citing, and analyzing evidence from whatever the required material. As well, to foster our conversations about these readings, you will be required to comment on at least two of your peers' posts. While these comments may be more informal than original posts, they must add something to the conversation at hand, rather than just agree with or repeat information. So, one original post per reading and two responses per unit.

Unit One: Parks, Monuments, & Memorials
The first unit will draw our attention to the big, public presence of Parks, Monuments, and Memorials as well as to seemingly mundane, everyday aspects of such institutions. As we read, talk, and draft, we will consider such questions as: Who makes parks, monuments, and memorials? Who ruins them? Who funds them? Who really funds them? Who are their intended audiences? Who are their real audiences? Where are they? Where aren't they? We can ask these types of questions of a range of outdoor spaces from Mount Rushmore to roadside memorials to the statue on the statehouse to home altars.

Documents
Depending on your topic, the documents you write will probably vary greatly from your classmates'. But, here's an example to get your own ball rolling. Say my topic is the newly refurbished Vietnam Memorial Park in my city. What could I possibly write? A short list might include:

- a letter to the editor of the local paper suggesting the ways in which the city could have and should have consulted citizens during the park's planning and construction
- a personal essay about the connection between one's visit to the park, a Vietnam vet near and dear to one's heart, and oneself
- a proposal and blueprint for an addition to the park in 2015. Try a free floor-plan/layout program such as Google's SketchUp8 (awesome for 3D stuff) or

Floorplanner.com
- a placard listing the park's rules upon entering (and perhaps some clever graffiti for the placard)
- a photo essay emphasizing its beauty and pride in the city's veterans, we well as championing the city's continued commitment to municipal spaces
- a descriptive entry for a travel guide with a photograph

Unit Two: Eat, Drink, and Be Merry
This unit will ask you to consider food and drink as cultural activities. Here, our attention to national and ethnic differences, as well as reading a range of haute and low media, will reveal the relationships between food, its ingredients, the tools necessary to prepare it, its cooks, the stomachs it ends up in, and, of course, writing.

Documents
Depending on your topic, the documents you write will probably vary greatly from your classmates'. But, here's an example to get your own ball rolling. Say my topic is a single ingredient, the chickpea, a food that has recently become central to my and my family's diet. What could I possibly write? A short list might include:

- a friendly letter sharing my fondness for a certain recipe, along with a recipe card
- a brief, animated history (it's the oldest food, some say) of the chickpea (Web site or timeline suitable for a popular forum)
- a critique of food trends (like clean eating, organics, low-carb, etc.)
- a menu for a Middle Eastern restaurant

Unit Three: Writing a Gallery Exhibit (A Group Project)
For this unit, your group will create a gallery exhibit of a visual art. Your purpose can range from exhibiting a specific artist, or a specific medium across a range of artists, or a specific time period across a range of media. In reading about and discussing visuals and images, visiting the university's Fine Arts Gallery, and conducting fieldwork, you will attempt to link rhetorical conceptions, design elements, and beautiful works of art with writing.

Documents
Depending on your topic, the documents your group writes will probably vary greatly from other groups. But, here's an example to get your own ball rolling. Say my group's topic is Dadaism, an anti-WWI cultural movement partly comprised of a style of art closely related Surrealism and Cubism. A well-known example of Dadaist art is Marcel Duchamp's LHOOQ, or the Mona Lisa with a mustache. During its heyday, Dadaism was written off as foolish and derivative, though it gets more respect and attention today. My gallery exhibit will acknowledge the changes in its status in the art world. What could I possibly write? A short list might include:

- a proposal for such a show, demonstrating its relevance to your audience, a

logistics plan, and a budget
- a letter of inquiry to secure grant funding for your show
- descriptive placards annotating the pieces chosen for the show
- an introduction for the program with sections such as "Brief History," "Major Artists," "Exhibits in the Late 20th Century," "The Future of Dada"
- a review of the show for the paper
- a profile of a Dadaist (living)
- a companion Web site with a selection of the works exhibited
- an event poster

Unit Four: Writing a Public Performance or Event

Consider this unit a grand finale. Since our readings suggest that people's interests lie in making the most of their time with their families, humans and animals alike, your task is to put on an enjoyable show or event—"something for the whole family," as they say.

Documents

Depending on your topic, the documents you write will probably vary greatly from your classmates'. But, here's an example to get your own ball rolling. Say my topic is a festival to promote the concept: "Our State Recycles." What could I possibly write? A short list might include:

- a proposal for such an event, describing the features of the event, a logistics plan, and a budget
- a leaflet promoting the event including directions and parking info
- an informative pamphlet to hand out at the event, including the day's schedule and map
- a logo and slogan for the festival with prototypes of a t-shirt, banner, and bumper sticker
- a script for a puppet show at the festival

Final Portfolio

The final assignment of the course is a Final Portfolio, worth 40% of your grade, which includes:

- Three of your documents, revised with peer and instructor feedback, polished and delivered as final products
- A reflective essay (3-4 pages) outlining your rhetorical and design choices for each, as well as the relevant contributions from your field analyses, feedback from classmates, the readings, or other aspects of the course. This essay should be organized around a theme or central feature of the chosen pieces.

Final Portfolio Presentations will be held during finals. Students will read aloud a section of their essays or describe a document of which they're particularly proud from any project.

Course Design

UWP 011: Popular Science & Technology Writing

Sarah Perrault

Course Description

UWP 011: Popular Science & Technology Writing is a sophomore-level course designed as an introduction to rhetoric of science at UC Davis, a science-focused land-grant university. The course fulfills the general education requirements for written literacy and for topical breadth in arts and humanities. The catalog describes the course as investigating the "positioning of science and technology in society as reflected and constructed in popular texts" (University of California, Davis, *General* 521). A main goal of the course is to foster students' critical scientific literacy and ability to read texts rhetorically.

Institutional Context

UWP 011 was created in the context of needs that, while especially strong at UC Davis, generalize to writing programs across the country. First, the course is intended to help define the University Writing Program's disciplinary identity, a perennial issue faced by Writing Studies programs of all kinds.[1] Second, the course addresses UC Davis's need for increased scientific literacy (SL) among graduates.

The University Writing Program (UWP) at UC Davis is an independent academic unit within the Division of Humanities, Arts, and Cultural Studies (HArCS). UWP separated from the English department in 2003, and since then our mission has shifted from an exclusive teaching focus to a shared teaching and research focus. This shift has taken two forms. First, the composition of the faculty has broadened. Prior to independence, all the UWP faculty were lecturers, mostly full time, with teaching appointments, whereas today the faculty also includes five professors (three full and two assistant) who have combined teaching/research appointments. In addition, we also have gone from having no minor, major, or graduate degree to having an undergraduate minor and a graduate Designated Emphasis in Writing, Rhetoric, and Composition Studies. We are working toward having a major and a Ph.D.

Despite these changes, we are still mainly focused on composition with the required lower and upper division writing courses making up over 90% of the program's offerings. As this figure suggests, we are in the early stages of defining what kind of department we will be and what kinds of degree programs we will develop. In creating courses, therefore, we are not only expanding our curriculum, but making early steps toward deciding and signaling to others what our disciplinary identity or identities will be. We are especially working to complement our existing composition focus by adding courses on theory, history, and research methods, and UWP 011 is our first rhetorical theory course at the undergraduate level.

As we add courses, we also are thinking and talking about the future stability of the program. Our success so far as an autonomous unit springs, to a great deal, from our program's Writing the Disciplines (WID) and Writing in the Professions (WIP) focus and the visibility this gives us across campus, and we know that to continue growing while maintaining the support these courses bring us, we need to heed Richard Young and Edwin Steinberg's advice that an academic program is most stable when it is "responsive to durable needs of society" (395). As Young and Steinberg point out,

> in the case of rhetorical studies, the durable social needs are obvious. Rhetoric has long sought to address the need for literacy and the need to participate reasonably and effectively in the social conversation; that is, rhetoric has always been concerned with the use of language in community-sustaining action. (395)

I would amend this only to say that Rhetoric today concerns itself not with literacy, but with *literacies*; indeed, our emphasis on WID/WIP reflects the diversity of discourse communities students are expected to visit or to inhabit professionally. These courses meet university and social needs by teaching disciplinary and professional rhetorics, and in doing so they also provide the UWP with a stable institutional mission and standing. However, as much as students need literacy in particular discourses, they need broader literacies as well, including one that UWP 011 is designed to address: critical scientific literacy.

UC Davis was founded as the University Farm School (an extension of UC Berkeley) in 1908 and has focused on sciences, especially applied sciences such as plant biology and agricultural engineering, from its earliest years. In 1959, it became a "general campus," separate from UC Berkeley, with the understanding that it would maintain a focus on teaching and research in agriculture. In this context, it makes sense that concern for *scientific literacy* (or SL) is stated clearly in the UC Davis "Revised General Education Requirement" document:

> The objective is to create graduates who understand the fundamental ways scientists approach problems and generate new knowledge, and who understand how scientific findings relate to other disciplines and to public policy. (University of California, Davis "Revised")

But SL is not just important to science students or future scientists. One of the most common arguments for SL—that it enhances citizens' decision-making abilities—applies to everyone, regardless of their career paths. Thus, SL matters as much in a humanities-focused program or campus as it does in an agricultural school like UC Davis. This is especially true of the second aspect of SL, the understanding of "how scientific findings relate to other disciplines and to public policy."

The problem, at Davis and elsewhere, is that science classes teach students how to solve scientific problems and create scientific knowledge, but many do not address the sciences' relationships to other areas of study and to society as a whole. Even when science classes do address this broader scope, they necessarily do so from an internal perspective. However, to truly understand these broader issues, students need to look at science from vantage points outside of STEM (Science, Technology, Engineering, and Math), vantage points provided by Science and Technology Studies (STS) disciplines such as sociology, history, philosophy, and rhetoric of science.

Even science educators agree that SL often is not, and cannot be, addressed solely within STEM disciplines. Science Education professor Jonathan Osborne writes in a 2010 issue of *Science* focused on SL that "[a]rgument and debate are common in science, yet they are virtually absent from science education" (463), and that

> Typically, in the rush to present the major features of the scientific landscape, most of the arguments required to achieve such knowledge are excised. Consequently, science can appear to its students as a monolith of facts, an authoritative discourse where the discursive exploration of ideas, their implications, and their importance is absent. Students then emerge with naïve ideas or misconceptions about the nature of science itself… (464)

Although it is understandable that many science courses emphasize content over critique—it is, after all, the point of "the programmatic goals of disciplinary classes—to become familiar with the content and issues that are salient in a given field" (Greene & Orr 149)—critical depth is exactly what is needed if students are truly to become scientifically literate—that is, if they are to attain a critical, not just an instrumental, scientific literacy.

At this point it is important to distinguish between different aspects of SL. The first, Instrumental SL, is a knowledge-centered approach characterized by most undergraduate science classes. As Bryan Brown, John Reveles, and Gregory Kelly explain, knowledge-centered perspectives on SL "value students' developing scientific knowledge, practices, habits of mind, and ways of using knowledge as citizens or individuals acquiring literacy for some extrinsic purposes" (780). Instrumental SL includes the kind of learning described in the first half of the UC Davis General Education requirements: how to "approach problems, pose questions, gather data, make conclusions, and then generate new hypotheses for testing" (*General* 3).

Instrumental SL, which is "confined to a surface-level recognition of scientific vocabulary and principles" (Zerbe 91), is good as a starting point. However, Zerbe points out that much science education stops here: "By and large, the contemporary curricular structure of science education leaves little room for studying science as more than learning its experimental and observational methods" (91). Returning to Brown, Reveles, and Kelly, in such an outlook "scientific literacy remains abstracted from experience and ultimately disconnected from the lives of people engaged in their world" (780). To go beyond Instrumental SL,[2] it is necessary to situate science in its broader epistemic and social contexts by engaging in *critical scientific literacy* (CSL).

This second approach, CSL, is rooted in a sociocultural-centered perspective that "seeks to situate any definition of scientific literacy in the actions of accomplishing everyday life" and in so doing, "considers how literacy is relevant to particular tasks at hand in some relevant social context" (Brown, Reveles, and Kelly 780). They continue:

> The task of using knowledge to accomplish a particular undertaking requires consideration of the modes of interaction and sociohistorical contexts brought into play in the construction of the literacy event. (780)

Although it is possible to go into more depth about variations within sociocultural-centered SL, such fine-grained taxonomy is less important here than the general concept of distinguishing instrumental from critical SL. Therefore, for the purposes of this article, I lump together the various aspects of the sociocultural-centered perspective—critical, epistemic, and ideological SL (see Zerbe 93-96)—under the heading Critical Scientific Literacy, or CSL. What these different aspects of CSL have in common is attention to knowledge-making processes in science, to the construction of scientific authority, and to the interplay of science and society.

Explaining why CSL matters does not explain why I think Writing Studies is well positioned to foster CSL. Here I offer two reasons, one general and one specific. First, on a general level, much of what is touted as CSL is actually critical thinking, an area where Writing Studies curricula have long excelled. In 2010 *Science* article, P. David Pearson, Elizabeth Moje, and Cynthia Greenleaf acknowledge the overlap when they write that "Science and literacy use many of the same reasoning processes: setting purposes, asking questions, clarifying ambiguities, drawing inferences from incomplete evidence, and making evidence-based arguments" (460). Similarly, Osborne suggests that students need not only "explicit teaching of how to reason" but also "a knowledge of the meta-linguistic features of argumentation (claims, reasons, evidence, and counterargument) to identify the essential elements of their own and others' arguments" (466)—curricular needs that clearly fall within the domain of Writing Studies.

Second, more specifically, Writing Studies is uniquely suited to foster CSL because of its interest in critical literacies. The *National Science Education Standards* (*NSES*) state that scientific literacy "includes understanding the nature of science, the scientific enterprise, and the role of science in society and personal life" (Center for Science, Mathematics, and Engineering Education 21). A rhetorical approach can help reveal the discursive nature of science and the role that texts play in mediating knowledge in and about science. In addition, as Zerbe notes, Rhetoric has a tradition of questioning dominant discourses and "a constant dedication to keep a close eye on powerful discourses" (2). He adds that in the early centuries of Rhetoric, the powerful discourse was the law. Later, religious discourse came to dominate, and rhetoricians focused their attention on the church. Today, science is one of the most powerful discourses—if not *the* most powerful discourse—in the world, and as such merits our scholarly and pedagogical attention.

Theoretical Rationale

I designed the curriculum with three main goals. The first goal was for students to see science as a sociocultural phenomenon, to see how it shapes and is shaped by the larger culture of which it is a part. The second goal, specific to rhetoric of science, was for students to recognize the discursive nature of science-related texts, and to be able to identify and critique the rhetorical moves in those texts in terms of how those moves construct popular understandings of science. The third goal, not specific to CSL, was for students to engage in scholarly practices: engaging in intellectual inquiry, seeking out and questioning evidence, understanding and questioning their own and others' perspectives, and articulating their findings and positions in clear and coherent prose.

In approaching the first goal, to help students see science as a sociocultural phenomenon, I was aware that a truly critical scientific literacy is interdisciplinary, characterized by knowledge and understandings not from the sciences but also from sociology, history, and philosophy of science (to name the most established science studies disciplines). Given the science-and-technology-oriented nature of the UC Davis student body, I could assume that most students had already begun acquiring instrumental scientific literacy. However, because UWP 011 is a lower division elective I could not assume students had any previous exposure to science studies. Therefore, I needed to provide some Science and Technology Studies (STS) perspectives, which I did during the first two weeks. To place our guiding questions in a historical context, I spent half of each class session explaining the history of science writing and of science popularization. I also introduced the two models of science popularization we would be using all term, models based on STS scholarship in Rhetoric, Communication, and sociology.

The first model goes by various labels, including the "deficit" model, the "Public Understanding of Science and Technology" (PUST) model, or in my own coining, the "Public Appreciation of Science and Technology" (PAST) model.[3] In this model, science communication is characterized as a one-way flow of reliable information from the scientific sphere to the public, with that public viewed as a "blank slate of ignorance on which scientists write knowledge" (Myers 266). The model is characterized by an uncomplicated view of science that promotes a "positivist view of the inexorably rational and progressive nature of scientific knowledge" (Taylor 115). It is also based on "a pervasive but outdated and overly simplistic model of communication as a simple linear process" (Hansen 107) in which scientists produce knowledge, the knowledge is packaged in language, and the packages are opened by the public and the knowledge in them absorbed in its original form.

One especially problematic aspect of the PAST model is the way it fails to distinguish between hot and cold science. Cold science (a.k.a. "textbook" science) is certain. It's the knowledge that has stood the test of replication and peer review and time. Hot science (a.k.a. "frontier" science) is much less certain; it is science in the making. This distinction was important in UWP 011 for two reasons. First, it helped students see the difference between what happens in classrooms and what happens in reality. Science classes, especially foundational undergraduate classes, teach cold science. Reducing science literacy to this level tends to promote "a damaging illusion that real science is somehow like school science" and so risks "communicating naively inductivist and empiricist misunderstanding of how science creates knowledge" (Turner 63). Second, it circumvented a miniature replay of the science wars by acknowledging all the ways that science has contributed solid understandings of the world while also admitting that not all science is equally reliable. In other words, it gave us a way to talk about science as *both* certain and uncertain, a key element of the second model of SL.

The second model, dubbed the "Critical Understanding of Science in Public" (CUSP) model by Peter Broks, focuses on both of the "twin duties" of science communication: "to inform and educate the public about science on the one hand, but also to probe and criticize it on the other" (Russell xiii). In contrast with the deficit-minded PAST model, the CUSP model evaluates popular science texts in terms of how well they bring to discussions of science a much-needed set of "citizen views, which bring in notions of equity and access, ethics, control and sustainability" (Einsiedel 181). Given the importance of understanding hot science, a primary aim in UWP 011 was to help students see science and its institutions in context, and to begin thinking about how many aspects of science are socially constructed. Becoming aware of the constructedness of knowledge "changes the geography of all previous categories; it denatures them as heat denatures a fragile protein" (Haraway 157). This denaturing, or denaturalizing of what seems natural and inevitable, opens up texts to critical questions about demarcation (e.g., What is science? What distinguishes science from other knowledge-making endeavors?) and about science in society (e.g., What is the role of science in society, and the role of society in relation to science?). Asking such questions helps to break down a monolithic view of science and allows students to build more complex understandings of science as a set of practices, institutions, and relationships. In other words, the CUSP model of SL eschews the reductive distortions of the PAST model and offers a more useful framework for critical engagement.

The two models of scientific literacy informed how I approached the second goal—for students to be able to identify and critique the rhetorical moves in texts about science—in terms of my text choices and the rhetorical lenses we used to analyze those texts.

The main course text was *The Best American Science and Nature Writing 2010* (*BASNW 2010*), a collection of 27 essays and articles edited by renowned physicist Freeman Dyson. A few supplemental articles from other sources were provided via the course SmartSite. I focused the course on popular science texts because these texts serve as "important components of the perception and practice of the contemporary cultural institution of science" (Zerbe 105) and therefore offer relatively easy insights into that cultural institution. Also, in contrast with primary scientific literature, popular science texts often show scientific issues in their social contexts while also being more accessible than scientific journal articles. As Zerbe argues, "in many ways, efforts to achieve a culturally informed, meaningful scientific literacy can be recognized and realized more quickly in popularizations than in original research" (106). Popular science texts allow students to engage with texts at the rhetorical level more readily than they would if they were struggling to learn the background science first.[4]

To teach a CSL-specific approach to rhetorical analysis, I introduced five analytic lenses[5] that are useful for identifying where popular science texts fall on the PAST/CUSP continuum. These lenses, in the order used in class, were demarcation, expertise, modes and stases, ethos and persona, and certainty/uncertainty and risk.

- The demarcation lens looked at how texts create a relationship between science and society. Using this lens, we looked at whether a given text supported the dominant view of science as something apart, or a critical view that situates science in its sociocultural context.
- The modes and stases lens illuminated how texts create subject positions, that is, the relationship between readers and science. This lens looks at what kind of stance readers are invited to take toward science.
- The expertise lens built on the modes and stases lens by showing how texts create a narrow or broad scope of participation in science-related decision-making.
- The ethos lens looked at how the relationship between the writer and science, that is, how a text creates the writer's technical credibility on science topics. Balancing this is the "persona" lens, which looks at how the writer creates a relationship with the reader.
- The certainty/uncertainty and risk lens revealed a writer's use of hedging, identified when hot science is being presented as more certain than it is, and helped students judge socioscientific issues such as the costs and benefits arising from particular courses of actions.

Explaining all five lenses would take more space than I have here, so I will focus on expertise as an example.

A PAST depiction reduces expertise to a binary in which scientists have it and non-scientists don't. In contrast, a CUSP depiction represents expertise as coming in different forms, with formal scientific training being one among several legitimate ways to learn about the world. Drawing on work by H. M. Collins and Robert Evans in sociology of science and Beverly Sauer in technical communication, I presented six categories of expertise. The first four come from Collins and Evans:

- Contributory expertise: The ability to do something well, or add to a body of knowledge. Researchers have contributory expertise within their research areas.
- Interactional expertise: The ability to use the language of a domain, but without "practical competence" (Collins and Evans 14). For example, a software project manager might not know how to program, but will know how to talk about programming well enough to communicate with programmers.
- Meta-expertise: The ability to judge others' expertise without having it oneself. An NSF grant committee includes members who do not have knowledge in the specific area of any given grant proposal but can still evaluate the quality of the proposal.
- Referred expertise: The "use of an expertise learned in one domain within another domain" (15). A student who learns good study habits in one discipline can apply those habits to another discipline after changing majors.

From Sauer, who argues for a greater understanding of "the interdependence of scientific knowledge and local experience, and the rhetorical presence of tacit knowledge" (20), I drew two additional concepts:

- Local expertise: The knowledge of "interested citizens" (79). Many California students have developed local expertise regarding the state budget and education funding.
- Experiential expertise: "Tacit or craft knowledge" (79). Many laboratory skills—for example, pipetting, preparing slides, and adjusting microscopes—require hands-on experience that cannot be provided via lectures or textbooks.

In deciding how to identify a text's representation of expertise, we asked questions such as: Who gets quoted? Are different kinds of experts quoted and critiqued in the same way? For example, whose contribution is given a positive label? A negative label? Whose assertions are weighted for their soundness, and whose are accepted as given? Authority comes in part through use of a specialized vocabulary. Who has one? Only scientists?

Others as well? Whose vocabulary is quoted? We asked these questions in class about Trevor Corson's "Stalking the American Lobster," a text that contains several kinds of expertise, then students applied them in their responses to a similarly broad-minded article, Burkhard Bilger's "Hearth Surgery." Asking such questions helps support SCL by looking at how "writing works in the world and how the 'tool' of writing is used to mediate various activities" (Downs and Wardle 558) and thereby encouraging readers to consider not only what a text says about its topic, but also how it construes scientific authority, and what kind of relationship between science and society it presents as normal.

Students responded to texts using the different lenses in classroom discussions and in their written assignments, the latter also supporting the third course goal: for students to engage in scholarly research and writing. Students wrote six responses and a research paper. The response assignments included three parts: a summary, a response, and an analysis.

The 200-300 word objective summary of the popular science text encouraged students to read for the writer's point of view, and it allowed them to practice summarizing, a foundational skill on which more critical skills are built.[6]

The 200-300 word response asked for their subjective reaction to any aspect of the text. Education experts suggest that good teaching helps students "see connections between what they are learning and their personal goals" (Glynn, Aultman, and Owens 164) or interests, and this part of the assignment was intended to help students make those connections. Additionally, the responses helped foster the critical aspects of scientific literacy. Given that science classes often train students to passively accept information, it was important to create a space in which they could break the sometimes-tacit rules of academia by saying whatever they wanted to about a text or an idea. I wanted to break them out of a passive reception mode and encourage opinions, no matter how subjective.

The 200-300 word rhetorical analysis gave students a chance to use that week's theoretical lens in practicing critical reading and analysis. Through this part of the Summary/Response/Analysis (SRA), students "become much more used to critical maneuvers with texts" (Downs and Wardle 572) such as asking about the writer's possible motives. For example, in the SRA using the expertise lens, students not only identified what kinds of expertise were represented in an article, but also speculated about why the writer might have chosen to cite those particular experts and about what effect those choices had on readers' perceptions of the scientific enterprise described in the article.

The overall idea behind the SRAs was to give students repeated opportunities to practice taking different stances toward texts, and to do so in a relatively low-stakes manner. Therefore, the grading criteria were geared toward clarity of expression, and I dropped the lowest of the six SRA grades.

The research paper included all three aspects of the SRA and added a research component. Each student chose a text from *BASNW 2010*, used one of the lenses to identify PAST elements in the text, and wrote about how the author could have made that aspect of the text more CUSP. This involved research, as the student had to find information the author had not included. Beyond requiring that students consult a range of sources and discuss them with me and with my TA, I wanted to leave open as many parameters as possible because "[w]hen students have the opportunity to help design their educational activities... they are more likely to benefit from them" (Glynn, Aultman, and Owens 158). Allowing students to choose any text, any aspect of that text, and any lens allowed them to pursue whichever of their own intellectual interests were sparked by the texts they had read and the concepts they had learned. The 27 pieces in Dyson's collection offered students a wide range of texts to choose from, while limiting their choices to those pieces ensured that students' workshop peers were familiar with the piece that any one student wrote about. The assignment included four stages—proposal, research report, draft, and final revision—with feedback at the proposal and draft stages.

I had two specific goals for this assignment. First, I wanted students to see texts as *rhetorical*, as being the result of a series of decisions the writer made. Looking at texts in terms of what the writer might have done differently really brought home to them that writers leave things out. Articulating those decisions in terms of the rhetorical concepts made students connect those textual decisions to social dynamics beyond the text. Thus, they became more able "to recognize texts not as information but as the words of real people" (Downs and Wardle 572).

I also wanted the assignment to help students see science, in Zerbe's words, "as more than learning its experimental and observational methods" (91). In the research paper, each student delved more deeply into a specific aspect of science. Those who chose to look at texts in terms of demarcation learned more about how texts create expectations about what the relationship between science and society is or should be. Those who chose to look at texts in terms of modes/stases, or in terms of certainty/uncertainty and risk, learned more about knowledge making in science. Those who chose to focus on textual representations of expertise, or on ethos and persona, learned more about constructions of scientific authority and of its relationship to other forms of knowledge. No matter which lens they selected, students had to find out more about the broader epistemic and social contexts for the science in their chosen articles.

Critical Reflection

Based on changes I saw in students' work and in class discussions, I think the class met its two main pedagogical goals—to increase students' CSL and their rhetorical understanding of texts—quite well. Although I don't have IRB approval (which I did not think of getting) and so cannot quote directly from student writing or evaluations, I can talk about the *kinds* of changes I saw.

The first major change was that students started asking critical questions about the readings and about science such as: What is the author's background? Where was this article first published? How might that have affected the writer's focus? Where was the scientific study published? Has the study been replicated? Has it been refuted? And what is the "n" on this study?

These kinds of questions are essential for critical literacy in general, but especially for scientific literacy. The *NSES*, whose definitions of SL I quoted earlier, also defines SL in terms of "being able to read with understanding articles about science in the popular press and to engage in social conversation about the validity of the conclusions... [and] to evaluate the quality of scientific information on the basis of its source and the methods used to generate it" (Center for Science, Mathematics, and Engineering Education 22). As a group, the class moved from a generally one-dimensional view of scientific studies as either right or wrong, to a more nuanced understanding of science as a process in which there are varying degrees of accuracy that must be judged in context.

The second change was that students grew comfortable using the lenses as a heuristic and approaching texts analytically. For example, when reading an expert's comment on a topic they would ask questions like "Is the scientist being quoted on a topic a contributory expert in that area? If not, does the scientist have some other kind of relevant expertise (e.g., metaexpertise or referred expertise) that makes the scientist credible on this topic?"

They also learned to read rhetorically, considering authors' choices and asking questions about a text's composition. They also, in the words of Downs and Wardle, "became much more likely to recognize texts not as information but as the words of real people" (572). Their research papers were especially revealing on this front as, in searching for answers to some questions, they sometimes found answers to questions they hadn't thought to ask. In a few cases, those unexpected findings turned out to be more interesting to them than their original queries had been. One student, looking for information on the research methods used in a study, was surprised to learn that the research team included not just Americans, as the *BASNW 2010* article had implied, but people from several other countries as well. This discovery prompted an interesting discussion of nationalism (or provincialism) in science popularization and a new look at other texts to see if they did the same thing.

As they grew more comfortable looking at science critically and at texts rhetorically, students also increased the complexity of the views they adopted and expressed during class discussions and in their writing. Specifically, their textual analyses grew more nuanced as they moved from blanket reactions to texts, labeling a given text as PAST (bad) or CUSP (good), to discussing texts in terms of a combination of PAST and CUSP elements.

The writing assignments helped students develop a critical stance toward texts and toward science. With the weekly SRAs, I showed students that any thoughtful, well-supported claim was acceptable by playing Elbow's "believing game" as I read and responded. In one early SRA, a student talked about how little he cared about the topic, a comment I considered just as valid as other students' more enthusiastic responses. Allowing students to express themselves freely in the "response" sections, and making sure to respond positively to any response, reinforced the message that challenging dogma was acceptable, and even favored.

The SRAs also helped students learn and/or practice foundational skills such as summarizing texts and conducting rhetorical analyses. This practice was helpful when they wrote their research papers because they were already in the habit of thinking about texts in terms of the writer's choices. The research paper then built on this foundation by having them do an inquiry-driven investigation into what writers weren't saying. The stages described above—proposal, research report, draft, and final revision—worked well. None of the students had trouble choosing an article, topic, or lens, and collectively they chose the full range of lenses. For example, some students selected highly epideictic texts and explored the forensic detail that the author might have included. In some cases, the students showed how that detail would have supported the author's claims; in other cases, the students showed how the epideictic prose was hiding some unsavory facts. Other lenses were similarly used to guide students' research and to help students critique the primary texts.

I will make changes in the concepts I cover when I teach the course again. Shawn Glynn, Lori Aultman, and Ashley Owens suggest that faculty engage students' interest "by introducing them to concepts that are moderately novel and moderately complex… [to] pique the students' curiosity, while avoiding boredom or anxiety" (164). In designing the course, I had tried to aim for a middle ground between boredom (too little complexity) and anxiety (too much), and at the end I felt I had aimed too far toward the anxiety end of the spectrum. There were a few reasons I felt this way. First, on a purely subjective level, I felt rushed. Perhaps in response to this feeling, during the course I found myself merging some concepts that seemed close enough to warrant their not being taken separately. More importantly, many students didn't quite grasp a fundamental concept of the course, a rhetorical understanding of genre in which texts are viewed as "mediating artifacts rather than things in themselves" (Bazerman and Russell 1). It was clear in retrospect that I need to slow down and give more time to the concept of genre. At the same time, I want to keep the course complex, not only to hold students' interest but also to accurately convey the complexity of the popular science writing genre and of issues of science in society.

Ultimately, I have decided to maintain the basic framework of the course, but to streamline it by removing one concept, merging two others, and changing the order in which we use the lenses. The topic I removed is the distinction between science and technology (not mentioned on the syllabus but brought up in the initial lecture); we didn't have enough time to address it well, and the distinction turned out not to be germane for the issues we discussed. As physicist and philosopher Gerard Fourez notes, although science and technology are different, the importance of the difference depends on the context; sometimes the differences matter and other times the similarities matter (909).

The topics I merged, in action last Winter and in the plan for this Winter, are risk and certainty/uncertainty (week 6 in the syllabus). I also plan to move these from the end of the course to near the start. That is, after the opening material (sociohistorical context, the PAST and CUSP models, and hot versus cold science, covered in weeks one and two), I will move directly to talking about risk and uncertainty. Addressing risk and uncertainty together makes sense as the two generally blur into each other—uncertainty matters most when there is something at risk, and risk is harder to talk about in conditions of uncertainty than when likely outcomes are known. Addressing these first makes sense because in Winter 2011, these were the concepts that really cemented students' understanding that science is not just something that happens in a lab but instead is an inseparable part of our lives. Having that understanding come in week two or three, instead of in week six, should result in more productive discussions earlier in the quarter. If we can reach a level of critical understanding in week three that last time came in weeks six and seven, we should be able to push the critical reading and analysis aspects of the class even further.

Shifting the risk and certainty/uncertainty lens earlier also makes sense because talking about risk and uncertainty immediately after introducing the idea of hot and cold science will demonstrate why the distinction matters when discussing science in society; distinguishing hot from cold science lets us acknowledge the many contributions of science while maintaining a critical perspective. Or, as Michael Ford puts it, seeing science in these terms allows us to escape from the "positivist endeavor" that "casts the success of science in terms of universal logic and scientific methods" (Ford 406), while still realizing that the various sciences have, over the years, "resulted in considerably reliable knowledge claims" (407).

Along with changing the order of the lenses, I plan to change the order of the readings. In Winter 2011, I started with some models of good (CUSP) popular science writing, thinking they would provide a positive benchmark against which students could measure other texts. That turned out to be a mistake; until they saw the problematic aspects of popular science writing in the PAST model, students were confused about why the PAST/CUSP distinction mattered. When they did read an overtly PAST-model text, they expressed immediate comprehension and they became more actively engaged in exploring where other texts fell on the PAST-CUSP continuum.

A quick illustration comes from the first article in *BASNW 2010*, Andrew Corsello's "The Believer," which we read in week eight. Although we had talked and read *about* the problem of popular science writing that describes scientists in godlike terms, the class didn't fully appreciate this problematic trope until they read descriptions of the scientist-entrepreneur Elon Musk that cast him in blatantly religious terms. For example, in his childhood, when his siblings and cousins were afraid of the dark, six-year-old Musk knew better, and Corsello shows the scene through the eyes of Musk's aunt Maye:

> The light has mostly waned, but Elon, he's so *white,* skin as pale as a fish's belly, and Maye Musk can see his face so clearly. Beaming. Euphoric. Because he *knows.*
>
> Elon hasn't been bickering with his sister and brother; he has been evangelizing. And now he raises both arms to make sure they can see, as well as hear, the good news.
>
> "Do not be scared of the darkness!" Elon Musk calls out to them from the wilderness. "There is nothing to fear—it is merely the absence of light!" (3, emphasis in original)

From his early years as miraculous child, "a child with freakish talent" (3), to his adult mission "to give the human race its biggest upgrade since the advent of consciousness" (5), Elon is shown as nothing less than godlike in his abilities and his scope. Once students had read and discussed the problems with this kind of presentation, including the fact that setting up scientists as gods can easily lead to disillusionment when they fail to produce miracles, they had a better sense of how other texts better served science and readers of popular science texts by presenting scientists in more measured, reasonable, and human terms. In Winter 2012 I plan to use a similarly blatant example from the *Best American Science Writing 2011*, assigning it during week one so I can refer to it while explaining the PAST model of scientific literacy.

Having narrowed the course's conceptual breadth and reordered the readings should let me add a few secondary sources to the mix. Not having taught this kind of class before, and being new to teaching lower division courses at UC Davis, I was initially unsure about what kinds of secondary texts would be appropriate, or whether they would fit into a quarter already stuffed full of reading popular science texts. After teaching the class, I think that my initial instinct to focus on primary texts was sound, but that I can work in some secondary sources. In particular, I plan to add two articles.

The first article is Kelly Dirk's 2010 "Navigating Genres" article from *Writing Spaces: Readings on Writing*. Unlike more theory-heavy genre texts I considered and rejected as being at too high a level for UWP 011—for example, Carolyn Miller, Amy Devitt, and Anis Bawarshi and Mary Jo Reiff—Dirk's article introduces the concept of genre in terms suitable for an undergraduate course. It also uses easily grasped examples to illustrate how genres function socially and epistemically (without ever resorting to the word "epistemically"!). I also plan to use "Science's New Social Contract with Society," a short (four-page) *Nature* article in which physicist Michael Gibbons argues that scientists need to be more concerned with how their work affects others, and should "ensure that scientific knowledge is 'socially robust', and that its production is seen by society to be both transparent and participative" (C81). While the article by Dirk should help students better understand genre, Gibbons' article shows that scientists as well as humanities scholars care about open communication between scientists and the public.

UC Davis is on the quarter system, and the limitations of a ten-week term meant I had to leave out assignments I would like to have included. If I had more time, I would make three significant changes. First, I would add more secondary sources. Second, I would add some scientific research articles. An ideal text for this is *A Century of Nature: Twenty-One Discoveries that Changed Science and the World* (Garwin and Lincoln), which brings together 21 original articles published in *Nature* during the twentieth century with commentaries written on them today. The book would be excellent because it reflects "a relatively common popularization goal... of promoting a more holistic view of science and highlighting its inextricable connections to culture at large" (Zerbe 109). And third, I would add a stylistic imitation exercise. I have done this in previous creative non-fiction classes, and it is immensely effective for helping students understand the way that tone and stance are created at the level of word choice. Basically, an imitation piece would do at the micro level what the research paper does at the macro level—show students how different decisions create different textual effects.

In terms of disciplinary identity, I would like to say that UWP 011 has helped establish the writing program as a disciplinary unit that is dedicated to but goes beyond its service function in teaching required composition courses, but I know better. Even the most well-received class is a fraction of the curriculum needed to create and sustain disciplinary status, and the struggle for recognition is much bigger than one class, or one professor, or even one program. That said, UWP 011 does complement and support our existing curriculum by adding a theory course that dovetails nicely with a WAC-based view of writing as always rooted in a particular context.

Over all, despite the bumpy aspects in Winter 2011, and the new bumps I am sure I will encounter in Winter 2012, I think that UPW 011 and courses like it are well suited to meet important social and academic needs for critical and rhetorical scientific literacy. Even though students in UWP 011 did not fully grasp a central concept of the course (genre as social action), they did learn to view texts as rhetorical artifacts, and to see science as embedded in and influenced by its sociohistorical context. And while I initially resisted paring back what seemed like an overly narrow conceptual toolkit, reviewing student papers to write this Course Design has reminded me that the goal is not to teach students to do everything. Rather, it is to broaden their understanding of what can be done, and to teach them to do some aspects of it well in the hope that they will maintain and build on those skills.

Notes

1. I use "Writing Studies" as an umbrella term that includes Writing, Rhetoric, and Composition Studies.
2. As Brown, Reveles, and Kelly note, valuing sociocultural-centered SL does not devalue information-centered SL, and vice versa. Thus, my emphasis on CSL does not reflect a desire to get rid of instrumental SL, but rather a recognition of its limitations.
3. I started out referring to it as PUST, but changed the label to the more accurate "Public Appreciation of Science and Technology" (PAST) after explaining for the umpteenth time that the "understanding" part of PUST was really about appreciation.
4. Zerbe does discuss ways to use scientific texts in first-year composition, and I refer interested readers to his excellent book.
5. Other concepts introduced during the course included: anthropomorphism and mechanomorphism, eugenics, the Mertonian norms, and various kinds of scientism (axiological scientism, epistemic scientism, existential scientism, ontological scientism, and political scientism).
6. Roger Ochse notes that "Single system reasoning is prerequisite to higher level reasoning, since reading comprehension and understanding of texts is the very basis of forming judgments and assessments in a multi-system reasoning environment" (4).

Works Cited

Bawarshi, Anis S., and Mary Jo Reiff. *Genre: An Introduction to History, Theory, Research, and Pedagogy*. Reference Guides to Rhetoric and Composition. West Lafayette, IN: Parlor Press, 2010. Print.

Bazerman, Charles, and David R. Russell, eds. *Writing Selves, Writing Societies: Research from Activity Perspectives*. Fort Collins: WAC Clearinghouse, 2003. Print.

Bilger, Burkhard. "Hearth Surgery." Dyson 311-33.

Broks, Peter. *Understanding Popular Science*. Maidenhead/New York: Open UP, 2006. Print.

Brown, Bryan A., John M. Reveles, and Gregory J. Kelly. "Scientific Literacy and Discursive Identity: A Theoretical Framework for Understanding Science Learning." *Science Education* 89.5 (2005): 779-802. Print.

Center for Science, Mathematics, and Engineering Education. *National Science Education Standards*. Washington: National Academies, 1996. Print.

Collins, H. M., and Robert Evans. *Rethinking Expertise*. Chicago: U of Chicago P, 2007. Print.

Corsello, Andrew. "The Believer." Dyson 3-15.

Corson, Trevor. "Stalking the American Lobster." *The Best American Science Writing 2003*. Ed. Oliver Sacks. New York: Harper, 2003. 138-59. Print.

Devitt, Amy J. *Writing Genres*. Rhetorical Philosophy and Theory Series. Carbondale: Southern Illinois UP, 2004. Print.

Dirk, Kerry. "Navigating Genres." *Writing Spaces: Readings on Writing*. Ed. Charles Lowe and Pavel Zemliansky. Vol. 1. Anderson: Parlor, 2010. 249-62. Print.

Downs, Douglas, and Elizabeth Wardle. "Teaching About Writing, Righting Misconceptions: (Re)Envisioning 'First-Year Composition' as 'Introduction to Writing Studies.'" *CCC* 58.4 (2007): 552-84. Print.

Dyson, Freeman, ed. *Best American Science and Nature Writing 2010*. New York: Houghton Mifflin Harcourt, 2010. Print.

Einsiedel, Edna F. "Public Participation and Dialogue." *Handbook of Public Communication of Science and Technology*. Ed. Massimiano Bucchi and Brian Trench. New York: Routledge, 2007. 173-84. Print.

Ford, Michael. "Disciplinary Authority and Accountability in Scientific Practice and Learning." *Science Education* 92.3 (2008): 404-23. Print.

Fourez, Gérard. "Scientific and Technological Literacy as a Social Practice." *Social Studies of Science* 27 (1997): 903-36. Print.

Garwin, Laura, and Tim Lincoln. *A Century of Nature: Twenty-One Discoveries That Changed Science and the World*. Chicago: U of Chicago P, 2003. Print.

Gibbons, Michael. "Science's New Social Contract with Society." *Nature* 402 (1999): C81-C84. Print.

Glynn, Shawn M., Lori Price Aultman, and Ashley M. Owens. "Motivation to Learn in General Education Programs." *JGE: The Journal of General Education* 54.2 (2005): 150-70. Print.

Greene, Stuart, and Amy J. Orr. "First-Year College Students Writing across the Disciplines." *Blurring Boundaries: Developing Writers, Researchers, and Teachers*. Ed. Peggy O'Neill. Cresskill: Hampton, 2007. 123-56. Print.

Hansen, Anders. "Science, Communication and Media." *Investigating Science Communication in the Information Age: Implications for Public Engagement and Popular Media*. Ed. Richard Holliman et al. New York: Oxford UP, 2009. 105-27. Print.

Haraway, Donna J. *Simians, Cyborgs, and Women: The Reinvention of Nature*. New York: Routledge, 1991. Print.

Myers, Greg. "Discourse Studies of Scientific Popularization: Questioning the Boundaries." *Discourse Studies* 5.2 (2003): 265-79. Print.

Ochse, Roger. *Critical Thinking: A Model for Collaborative Research*. 1996. Paper presented at the Annual International Conference on Critical Thinking and Educational Reform (Sonoma, CA, July 28-31, 1996). *ERIC*. Web. 19 Sep. 2012.

Osborne, Jonathan. "Arguing to Learn in Science: The Role of Collaborative, Critical Discourse." *Science* 328 (2010): 463-66. Print.

Miller, Carolyn R. "Genre as Social Action." *Quarterly Journal of Speech* 70 (1984): 151-67. Print.

Pearson, P. David, Elizabeth Moje, and Cynthia Greenleaf. "Literacy and Science: Each in the Service of the Other." *Science* 328 (2010): 459-63. Print.

Russell, Nicholas J. *Communicating Science: Professional, Popular, Literary*. Cambridge: Cambridge UP, 2010. Print.

Sauer, Beverly J. *The Rhetoric of Risk: Technical Documentation in Hazardous Environments*. Mahwah: L. Erlbaum, 2003. Print.

Taylor, Charles Alan. *Defining Science: A Rhetoric of Demarcation*. Madison: U of Wisconsin P, 1996. Print.

Turner, Steven. "School Science and Its Controversies; or, Whatever Happened to Scientific Literacy?" *Public Understanding of Science* 17 (2008): 55-72. Print.

University of California, Davis. *UC Davis General Catalog: 2012-2014*. Davis, CA: University of California, Davis, 2012. Print.

University of California, Davis. "Revised General Education Requirement." Davis, CA: University of California, Davis, 2008. Web. 24 Sept. 2011.

Young, Richard E., and Edwin R. Steinberg. "Planning Graduate Programs in Rhetoric in Departments of English." *Rhetoric Review* 18.2 (2000): 390-402. Print.

Zerbe, Michael J. *Composition and the Rhetoric of Science: Engaging the Dominant Discourse*. Carbondale: Southern Illinois UP, 2007. Print.

SYLLABUS

UWP 011: Popular Science & Technology Writing

Course Description

The positioning of science and technology in society as reflected and constructed in popular texts. Topics include genre theory, demarcation, rhetorical figures, forms of qualitative and quantitative reasoning, and the epistemic role of popularization in science.

Course Texts

Dyson, Freeman, ed. *The Best American Science and Nature Writing 2010.* New York: Houghton Mifflin, 2010.

Articles on SmartSite (in the Resources à Readings folder):

Corson, Trevor. "Stalking the American Lobster." *The Best American Science Writing 2003.* Ed. Oliver Sacks. New York: Harper, 2003. 138-59. Print. (on SmartSite)

Franklin, H. Bruce. "The Most Important Fish in the Sea." *The Best American Science and Nature Writing 2002.* Ed. Natalie Angier. New York: Houghton, 2002. 80-88. Print.

Hirsh, Aaron E. "Signs of Life." *The Best American Science Writing 2004.* Ed. Dava Sobel. New York: Harper, 2004. 79-88. Print. (on SmartSite)

Margulis, Lynn, and Emily Case. "The Germs of Life." *The Best American Science and Nature Writing 2007.* Ed. Richard Preston. New York: Houghton, 2007. 123-26. Print.

Assignments

Assignment	%
Participation	10
Summary/Response/Analysis (SRA) on six essays (lowest grade dropped)	25
Midterm exam	15
Paper (proposal = 5, draft = 5, revision = 20)	30
Final exam	20
Total	100

Calendar

W = Week

D = Date ("J.04" = January 4th)

SRA = Summary/Response/Analysis

W	D	Reading Due	Writing Due
01	J.04		
	J.06	Dyson, "Introduction" Franklin, "The Most Important Fish in the Sea" (on SmartSite)	
02	J.11	Kolbert, "The Catastrophist" Osnos, "Green Giant"	SRA 1 = Demarcation (a.k.a. Science and Society, or Context)
	J.13	Corson, "Stalking the American Lobster" (on SmartSite)	
03	J.18	Bilger, "Hearth Surgery"	SRA 2 = Expertise
	J.20		
04	J.25	Kolbert, "The Sixth Extinction?" Weinberg, "The Missions of Astronomy" Hirsh, "Signs of Life" (on SmartSite)	SRA 3 = Stases/Modes
	J.27		
05	F.01	Carrier, "All You Can Eat" Manning, "Graze Anatomy" Margulis & Case, "Germs of Life" (on SmartSite)	SRA 4 = Ethos/Persona
	F.03	MIDTERM EXAM	
06	F.08	Stap, "Flight of the Kuaka" Stover, "Not So Silent Spring" Flannery, "The Superior Civilization"	SRA 5 = Certainty/Uncertainty & Risk
	F.10		
07	F.15	Kunzig, "Scraping Bottom" Specter, "A Life of Its Own"	SRA 6

W	D	Reading Due	Writing Due
	F.17		Paper Proposal
08	F.22	Corsello, "The Believer"	
	F.24		Paper Research Report
09	M.01		
	M.03		Paper Draft
10	M.08		
	M.10		Paper Revision

Supplemental Materials

Instructions and Evaluation Criteria for the SRAs

Description

For each article, write:

- A 200-300 word objective summary of the article. Include its main point(s), and write this entirely in your own words (no quoting).
- A 200-300 word response to the article in which you share your personal reactions to or thoughts about any aspect of the article.
- A 200-300 word analysis of the article using the theoretical lens assigned for that SRA (see below).

Use the following headings to separate the sections: Summary (# words), Response (# words), Analysis (# words). For "# words," include the number of words in that section. Write each section separately, without any overlap.

Writing SRAs will help you:

- Practice shifting between three stances toward a text: An objective stance in which you simply report, a subjective stance in which you offer personal reactions, and a scholarly stance in which you evaluate the text.
- Practice writing concisely and clearly.

Evaluation Criteria

SRAs will be evaluated on content and professionalism.

Content:

- The summary is objective and includes the article's main points/ideas.
- The response includes your subjective reactions to or thoughts about the article.
- The analysis is insightful and is well supported with examples from the article.
- The writing throughout is clear and unambiguous.

Professionalism:
- The document heading includes your name, the date, and the title of the article you are writing about.
- The SRA file is named according the file naming conventions described in the syllabus.
- The SRA is written and formatted according to instructions.
- Grammar, mechanical, or spelling problems (if any) are minor and do not interfere with meaning.

Instructions and Evaluation Criteria for the Research Paper

Proposal

The proposal should be 1-2 pages (300-500 words) and answer these questions:
- What text you will examine from *The Best American Science and Nature Writing 2010*?
- Why are you are interested in that text?
- What lens will you use?
- Why is that an appropriate lens for your analysis? That is, what PAST element of the text does that lens allow you to see? Provide at least 2 examples from the text to show why this lens is appropriate for this text.
- What sources do you expect to use in your research? (This can be speculative, but please list at least 3-4 potential sources.)

Research Report

Write about a page (300 or so words) sharing the information you have found through your research. Please include citations.

Draft and Revision

The draft should be a *complete* draft of 4-5 pages (1200-1500 words) and should include:
- A brief summary (200-300 words) of your chosen article.
- An analysis of the article using your chosen lens, clearly explaining how that aspect of the article is more PAST than CUSP.
- An explanation, using your research, of how that aspect of that article could be more CUSP.

Evaluation criteria for the research paper:
- The draft is complete; it is 4-5 pages, and it includes all the elements listed above.
- The summary is objective and includes the article's main points/ideas.
- The analysis is insightful and is well supported with examples from the article.

- The research findings are used to support your explanation of how the article could be more CUSP.
- The writing is coherent, with explicit connections between points, evidence, and explanations.
- The writing is clear and unambiguous throughout.
- Sources are cited in an academic citation format.
- Grammar, mechanical, or spelling problems (if any) are minor and do not interfere with meaning.
- The revision thoroughly responds to and incorporates feedback given on the draft.

Remixing Composition: A History of Multimodal Writing Pedagogy, by Jason Palmeri. Carbondale: Southern Illinois UP, 2012. 194 pp.

Reviewed by Andrew Davis, The University of Mississippi

In *Remixing Composition: A History of Multimodal Writing Pedagogy*, Jason Palmeri both reconstructs and remixes the historical role multimodality has played in the teaching of composition. Whereas much contemporary scholarship on the subject of non-alphabetic composition, whether digital or not, expresses both excitement for the capacity of these forms to revolutionize the field and fear that they introduce elements into our classrooms that fall outside our realm of expertise, Palmeri highlights the fact that multimodality has been a constant thread in our teaching for the last several decades and that we are the most qualified to teach multimodal composition in the structure of the academy. His extensively sourced historical "remix" highlights points throughout recent movements in Composition Studies where multimodality has played a significant role, and uses them to argue that multimodality is not only a natural part of the teaching of composition, but that to exclude it from our curriculum also excludes the voices of students (and cultures) falling outside of the dominant model of alphabetic literacy.

Palmeri divides the book into two parts, each consisting of two chapters. Each chapter is subsequently divided into several "tracks" and "refrains," thus maintaining the structural metaphor of the "remix." Part 1, entitled "Composition has Always Already Been Multimodal," associates multimodality with specific movements from the last four decades of Composition Studies. Palmeri makes it clear that multimodality does not rest on a specific theoretical model, as he charts its relevance to schools of thought ranging from current traditionalism to critical pedagogy. Both chapters in part 1 make the argument that compositionists both have a history of engagement with multimodality and have the expertise to teach it.

The first chapter of part 1 reconsiders the early process movement, which Palmeri defines as ranging from 1971 to 1984. His goal is to highlight that some of the core goals of the process movement rely upon multimodal thinking. He begins with two fundamental questions around which the chapter is framed: one, "[a]re there similarities in the creative composing process of writers, visual artists, designers, and performing artists?" and two, "[w]hat role do nonverbal modes of thinking play in the invention and revision of alphabetic texts?" (25). Palmeri presents three tracks in response to these questions. The first and second tracks explore the relationship between the alphabetic writing process and the composing process in the allied arts, based on the work of Janet Emig, Linda Flower, and John Hayes. He notes that, despite the fact that the writing process is multimodal at its core, teachers of composition receive little training in non-alphabetic ways of approaching it (27). This gap ignores students whose creative process is naturally multimodal. Palmeri extends this argument throughout tracks two and three. He asserts provocatively in track two that multimodality can be both a method and a product: the "ultimate goal" of this being the "rhetorical choice about which modalities are best" given the context (38). The claim culminates with Palmeri's call for "composing" across the curriculum programs that do not place value in print alone, but encourage and promote true multimodal literacy.

Chapter 2 further explores the presence of multimodal thinking in historical pedagogy. Here Palmeri pays special attention to the metaphorical and literal exploration of "voice" in expressivist, rhetorical, and critical pedagogy. By beginning the first track with the work of Peter Elbow, he distinguished metaphorical "voice" in student writing and their actual auditory voice. Words, he argues, are "both sounds and alphabetic signs," and thus are themselves multimodal (55). The division between sounds and signs is entirely artificial, originating with the disciplinary divorce of English studies and speech in 1914 (52). Building on the foundation of auditory words, subsequent tracks in the chapter explore the connections between composition and acting, dialogue, and dialect. Each track points specifically to the ways these modalities provide a path for student access beyond written words. The chapter concludes with a call for a new literacy that values more than just print, and reminds readers that only traditionally privileged knowledge is best expressed through words on the page alone. (84).

While part 1 engages primarily with theoretical models and broad trends in the field of composition, part 2, entitled "'All Media Were Once New,' or 'The Technologies Composition Forgot'" takes a practical turn to explore specific instances of multimodal practice in the historical composition classroom. Palmeri parallels specific examples with the delineation expressed in part 1 between scholars and teachers who viewed multimodality as a means to augment traditional alphabetic literacy, and those who saw it as an opportunity for new forms of expression. Additionally, part 2 demonstrates a continuity between the cautionary forecasts compositionists made in past decades about the effect of multimedia on the field with claims appearing today about digital media. In highlighting the "limitations and contradictions" of that historical alarmism, Palmeri frees the contemporary multimodal turn from the same arguments (18).

Chapter 3 surveys the multimodal trends that occurred in Composition Studies between 1967 and 1974. This period, Palmeri suggests, parallels the conversations we have today about the role of different modalities in our teaching. He takes some issue with Kathleen Blake Yancey's 2004 assertion that the current shift towards digital literacy is unique. The late 1960s and early 1970s, like today, saw composition scholarship focused both on the analysis of multimodal texts and their production. It also saw a minority of scholars disputing the privileging of academic print, and calling for multimodal, mixed-media forms of expression, and the teaching of such (88).

Palmeri emphasizes that the digital compositions we ask of our students today are just a remix of what we asked them to do in the past, and that students have always preferred multimodal composition to essayistic composition (98). Though for the most part the chapter serves as a historical survey of specific instances of multimodal composition in the early 1970s, the conclusion makes two important points that stand out as particularly important. One, as we develop new digital media and multimodal composition curricula for our students in the 21st century, we would do well to consider the "successes, failures, and contradictions" of the past (108); and two, simply adding a multimodal component or layer to a curriculum that is rooted in fundamentally ineffective pedagogy cannot "reinscribe" that pedagogy (109).

In the final chapter, Palmeri continues his practical recovery of instances of multimodal thinking in the history of composition pedagogy, this time focusing on the integration of visual media with print between 1971 and 1984. This chapter has a much narrower focus, and explores specifically the kind of multimodal composition that utilizes images and video. In exploring the careful balance between the teaching of composition and the teaching of production, Palmeri reveals that not only is it possible for composition teachers to develop a rich, multimodal pedagogy involving photography and video, but that teachers did it twenty years before contemporary digital tools that made the production process much simpler. The chapter concludes with a call similar to the preceding three; that expanding the teaching of composition to include the critical adaptation of different modalities ensures that our students will be able to communicate robustly in a diverse and multicultural world (148).

The epilogue highlights three goals that Palmeri believes should frame future conversations about multimodality. First, he advocates that we continue to use multimodal tools to enhance traditional alphabetic composition. He suggests that the incorporation of multimodality into this process can make writing more relevant in an increasingly non-alphabetic age. Secondly, Palmeri calls upon teachers of composition to reclaim multimodal composing, and to apply to it the same theories of process and rhetoric that we value for print. Finally, the third goal broadly predicts that opening the field to multimodal composition can not only make it more relevant, but can provide a way in for diverse cultural perspectives, and break down the limited cultural range of the print hegemony.

This book adds an important perspective to the ongoing disciplinary conversations about multimodality, and the role of non-alphabetic composition in our classrooms. Palmeri makes it clear that we are overlooking several decades worth of experience and knowledge about multimodality when we say that the challenges and opportunities posed by digital media to be completely new. In fact, digital technologies represent only the latest in a series of tools that arose to facilitate multimodal composition. In highlighting the myriad ways multimodality has enhanced and augmented the teaching of composition in the past, Palmeri makes a compelling argument that compositionists are not only well suited, but the most well qualified in the academy to teach non-alphabetic literacy, whether it is in support of traditional writing, parallel to it, or entirely independent.

Oxford, MS

To Know Her Own History: Writing at the Woman's College, 1943-1963, by Kelly Ritter. Pittsburgh: U of Pittsburgh P, 2012. 256 pp.

Reviewed by Annie S. Mendenhall, The Ohio State University

With local historians heeding Linda Ferreira-Buckley's call to "rescue the archives," our historical depiction of Composition grows increasingly varied and complex. We now know more about institutions where composition instruction survived, and even thrived, at times when a prior generation of historians assigned it a dismal fate. Continuing this trend of local archival research, Kelly Ritter's *To Know Her Own History: Writing at the Woman's College, 1943-1963* addresses two historical oversights: first, the relative dearth of information on women's education in composition, especially at public women's colleges; and second, the lack of attention to the interwoven histories of composition and creative writing. To do this, she provides an extensively documented, multi-frame picture of the Woman's College of the University of North Carolina (W.C.), today the University of North Carolina-Greensboro (UNCG). Ritter's overarching argument is that the W.C. balanced the local desires of students and faculty with national trends in composition, creative writing, and general education as it maintained a commitment to rigorous and progressive composition instruction.

To Know Her Own History begins in chapters 1 and 2 by connecting the normal school origins of the W.C. to its later curricular focus on writing. Founded as the State Normal and Industrial School in 1891, the institution later transformed into the W.C. in 1931, finally becoming the coeducational UNCG in 1964. Ritter contextualizes the role of English—and writing instruction specifically—within the history of normal schools' concern for training teachers to address the literacy needs of primary and secondary school students. In contrast to elite women's colleges, normal schools valued writing and rhetoric courses for the professional preparation they offered women. But Ritter contends that institutional type did not solely determine pedagogical focus. Within its larger mission to train white women as appropriate model teachers in Southern culture, the State Normal and Industrial College provided extensive writing instruction, emphasizing the value of student writing and creative and expository assignments.

After transitioning to the W.C., these past practices informed the college's commitment to writing in the postwar era that is the focus of the remaining chapters. Ritter's assessment is supported by her reading of the W.C.'s first-year writing student publication, the *Yearling* (1948-1951). Showcasing student writing from the first-year course, the *Yearling* reveals the interconnected threads of creative writing and composition at the W.C. Often blurring expository, argumentative, and creative genres, students' texts consider literary, personal, and political topics—from nature poems to stories exploring race and gender constructs. To fill out this picture, Ritter interviews three women who published in the *Yearling*, noting they valued the W.C.'s investment in creative writing and student leadership, even though they encountered restrictions there. One anecdote, from Elizabeth Poplin Stanfield-Maddox, about a male professor blocking her library request of a risqué Mark Twain story is humorous, but also hints at the complex gender dynamics these students confronted. Their perspective challenges us to acknowledge what students, past and present, appreciate in writing courses, and the interviews provide a model for supplementing historical material with individuals' narratives.

Maintaining focus on how the institution adapted to national trends, chapter 3 provides a history of general education reform, arguing that in the heyday of such reforms nationwide the W.C. resisted abstract recommendations in favor of local considerations. Ritter contrasts the 1945 Harvard publication, *General Education in a Free Society* ("the Redbook"), with a failed attempt to apply its recommendations at the W.C. from 1951-1953. Her analysis employs committee reports, meeting minutes, and surveys to show how the Redbook overlooked perspectives from different disciplines and institutions in its vague recommendations for curriculum reform. In doing so, the Redbook also devalued the content of composition and the arts—both central to the W.C. The W.C. faculty resisted Redbook-inspired reforms; instead the English department conducted an independent review of first- and second-year sequence, integrating the courses' content and reasserting their merit, rather than—as Harvard suggested—subordinating writing to other general education approaches (e.g., "Great Texts" or Western civilization). The W.C.'s resistance to Harvard demonstrates why that university should not be the barometer for historical composition. Instead of adopting sweeping reforms, the faculty assessed courses locally in the context of their institutional approach to writing—a desire that may feel relevant for writing program administrators negotiating state and federal mandates impacting writing programs today.

The final two chapters of the book turn a critical eye on Ritter's earlier, largely positive, narrative of the W.C. Chapter 4 complicates her earlier depiction of creative writing and composition as symbiotic by detailing the disparate career paths of writing program administrator May Bush and esteemed poet Randall Jarrell. Ritter argues persuasively that the W.C.'s multiple attempts to retain Jarrell on faculty and boost its creative writing program inadvertently resulted in Bush's delay of raises and promotion several times. Ritter astutely calls attention to the disparity between Bush's and Jarrell's careers because of gender differences and the power differential between creative writing and composition. Significantly, this history offers a way out of the literature/composition binary dominating the portrayal of composition as "the sad women in the basement," always subordinated to English literature. Ritter instead posits that, in this case, composition's relationship to other writing pedagogies and programs impacted its prominence in the college.

Then, in chapter 5, Ritter troubles her initial assessment of the W.C. as a progressive force in women's education, discussing the institution's transformation into a comprehensive, coeducational university. She asks, "What, indeed, does it mean to see such a dedicated plan for writing and the arts for women students collapse into the background of yet another large, generic university?" (195-96). How do we interpret this history, when the institution dismissed its special mission for women, yet maintained strong creative writing and composition and rhetoric programs? Ritter's analysis of alumni letters and administrative statements regarding the W.C.'s fate highlights differences between administrative visions for a coeducational university and student and alumni attachment to the institution's unique identity. Institutional decisions emerge from a cacophony of student, public, and administrative voices and resist easy labels like progressive or conservative; institutional histories, too, must recognize this complexity.

Ritter's major contribution, I would argue, is historiographical. In exposing dissonances among archival documents, Ritter reminds us that history is narrative imposed on messiness. Frequently, to end a chapter or section, she offers multiple interpretations of her documents. For example, in understanding the intersection of creative writing and composition at the W.C., she suggests we might view creative writing either as an extension of the university's attentiveness to writing instruction and student desires, or as ultimately limiting the composition program (or, likely, as both). This rhetorical move avoids reducing local history to mere lessons, polemic, or unqualified recovery—an important step for scholarship in the field. However, Ritter's discussion of historiography, while generally engaging, did lose me toward the book's end when she suggests that we view archival research of writing programs as an "ethnographic practice" (209). Given the larger disciplinary debates over ethnography, I thought the term, which seems to be used metaphorically, deserved additional definition to seem justified in this context.

Additionally, one gap in the text might suggest further work for composition historians. As I read, I noticed that community and public perspectives of the W.C. lurk unexplored in the book's background. At one point, Ritter hypothesizes that some may have viewed the W.C. as "a step removed from a finishing school, or a training site for wholly domestic careers" (205). Yet those opinions are largely absent from her analysis, as they are from many composition histories. How might public voices be included in our archives to help us better articulate the history of public and academic relationships?

These criticisms are relatively minor, however. Ritter's book articulates the value of history to disciplinary, administrative, and pedagogical concerns. For me, her point hit home when I recently heard Kevin Carey, director of Education Policy at the New America Foundation, discuss rising college tuition costs on NPR's *Fresh Air*. Carey rehearsed the history of higher education through the lens of Harvard and Johns Hopkins, arguing that college tuition was doomed from the moment it adopted the German research model, and privileged expensive research over teaching obligations. Carey's argument relies on more than just poor history, but his failure to acknowledge various institutional types and their responsiveness to local communities seems inexcusable. Acknowledging the complexity of institutional life, Ritter's analysis nevertheless proves the point that Carey misses—that institutional history *is* varied and important. Education means more to teachers and students than simply an "exchange of information," as Carey puts it. Ritter's book demonstrates how composition, aware of its local histories, might be well positioned to fight such reductive claims.

Columbus, OH

Works Cited

Ferreira-Buckley, Linda. "Rescuing the Archives from Foucault." *College English* 61.5 (1999): 577-83. Print.

"What's Driving College Costs Higher?" *Fresh Air*. Natl. Public Radio. WHYY, Philadelphia, 26 June 2012. Radio.

The Promise of Reason: Studies in The New Rhetoric, edited by John T. Gage. Carbondale: Southern Illinois UP, 2011. 244 pp.

Reviewed by Abigail L. Montgomery, Blue Ridge Community College

In common with many composition teachers, I have in recent months drawn students' attention especially carefully to public rhetoric. While covering persuasive argument, I have said several variations of, "We are in an election year. Pay attention in the next few months to how political ads and debates are constructed. Who is shaping the messages, and for what reasons? Who seems to be the target audience? How are emotions, facts, and values being used to persuade? Are these things being used unscrupulously or manipulatively?" In every class, at least a few students nod or laugh in wry recognition. We and our students recognize something missing from our public discourse, and many of us regard the study and teaching of argument as ways to be and train better citizens and thus possibly to create a better world.

John Gage, editor of the sixteen-essay collection *The Promise of Reason: Studies in* The New Rhetoric, tells us that Chaïm Perelman and Lucie Olbrechts-Tyteca's 1958 *Traité de l'argumentation: La nouvelle rhétorique* (*The New Rhetoric*), the product of a decade of research amid the tumult of World War II-era Europe, recognized a similar lack and held a similar aspiration: to create "a new place for reason in a postwar world in which logical positivism and science seemed to some to have demonstrably failed to fulfill the promise of freedom" (1). Perelman and Olbrechts-Tyteca themselves had the not inconsiderable goal of "a *break with a concept of reason and reasoning due to Descartes* which has set its mark on Western philosophy for the last three centuries" (1, emphasis in original). This collection, stemming from a 2008 conference at the University of Oregon marking *The New Rhetoric*'s fiftieth anniversary, brings together celebrations of, reflections on, and applications for this ambitious and influential text.

After Gage's introduction and a biographical tribute from Perelman's daughter, the essays fall into four sections. The first, "Conceptual Understanding of *The New Rhetoric*," highlights Perelman and Olbrechts-Tyteca's key concepts and probes the history of their writing of *The New Rhetoric*. Barbara Warnick highlights Perelman and Olbrechts-Tyteca's innovative approach of studying arguments in their own contexts rather than privileging established formal frameworks. Jeanne Fahnestock assesses the strengths and weaknesses of their discussion of the intersections of style and content in argument. Loïc Nicolas adds a brief précis of Perelman's "universal audience" concept. David Frank and Michelle Bolduc's examination of the collaboration between Perelman and Olbrechts-Tyteca, which focuses on how Olbrechts-

Tyteca's contributions have sometimes been minimized and applies *The New Rhetoric* to an understanding of collaborative writing, closes the section.

The second section, "Extensions of *The New Rhetoric*," places Perelman and Olbrechts-Tyteca in conversation with Charles Darwin, Kenneth Burke, and today's French linguists. For Alan Gross, Darwin's work demonstrates a way to expand *The New Rhetoric*'s notions of presence and visual argument. Richard Graff and Wendy Winn synthesize Burkean form-based Identification and Perelman/Olbrechts-Tyteca's value-based Communion as different but connected ways of both constructing and addressing audiences. Roselyne Koren praises *The New Rhetoric* for providing a theoretical way to discuss subjective and value-based arguments in scientific and journalistic writing, genres that, she contends, many models simply treat as entirely objective and outside the realm of argumentation.

Section three, "The Ethical Turn in Perelman and *The New Rhetoric*," reviews the World War II-era history surrounding *The New Rhetoric* and emphasizes argumentation's social implications, then and later. Ray Dearin's and Linda Bensel-Meyers's essays concentrate on Perelman's post-World-War-II work with UNESCO research on democracy, a term Perelman found problematic to define and vulnerable to manipulation by the unscrupulous. Jean Nienkamp argues that ethics proceeds by rhetorical means and that rhetoric has inherent ethical responsibilities, "that both are value-based action in the social world" (179).

The last and most wide-ranging section, "Uses of *The New Rhetoric*," offers several pedagogical possibilities inspired by *The New Rhetoric*. James Crosswhite critiques conventional, acontextual models for teaching argument, asserting that *The New Rhetoric* provides "a richer and truer account of argument than the simpler models that can fit on a board or a screen and be explained in a fifty-minute hour" (193). Maria Freddi applies Perelman and Olbrechts-Tyteca's analogical models to Richard Feynman's uses of argument to teach science; Paula Olmos employs their observations to discuss traditional use of classical proverbs alongside modern-day use of movie catchphrases as means of connecting with an audience. Finally, Mark Hoffmann, insisting that "not all arguments are limited to their rhetorical situations" (243), uses concepts from *The New Rhetoric* in a case study of Tolstoy's *The Kingdom of God Is Within You* as an essence-based argument.

This collection clearly aims to both honor *The New Rhetoric* and reinvigorate the research and teaching of such familiar and vital rhetorical concepts as audience awareness, ethos, figurative language, allusion, and social context. Respect for Perelman and Olbrechts-Tyteca's monumental work imbues the essays, as does a sincere desire to apply *The New Rhetoric* rigorously and meaningfully to researching and teaching argument. The essays demonstrate an equal commitment to thinking creatively and carefully about the rhetorical choices and aims implicit in that very research. *The New Rhetoric* is honored, interrogated, and expanded upon by the contributors. Even after more than 500 pages, Perelman and Olbrechts-Tyteca themselves felt they had "barely scratched its [argumentation's] surface" (509) and were eager for other scholars to carry that work forward. Just as they sought to expand rhetoric beyond purely rational, formal models, scholars inspired by them seek, in this volume, to expand its application to a broad range of fields, texts, audiences, and situations.

The Promise of Reason: Studies in The New Rhetoric is ambitious and sometimes unorthodox in its scope, and this varied, shifting focus can at times read as a weakness of the collection. Because the collection pursues several different avenues, the different sections do not necessarily cohere smoothly and treatment of some ideas feels a bit rushed. This same diversity, though, means that this collection will prove useful to scholars and students across composition and beyond. Beginning and advanced composition teachers will benefit from the theoretical, historical, and practical discussions of argumentation. Theorists and historians of composition, science writing, linguistics, philosophy, and ethics will likewise find valuable insights about uses and influences of rhetoric in their fields. The relevant individual chapters would fit smoothly on both graduate and undergraduate syllabi in all of these fields or be useful to researchers and students as supplemental resources. The collection as a whole would be a solid addition to the reading list of graduate rhetoric surveys as well as courses in composition theory and the history of composition. *The Promise of Reason*'s variety makes it a useful primer on the first fifty years of *New Rhetoric* scholarship. The sheer number of conversations this short collection manages to pursue bolsters that spirit and makes *The Promise of Reason*, as Gage hopes, a starting point for "the next fifty years" (2) of the same.

Weyers Cave, VA

Works Cited

Perelman, Chaïm, and Lucie Olbrechts-Tyteca. 1958. *The New Rhetoric: A Treatise on Argumentation*. Trans. John Wilkinson and Purcell Weaver. Notre Dame: U of Notre Dame P, 1969. Print.

From Form to Meaning: Freshman Composition and the Long Sixties, 1957-1974, by David Fleming. Pittsburgh: U of Pittsburgh P, 2011. 273 pp.

Reviewed by Jacob Babb, University of North Carolina at Greensboro

Scholars in Composition Studies have learned much by studying our disciplinary history. The work of authors such as James Berlin, Robert Connors, Susan Miller, and Steven Mailloux has proven to be vital for understanding the development of the field. More recently, scholars have turned to local histories rather than the large histories of the authors noted above, arguing that a better understanding of the field lies in constructing and examining narratives focused on individual composition programs. David Fleming's book fits in that trend, examining the rise, fall, and resurrection of the freshman composition program at the University of Wisconsin-Madison (UW), a large midwestern land-grant university. Fleming traces the development of the writing curriculum across the course of the century as it was adapted to meet the social and economic needs of the era. Specifically, the book focuses on the "long sixties," a tumultuous period in Madison and in the United States in general. That decade saw increasing tensions between students and faculty throughout the university; the book chronicles the especially tense interactions between graduate TAs and English faculty, culminating in 1969 in a vote by the English faculty to abolish the freshman composition requirement for incoming students, effectively ending the composition program at UW for twenty-five years. Several individuals and groups in the university and the community called for the English department to provide writing instruction, but freshman composition was not revived at UW until 1996, five years after the department launched a full-fledged Ph.D. program in Composition Studies.

Fleming's investigation of the composition program at UW was prompted by his interest in the lore surrounding the confrontation that still circulated among faculty when he joined the English department in 1998. Fleming's investigation involved numerous graduate students, including students in a seminar who helped him locate some of the first documents the book is based on as well as two research assistants, Rasha Diab and Mira Shimabukuro, who helped him delve into the archives and gather interviews with former TAs and faculty. The end result of their search is a compelling narrative of the growth and development of freshman composition and the subsequent abolition of English 102, a course that nearly all freshmen at UW were required to take.

Although the book focuses on the long sixties and the slow buildup to the battle between TAs and faculty, Fleming begins his history in the mid-nineteenth century with what he terms a "prehistory" of writing instruction at UW. Chapter 2 describes UW's shift from an antebellum curriculum that emphasized public oratory and studies in the classics to the research-intensive model that characterized most major American universities in the twentieth century. Freshman composition began at UW during this transition to the research model; Fleming argues that the course began in this time as society began to privilege education as cultural capital, making universities crucial to the development of the professional-managerial class (6). Fleming then briefly describes the many forms composition took in the early twentieth century in response to the rapid growth (or in the case of the Great Depression, the sudden collapse) of student enrollment, examining the different iterations of course objectives and descriptions written by a succession of composition directors.

The next two chapters provide the history leading immediately up to the confrontation between TAs and faculty. Chapter 3, "The Postwar Regime, 1948-1968," describes a remarkably stable period in the composition program, despite the explosive growth of the university's student population. The fixity of the course contributes to the angst and frustration of TAs in the mid-1960s, who wanted to engage in more pedagogical experimentation than the rigidly structured course allowed. Chapter 4 describes the English department's increasing dependence on TAs to teach the course as faculty dedicated their efforts to their individual specializations and their advanced undergraduate and graduate courses. As faculty withdrew from the teaching of writing, the TAs took on greater responsibilities for planning the writing curriculum, exemplified in early 1969 by a thorough revision of English 101, UW's basic writing course.

The next two chapters focus on the crisis between the TAs and faculty that led to the abolition of the composition requirement at UW. Chapter 5, "TA Experimentation, 1966-1969," co-written with Diab and Shimabukuro, recounts the TAs' new approaches to teaching writing—approaches that were seen by the faculty and some university administrators as challenges to the accepted writing curriculum that had remained relatively unchanged for twenty years. The chapter centers on *Critical Teaching*, published by the university's TA union in 1968 and 1969 with several essays contributed by English TAs, as an indicator of the TAs' dissatisfaction with the state of pedagogy in the university. The two volumes collectively call for teaching that is less corporatized for the needs of the state and the military and more relevant to the social and political needs of the individual students, concepts that demonstrate the publication's alignment with the general political discontent of the late 1960s. TAs began to reject the program directors' textbook choices, most notably when TA Joseph Carr attempted to adopt *Sense of the Sixties*, a reader that emphasized contemporary social problems. Other TAs also challenged accepted grading norms, assigning higher grades in part as a critique of the grading system in general and as a challenge to the political reality that students who received lower grades were more vulnerable to the draft as the United States increased its military presence in Vietnam.

Chapter 6 provides a detailed account of the TA and faculty meetings that led to the abolition of English 102. The confrontation, ignited by Carr's insistence on assigning the *Sense of the Sixties* and fueled by department chair Tim Heninger's concern over what he saw as TAs' increasing resistance to faculty oversight, began with a meeting between Heninger and the TAs in which the TAs asked for greater control over the composition curriculum. In a series of subsequent faculty meetings in which anger escalated until police were called on to guard the doors to prevent TAs from entering, the debate about English 102 centered around what the faculty perceived to be the TAs' attempts to undermine their authority over the course until finally the course directors called for the abolition of English 102. However, the TA-faculty confrontation is not cited as a reason for ending the course; instead, the argument the English department forwards to abolish the course is that faculty in the disciplines should provide writing instruction in their majors because, according to evidence from placement exams, incoming freshmen no longer needed further preparation in composition, having received enough writing instruction in high school. Fleming offers several accounts from memos, interviews, and newspapers (the English department's choice to abolish English 102 made the front page of local papers) that cite the confrontation with TAs as the chief cause of the department's action. In other words, although the official record does not reflect the conflict with the TAs, it was generally accepted that the TA-faculty confrontation was the cause of the course being abolished.

Fleming draws a number of observations from his local history and applies them to the field of Composition Studies. Fleming argues that freshman composition is unique because of the general perception that it is a course without content, making it vulnerable to attack from multiple stakeholders while it is simultaneously protected by society's perpetual fear of a literacy crisis. Fleming offers three terms to explore the "cultural resonance and institutional instability" characteristic of composition: *generality, universality,* and *liminality* (200). *Generality* emphasizes how composition appears to be devoid of content, a characteristic that makes the course incredibly flexible, illustrated by the many iterations it assumed at UW. *Universality* indicates the course's mission to meet the needs of all students in the university, regardless of their background and their majors. Finally, *liminality* points to how composition and its attendant discipline exist at the margins of the academy in seemingly permanent stasis, always grasping for institutional stability and intellectual legitimacy.

From Form to Meaning is a meticulously researched and engaging narrative about how easily freshman composition can be abolished. The book is especially useful for readers interested in the history of Rhetoric and Composition, and how that history is frequently defined according to the peculiar social and political climate of local writing programs. Fleming's introduction offers a focused and concise history of freshman writing in the United States that many instructors may find useful for introductory graduate courses in Composition Studies, while his archival work provides an excellent model of historical methodology. Yet while most of Fleming's book chronicles the historical events of the late sixties at UW-Madison, his terminology—*generality*, *universality*, and *liminality*—gives readers a cogent framework for reconsidering the historically troubled position of freshman composition in the university.

Greensboro, NC

Toward a Composition Made Whole, by Jody Shipka. Pittsburgh: U of Pittsburgh P, 2011. 179 pp.

Reviewed by Trent M. Kays, University of Minnesota

Multimodality as a buzzword is in vogue in the field of Composition Studies. The predominance of "multimodal texts" seems to only spread from writing program to writing program, yet the assessment, pedagogy, and theoretical framework governing multimodality in Composition Studies is stunted. Referring to the production of texts, broadly defined, one either engages in multimodal discourse or one does not. The middle way seems lost, and this dichotomy, false as it may be, still permeates composition curriculum at various levels.

Jody Shipka's *Toward a Composition Made Whole* offers the field of Composition Studies an opportunity to appreciate and critically reflect on the uses and governance of multimodality in assessment, pedagogy, and theory. This practice becomes important when we realize how little we know about the inherent multimodality of composition. Shipka begins her book with an introduction focused on basic but important thoughts about multimodality and communicative practice. The discussion presented is brilliant in its simplicity. Offering her readers the chance to understand her anecdotal perspective, Shipka regales us with a tale of a particular workshop experience. As is often the case, those outside of Composition Studies, and even some inside, often have a difficult time understanding the value of multimodality or, as a course, composition. She even suggests, "Whether implicitly, as was the case here, or explicitly stated, some of the questions lurking behind the reaction seem to be, 'How is *that* college-level academic writing?,' 'How can *that* possibly be rigorous?,' or 'How can allowing students to do *that* possibly prepare them for the writing they will do in their other courses?'" (2).

These questions are important, yet they seem to implicitly argue there isn't value in multimodality. Further complicating the notions of multimodality, we begin to see there is more at play than just curriculum. The nature of the multimodal outside the university environment and the nature of the multimodal inside the university environment are at odds insomuch the former and latter hardly seem to meet. Why is this? The relevancy of primary labeling of multimodal texts is of great concern, and it seems those inside the university and those outside the university have different understandings of the multimodal. Like so many arguments in Composition Studies over the past five decades, the conceptions of what constitutes a "text" seem to be of supreme concern of those *inside* the university, despite the promulgation of multimodality *outside* of the university. Text certainly is not dead, but it isn't what it once was either.

Moving through the text, Shipka provides a candid argument about what exactly Composition is and how composition scholars must rethink their assumptions. Too often, Composition is seen as a discipline stuck in the past and holding to conservative views of what constitutes text; the author aims to, and rightly so, destroy those long held and ill-formed assumptions by showing that the multimodality of text should hold primacy in the composition classroom. Held within ideas of the past and present, compositionists must take hold of their scholarship, research, and pedagogy in order to critically examine the dynamic presence of the multimodal text. The field of Composition Studies has too long held onto the notion of textually dominant composing practices without understanding said practices in relation to the mediated processes through which text is created.

Providing us a detailed discussion of the fragile union of the fields of Composition Studies and Communication Studies, Shipka shows that while this union was ultimately unstable, it underscored an important aspect of both fields: neither seems to have a clue about how to define "writing." Indeed, the discussion of these fragile unions should be read with bemusement as the discussion elucidates the seemingly pigheadedness and sheer uncompromising behavior of some scholars in both fields. This discussion provides both fields with a moment through which a new approach may be proposed, and the author does just that.

The sociocultural approach to communication often eludes those in composition courses, mostly because said approach is a stalwart pillar of the field of Communication Studies. However, Shipka suggests this approach to communication is necessary to the field of Composition Studies because it provides avenues to contend with the social and individual aspects of composing without throwing away the technologies often employed in the creation of texts. The author is deliberate and coherent in her argument, granting us an ability to understand how the multimodality of text can be employed in the composition classroom. Providing us with a discussion of past theory and then a discussion of her new approach, she shows while not completely inadequate, past theories of composition have often failed to recognize the technologies that have mediated text. Through the application of this new approach, the field of Composition Studies can rectify those past transgressions and begin to understand composition holistically, instead of just examining one particular act.

The author understands the need to consider what this approach might look like, and she delivers by highlighting data collected during two process studies. In perhaps the most interesting part of her book, Shipka shows us the majesty and simplicity of the ever-flowing composing process, as understood and enacted by students. The elements of a course show students becoming engaged with the material presented in ways that must seem unorthodox by the still dominant current traditionalist ethos in the field of Composition Studies. Performances of dance, illustration, mixed media composing, and others show the act of composition is far removed from the static nature of the page. In reading Shipka's description, one can't help but want to jump for joy and wish they had participated with and been witness of her students' telling experiences. How lovely it is to read of students enjoying the act of composition through embracing the multimodality of artifacts traversing university boundaries.

Taking this experience, Shipka moves to debates of curricula within institutions of learning and exactly what we can do to make things fit. She comes off as perhaps her most idealistic in this part of her book, and it should be applauded. We are provided with a framework on how to incorporate multimodal composing into our courses in ways that will engage students, both critically and reflectively. The framework the author proposes focuses on activity-based learning incorporating multimodal and mediate aspects of text. Fascinating and useful, the framework and examples highlight a great deal of negotiation with students as to the work that will be completed. Since the focus is on activity and ideas of text beyond the university, students are able to engage with artifacts foreign to them as compositional acts.

It seems evaluations and assessments are things we cannot escape. They dominate discourse in higher education, and Shipka does deliver and contribute to this dominant discourse by laying out a framework for assessing multimodal projects. Perhaps complicating the notion of multimodality, projects carried out through multimodal discourse cannot be subject to the same evaluation criteria to which a standard and, sometimes, boring traditional student essay is subject. It would not work because there are different issues at hand when experiencing a multimodal project versus reading a traditional essay. This framework, perhaps one of the best detailed and clear in the field of Composition Studies, should be the model for multimodal projects. Most importantly, the spirit of experimentation underscores the entirety of the evaluation framework, which provides students permission to do something they often are not encouraged to do in college-level coursework: fail. Much could be made for the usefulness of failure in composing, and while this spirit isn't exactly encouraged in fields outside Composition Studies, it should always be available to those who wish to give their students authority to be writers.

Earlier compositionists, from Berlin to Faigley to Elbow, gave birth to parts of Shipka's argument in one way or another; however, they were unable to put the pieces together because of their place and time within the field of Composition Studies. Fortunately, like many scholars before her, she has seized upon a vogue topic of critical importance to the entire field of Composition Studies. Riding the kairos-wave she has gathered, the author has offered us a chance to integrate the spirit and essence of multimodality into our courses and into our field. Indeed, we are provided a text worthy of any doctoral reading list, and one that should be a centerpiece of any composition scholar's bookshelf. Shipka has given us a treatise for an important element of 21st-century composition and provided us with a solid and clear framework for a composition truly made whole. We would do well to embrace it.

Minneapolis, MN

Conversational Rhetoric: The Rise and Fall of a Women's Tradition, 1600-1900, by Jane Donawerth. Carbondale: Southern Illinois UP, 2012. 205 pp.

Reviewed by Dara Rossman Regaignon, Pomona College

Conversational Rhetoric: The Rise and Fall of a Women's Tradition, 1600-1900 is in many ways the critical companion to Donawerth's excellent anthology of women's rhetorical theory, Rhetorical Theory by Women before 1900. Whereas that anthology begins in the fifth century BCE and includes authors from China as well as Europe and the Americas, this volume is focused on an English and American rhetorical theory that appeared during the seventeenth, eighteenth, and nineteenth centuries. Donawerth elaborates the 300-year history of a transatlantic rhetorical theory articulated by women about women's speech and writing—a theory carefully documented in Rhetorical Theory. Conversational Rhetoric offers careful and detailed analysis of numerous important texts of rhetorical theorists, and will serve as an important touchstone for students and scholars working on those women's work for some time to come. As a work of "revisionist and critical or 'constructionist' history of rhetorical theory" (xi), this book shows how women rhetorical theorists used conversation—intimate, informal, dialogic—as a "model for *all* discourse" (xi), offering a vision of communication that both complemented and challenged the masculinist emphasis on oratory, declamation, and argument.

The primary focus of the book is the female rhetorical theory that first started to appear in England between 1600 and 1800, in part through the influence of the work of the much-translated French author, Madeleine de Scudéry. This was a time when public speaking was particularly gendered, but during which access to education was becoming more and more widely available. As a result of both of these factors, writers were thinking about the nature and possibilities of women's speech (2-3). To varying degrees throughout the period (and depending on class position, as well as other factors), women's speech was restricted to private, interpersonal settings and to domestic, familial and often pedagogical, purposes. As a result, when women wrote or spoke to articulate their place in the *salon* culture of seventeenth-century Paris or eighteenth-century London, to justify girls' education, to defend women's rights, or to trumpet the cultural and political significance of feminine influence, they drew on the dialogic, consensus-based, and audience-focused nature of conversation for the framework that excused their speech (16). As Donawerth shows throughout the study, this model creates an ideal rhetoric that is relaxed rather than declamatory, intimate rather than formal, and peculiarly attuned to *kairos*.

The book is primarily organized by genre, although in several cases the genres map onto historical period, with detailed analyses of specific texts; this organizational scheme echoes that in the Introduction to *Rhetorical Theory* (see pp. xxi-xxxiii). Chapter one focuses on the dialogues of Madeleine de Scudéry, Margaret Cavendish, Bathsua Makin, and Mary Astell. These treatises make no pretensions to opening up space for women as orators, but instead focus on the importance of women's education given their central roles in childrearing and letter writing, and as *salon* hostesses (18). In the service of these goals they begin to justify and theorize women's (public) speech by describing it in the non-threatening terms of conversation. Chapter two builds on these insights to show how conduct books in Britain and the U.S. further developed this notion over the course of the nineteenth century. Referring to one another and to at least some of the authors discussed in the first chapter, writers such as Hannah More, Lydia Sigourney, Eliza Farrar, Florence Hartley, and Jennie Willing argue that conversation and letter writing are rhetorical activities of equal (if different) importance to oratory and essay writing. Coding such activities as female and yet still widely influential, these authors use the ideology of separate spheres to make space for women in public, civic discourse.

Chapters three and four describe how this conversational model was used even more directly to justify women's public speaking. The third chapter—which spans the historical period being studied—examines defenses of women's preaching. While offering revisionist interpretations of the Bible that include identifying a lineage of women preachers, authors such as Margaret Fell, Lucretia Mott, and Jarena Lee theorize preaching as an informal, intimate mode of communication—in essence, as conversation. Chapter four further charts the breakdown of the distinction between "conversation" and "oratory" in its study of late-nineteenth-century elocution textbooks. By the late 1800s, American sentimental culture had found an ideal expression in women's public display of emotion. Elocution textbooks provided an occasion to theorize bodily autonomy through their discussion of how to "perform... emotion through voice and body" (105). Authors (and professional elocutionists and actresses) Anna Morgan, Genevieve Stebbins, Emily Bishop, and Hallie Quinn Brown "offer women empowerment to resist traditional feminine roles through control over their own bodies" (108-9). While elocution helped bring women's rhetoric out of the parlor and onto the public stage, so to speak, it both used and rendered obsolete the conversational model. Theorists of elocution-as-feminine-rhetoric could draw on the same oratorical models that had dominated rhetoric for centuries; they no longer needed the more dialogic and informal model of conversation.

Donawerth opens her conclusion asking why the conversational model vanished:

> By the end of the nineteenth century, there was a firmly established women's tradition of rhetorical theory devised by women.... At the end of the nineteenth century, however, this women's tradition created by women rhetorical theorists simply disappeared, as thoroughly as the first English colony in America on Roanoke Island. What happened? (126)

She offers two answers. First, she points out that the conversational model had, for three centuries, been instrumental in justifying women's participation in public political and religious discussions. As it succeeded, however, and the separation of spheres began to break down, there was less need to code women's public speaking as private and hence conversational in nature. Second, Donawerth draws attention to the dramatic changes at the end of the nineteenth century in who attended and taught at the college level. Donawerth's conclusion examines several composition textbooks written by women and aimed at a co-ed audience. This becomes a suggestive meditation on the ways the conversational model migrated from a rhetorical theory into a pedagogical strategy, one that continues to shape the delivering of composition instruction.

This is an important and groundbreaking book. *Conversational Rhetoric* sheds light on an intersecting set of rhetorical theory texts that have hitherto gone under-examined. Scholars of nineteenth-century Britain may be disappointed to find that country and period comparatively under-represented, but given the contribution Donawerth makes both to the history of rhetorical theory and to the pre-history of American composition history and pedagogy, those scholars should be inspired to round out the picture. This text offers a compelling narrative for the rise and fall of a distinctively female rhetorical theory that was at once separate from and aware of the tradition of canonical male oratory. At the same time, the story Donawerth tells never feels teleological; the discussion of eighteenth-century authors, for example, does not seem constrained or limited by the aspects of their theory that influenced later authors. I find myself periodically frustrated in reading it, however, because I wish that Donawerth had theorized and historicized her notion of "conversation as a model of all discourse" (xi) more fully. While in the early chapters her analysis distinguishes between what *conversation* seems to mean in the various texts she discusses, these distinctions drop out later and the focus is on how the various authors mobilize a more monolithic concept of *conversation* to their various ends. But that is perhaps a task for future scholars, as they build on this generative work. In addition to being of interest and value to such scholars—of feminist theory, feminist rhetoric and rhetorical theory, rhetorical theory *tout court*, and the various genres Donawerth discusses here—this book makes a valuable contribution to composition historians' quest to better understand the conceptual genealogy of our discipline and its pedagogies.

Claremont, CA

Works Cited

Donawerth, Jane, ed. *Rhetorical Theory by Women before 1900: An Anthology*. New York: Rowman and Littlefield, 2002. Print.

I Hope I Join the Band: Narrative, Affiliation, and Antiracist Rhetoric, by Frankie Condon. Logan: Utah State UP, 2012. 189 pp.

Reviewed by Ryan Winet, The University of Arizona

Frankie Condon's *I Hope I Join the Band: Narrative, Affiliation, and Antiracist Rhetoric* addresses an immediate but complex question for teachers: how does one approach the problem of racism in the classroom? Condon's book does not provide easy answers to this exceptionally difficult question; instead, she reveals possible approaches through a series of essays that draw upon rhetorical theory and upon her experience as an associate professor and writing center faculty coordinator at the University of Nebraska-Lincoln. Although paraphrasing a book like *I Hope I Join the Band* threatens to be reductive, one could say that Condon aims to develop spaces for discursive borderlands, spaces where people of different racial backgrounds can voice their experiences, engage in critical self-inquiry, and imagine future conditions where solidarity, rather than hegemony, stands as the aim of educational practice. Condon's book, which is ultimately a successful addition to the scholarship on antiracist rhetoric, reads more as a meditation than a practical guide for instructors. Readers looking for easy steps will be disappointed; however, for readers who understand that the subject of race cannot be merely academic, Condon's book will remain a testament to the struggles and possibilities that lie before those who dare to engage with antiracist rhetoric.

Condon draws her book's title from an African-American spiritual with the same name. From her perspective, the lyrics of this spiritual present hope as the "necessary condition for justice struggles" (4); unlike utopianism and optimism, hope can resist injustice at the same time it sustains the imagination for a more equitable future. In chapter 1, readers will notice that Condon's sense of hope dovetails with her sense of antiracist rhetoric: both terms describe a condition that is at once activist and theoretical. In other words, Condon returns us to those borderlands always located between ideological positions. Condon makes clear that occupying such a position is difficult, alluding to the struggle she has suffered during her own experiences inside the borderlands with chapter titles evoking moments in the Old Testament. We have evocations of Jacob wrestling with the angel and the devout awaiting Elijah's return from heaven. For the professional writing instructor or administrator, Condon's first chapter at once encourages discussions of race while also warning that such discussions are difficult. To handle such difficulties, Condon deploys a vocabulary directed to professional instructors and administrators that aims to deconstruct racial assumptions.

In chapter 2, Condon develops this working vocabulary to talk about racist and antiracist rhetoric. Broadly conceived, racist rhetoric does not only define explicit claims of racial superiority, but also implicit assumptions that guide arguments and educational policies. Condon, following the example of Minnie Bruce Pratt and later Marilyn Frye, calls these implicit assumptions *whiteliness*, what Condon paraphrases as the "learned ways of knowing and doing characterized by a racialized (white) sense of oneself as best equipped to judge, to preach, and to suffer" (34). Because racism is often implicit within assumptions, antiracist rhetoric seeks to challenge and reframe assumptions. Condon uses the word "ideation" to describe the act of forming new ideas from different assumptions, identifying three forms of ideation as especially important for antiracist rhetoric: practical, critical and creative. The most promising form of ideation for antiracist rhetoric and practice, according to Condon, is creative ideation, or the capacity "to form thoughts about worlds not yet seen by building upon, but not limited by, history and lived experience" (47). Condon expands this definition into the field of composition practice when she argues that creative ideation is "relational at root," that the ability to form these kinds of thoughts is the "intellectual labor of future perfect" (47). Condon thus moves from a vocabulary for writing professionals to a vision for their students, claiming that the antiracist classroom encourages acts of invention and creativity in order to develop possible futures less burdened by racist thinking.

Chapter 3, "Wrestling with Angels," chronicles Condon's efforts to put antiracist rhetoric into practice. Condon immediately connects this struggle to the Biblical story of Jacob wrestling with the angel. We should not forget that late in this struggle, Jacob's hip is wrenched; despite suffering this injury, Jacob refuses to release the angel. Condon conceives of antiracist activism as a similar kind of wrenching, a subject position that accepts what Roland Barthes calls the punctum, the "accident which pricks me (but also bruises me, is poignant to me)" (80). Condon relates some of her own struggles with this punctum through narrative. We learn about Condon's last efforts to save her brother Rick, a child of the Sioux Nation who was "adopted" by Condon's biological white family as part of the Indian Adoption Project, from drug addiction: she would no longer "extract" her brother from his problems; rather, she would provide a "support structure" (58). At the end of the narrative, Rick throws a chair and directs a racial insult at Condon, leading her to affirm that "love, alone, is never enough" to do the work of antiracism (59). Rather than relying on love alone, the antiracist activist must also engage with the "epistemological and rhetorical practice of decentering" (62). The antiracist classroom is therefore not merely an open-ended, creative place. As Condon elaborates in this chapter, creative ideation must "decenter" mindsets to achieve a more liberated learning environment. In the classroom, students might encounter the epistemological experience of decentering through rhetorical assignments and exercises.

The writing instructor would be right to voice concerns about encouraging decentering in the classroom. Don't we face the risk of offending some students? Or even worse, losing control of the classroom environment?

Condon addresses many of these concerns in chapter 4, titled "Angels Before Thee." The major concept of this chapter is nuancing, which "scratches, teases, tears at the binaries between self and other, personal and social, subjective and objective, individual and collective" (87). Very much aware of how decentering and nuancing might worry instructors, Condon subdivides her chapter into five sections: "The Agon," "Whiteliness," "Disinterest and 'Objectivity,'" "White Guilt," and "Fear." Each of these subdivisions tackles a different concern that writing administrators and instructors might have in employing nuancing.

In chapter 5, Condon suggests that a failure to act in educational, rhetorical, and social spaces does not just threaten the present generation, but also threatens those who will inherit the world. The chapter title, "An Open Door for Elijah," comes from the tradition that the prophet Elijah will return to Earth at the end of days and answer "all of the unanswerable questions" (121). For Condon, the open door represents the sort of intellectual and experiential challenge for antiracist and social justice practice: "the opening, the joint, the articulation between peoples is as dangerous and fragile a place as it is a locus of possibility" (122). Such an opening requires practitioners to imagine a mode of listening and reflection much larger in scale than is usually at stake in agonistic rhetoric. Borrowing her terminology from the musician and essayist Brian Eno, Condon advocates thinking of this opening in terms of the "Big Here" and the "Long Now." For Eno, the Long Now marks the recognition "that the precise moment you're in grows out of the past and is a seed for the future" (126). Writing administrators and instructors might think of this "Big Here" and "Long Now" kind of thinking as an ideal mindset, a best-case scenario after students leave the classroom.

Scholars of rhetorical theory and instructors invested in handling the subject of racism in the college composition classroom will find Condon's book theoretically and personally valuable. Condon's narrative is gripping and her reassurances to fellow instructors that it is better to tackle racism rather than to ignore it are persuasive; however, it is less clear how one applies antiracist rhetoric as an institutional practice within writing programs. Perhaps Condon's relative silence on this matter fits into one of her larger points: because racism ossifies inside institutions, we should allow instructors and students the freedom to conduct their classes and write their narratives in a manner that cultivates decentering, nuancing, and ultimately, hope.

Tucson, AZ

The Megarhetorics of Global Development, edited by Rebecca Dingo and J. Blake Scott. Pittsburgh: U of Pittsburgh P, 2012. 266 pp.

Reviewed by David Dadurka, University of Central Florida

As I watched the summer Olympics, a Best Buy commercial began playing in heavy rotation that, had I not read *The Megarhetorics of Global Development*, I might not have given a second thought. The advertisement features Kiva.org founder, Jessica Jackley, and her father, David, telling how the laptop he bought his daughter allowed her to start the first peer-to-peer microlending site "to lend twenty-five dollars or more to entrepreneurs around the world" (Future Innovators). The 30-second commercial features a few quick flashes of still photographs of these entrepreneurs—a group of Africans, a Latino man on what appears to be a farm, a single African woman standing in a muddy field and other people of color. This combination of understated corporate involvement, social responsibility and decontextualization of foreign aid in the commercial encapsulates what editors and contributors to *The Megarhetorics of Development* seek to unravel through rhetorical analysis: to challenge the commonplace assumption that "development always leads to growth, progress, one-way assistance, and empowerment" (3). This volume not only succeeds in providing new models for applying rhetorical analysis of contemporary texts but also effectively serves as a counter-rhetoric of its own.

After reading Rebecca Dingo's chapter titled "Turning the Tables on the Megarhetoric of Women's Empowerment," I began to understand the power of the rhetorical unraveling of megarhetorics the authors engage in. Dingo's analysis of CARE, another micro-lender, and Kiva.org reveals that both organizations provide little, if any, context for who their donations support nor do they educate donors about the limits of economic exchange to empower entrepreneurs. She argues that the megarhetoric of empowerment used in micro-lending is "short-lived" because it is uni-directional and simply reinforces a neocolonialist approach of white, wealthy Westerners helping impoverished people of color (196). In their introduction, Scott and Dingo appropriate anthropologist Arjun Appurdurai's term "megarhetorics of development" to describe a commonly accepted view "that wealthier nations will not be secured financially or geopolitically if the poor are not part of the modern, global, and capitalist economy" (2). These megarhetorics include God-terms such as "empowerment," "inclusion," "fair trade," "corporate social responsibility," and "sustainability," all taken up and taken apart by this volume's contributors.

A major strength of *Megarhetorics* is its intertextuality. Inspired by a 2009 CCCC workshop on transnational rhetorics, the contributors continually reference and link across the texts to develop a continuity among subject matter that on the surface might appear disparate but nevertheless remains interconnected.

Megarhetorics is divided into two sections. The first half of the book, titled "Extending Rhetorical Concepts and Methods," applies classical theories of rhetoric in novel ways. For example, Robert DeChaine examines Ethos Water's marketing campaign as a "humanitarian doxa, or structure of beliefs" around the megarhetoric of corporate social responsibility (77). His analysis advances a more complex understanding of ethos in the context of increasingly corporatized world. Matt Newcomb, in a chapter titled "Development Shifts: Changing Feelings about Compassion in Korea," expands the role of affect in rhetorical analysis of categories such as "developing countries" (109) used by NGOs that may shape the identity of a nation. The idea of extending rhetorical concepts also is evident in Jason A. Edwards and Jaime Wright's analysis of President Clinton's addresses on globalization. They not only examine the discourse he engages in, but also contrast it with the material consequences of his policies. The second half of the book, titled "Building Counter-Rhetorics of Resistance," helps cement it as a direct challenge to the assumption that development is inherently good. For example, Robert McRuer's "Enfreakment; or, Aliens of Extraordinary Disability," is perhaps the most powerful and entertaining example of complicating the megarhetorics of "inclusion" and "accessibility" through his reading of the 9-minute film *The Chain South*, produced by performance artist Nao Bustamente and videographer Rafael Calderon. In stark contrast to the mostly somber tone of other chapters in this volume, McRuer's writing as well as his subject matter is an energetic exploration of convivial rhetoric.

Geared toward students and teachers of transnational rhetoric, *Megarhetorics* illustrates the complex intertextual and "intercontextual" (Scott 18) layers of global rhetoric—Scott borrows media theorist Lev Manovich's "drifting 'global media cloud' of rhetoric" to describe the dynamics of tracking transnational rhetorics in his chapter titled "Tracking 'Transglocal' Risks in Pharmaceutical Development" (38). In Scott's analysis of pharmaceutical giant Novartis and its lawsuit to reverse the Indian government's rejection of its patent request for an anti-cancer drug called Glivec, there is no clear victor in the debate over issues of fair trade, sovereignty, and international patent law. Scott highlights a simple dichotomy that forms the basis for arguments surrounding various rhetorical events: patients versus patents. Drawing on the classical concept of *metis*, Scott's analysis traces the way that various parties shift and adjust this dichotomous phrase to their advantage. Similarly, Tim Jensen and Wendy S. Hesford discuss the shifting rhetoric employed by the Chinese government to win the bid to host the 2008 Olympic Games through appeals to human rights and their efforts to de-politicize and distance themselves from human rights issues once awarded host status. Their chapter, titled "Staging the Beijing Olympics: Intersecting Human Rights and Economic Development Narratives," provides examples of effective counter-rhetorics, particularly shaming tactics (human rights groups branded the 2008 Olympic Games as the Genocide Olympics), which succeeded in influencing China to change its policy toward human rights issues in Darfur, Sudan (134-36). These kinds of contrasts between megarhetorics and their counter-rhetorics are frequently juxtaposed in the book.

Moreover, many of the contributors focus on the visual as central to their rhetorical analysis. Scott and Dingo foreshadow this focus in their introduction through a description of a scene from the documentary *Life and Debt*, which focuses on Jamaica's economic troubles since the 1960s. Eileen Schell's chapter, titled "Framing the Megarhetorics of Agricultural Development," compares and contrasts the visual rhetoric of agribusiness giant Archer Daniels Midland (ADM) and the rhetoric used by feminist activist Vandana Shiva to promote sustainable agricultural development. Schell takes apart the visual rhetoric employed by ADM in its television and online marketing, demonstrating how the company relies on an epideictic approach, one of praising farmers, as its chief rhetorical strategy. Schell, however, highlights ADM's role in price fixing in the 1990s, an "act . . . in direct contrast to ADM's rhetoric of partnerships" with farmers (157). She then turns to contrast ADM's epideictic rhetoric with Shiva's strategies of rhetorical identification through book publishing, online grassroots advocacy, and non-violent protests. Schell describes the Shiva-led protest against an act of "bio-piracy" in which a Texas company attempting to patent a species of Basmati rice native to India (166). Schell describes the cover of Shiva's casebook *Campaign against Biopiracy*, which uses the synecdochal symbol of a "fat, top-hatted white capitalist man in tux and tails running full speed with a bag of seeds in his hands" (167). Schell argues that this synecdochal image is an attempt to reveal a history of colonialism "continued under a new neoliberal 'hat'" and not simply target one company but the history of Western colonialism "as manifested in U.S. patent laws and WTO agreements" (167). Bret Benjamin's chapter "Making the Case: Bamako and the Problem of Anti-Imperial Art," focuses exclusively on analysis of the critically acclaimed film *Bamako*. *Bamako* is set in a Malian courtyard, where the World Bank and other institutions are put on trial for destroying Africa's social fabric. Building on literary theorist Frederic Jameson's Marxian analytical methods, Benjamin spends considerable time framing a theory of "imperialism" in historical and analytical terms, "rather than merely as a pejorative descriptor" (203). At the risk of oversimplifying, the problem with imperial art, in my read of Benjamin, is that it appears to be limited primarily to a role of provocation. "One film," he concedes, "cannot, of course, bring down the World Bank" (229). Benjamin's critique raises the question of how effectively art serves as counter-rhetorics. Of the more successful examples of counter-rhetorics described in this volume, those that actually appear to provoke action involve networks of campaigning activists and varying rhetorical strategies from re-branding and appropriating logos (Jensen and Hesford's description of activist tactics at the 2008 Olympics) or engaging in rhetorical events (Shiva's protest at the U.S. embassy in Delhi).

As a former marketer for an international non-governmental organization and now a teacher of rhetoric, I found *Megarhetorics* to be consciousness-raising. I found myself arguing aloud with Dingo and her critique of micro-lending and its role in empowerment, laughing at McRuer's celebration of "freakery," and contemplating whether I might have been complicit in perpetuating a neoliberal development agenda (243). *Megarhetorics* provides models for how other scholars might extend rhetorical concepts to a range of new media discourses. More importantly, what makes the book worth reading is its deft deconstruction of common assumptions about global development.

Orlando, FL

Works Cited

Future Innovators: Kiva. Advertisement. On Best Buy. 2012. Web. 2 Aug. 2012. http://www.bestbuyon.com/ces-2011/future-innovators-kiva

Words at Work and Play: Three Decades in Family and Community Life, by Shirley Brice Heath. Cambridge: Cambridge UP, 2012. 221 pp.

Reviewed by Stacy Kastner, Bowling Green State University

A forerunner of the New Literacy Studies, Shirley Brice Heath's 1983 *Ways with Words: Language, Life, and Work in Communities and Classrooms* profiled the language use of three hundred black (Trackton) and white (Roadville) working-class families in the Piedmont Carolinas from 1969 to 1978. Three decades later, still in contact with roughly 85% of the original three hundred families, *Words at Work and Play* follows the descendants of the Piedmonts, now scattered across the United States, from the early 1980s to 2007. In light of changes in work and family activities during these years, her present book considers the social, linguistic, and cognitive effects of dual-earning parents, middle-class aspirations, and after school activities and community organizations. A large portion of the narrative is concerned with the YMCA, 4H Club, youth theatres, and other local and national organizations designed with kids and teens in mind. Having found that "families [no longer] generate the human resources to provide the quantity and quality of talk and experience necessary to socialize children for adaptive competence" and that "[f]ormal schooling did not keep up with the rapid increase in scientific discovery or the accelerating interest of young people in technology, arts, and design" (65), *Words at Work and Play* conveys the importance of such "extracurriculars" in children's lives.

Chapter 1 offers a succinct summary of *Ways with Words* that registers the cultural and economic changes in family and work life that characterize the forty years comprising Heath's research. The original families from Trackton and Roadville did not have checking or savings accounts, likely did not have high school diplomas or higher education, did not own homes or automobiles, lived segregated by train tracks, and drew incomes from mill work, farming, or a combination of both. In contrast, the second and third generations of these communities had checking and savings accounts for adults and children, card credits, loans, mortgages, and jobs requiring special training or college.

The first of several of what Heath calls "relay race[s] of then-and-now stories" (1), chapter 2 introduces Jerome. When we meet Jerome (born in Trackton), he has made his way to Chicago. For a small financial incentive, Jerome and his friends from the local theatre company recorded many of their own conversations, kept track of them using "Script Time Data Sheets," transcribed and annotated them, tracked language structures on a "Linguistic Research Chart," and met with Heath to discuss and interpret the data collected (29). Moving deeper into the book, we understand Heath is not the ethnographer observing from a distance. Her research is dependent upon the co-researching capabilities of families, particularly teenagers like Jerome and his friends, who contemplated what it meant for them when the present tense columns continued to outweigh the past tense columns on their research charts: "'Our kids gonna grow up just like us—stuck in NOW'" (32-3). Heath uses the appendices to explicate the broad changes in social history- and ethnography-based research disciplines that explain the contrast between the distanced narrative that characterized *Ways with Words* and her current work, within which she plays a critical role. Testament to such changes, her first appendix offers her own backstory.

Chapter 3 transports us to the suburbs of Boston where we reconnect with Martin, a child of Roadville, who is now married with two children, Rebecca and Mark. Rebecca and Mark's nanny, and the thirty hours or more a week each child dedicates to after school activities introduces Heath's concept of "intimate strangers," a phrase she uses to characterize coaches, choir directors, and other non-family adults children's extracurricular activities bring them into contact with. We also reconnect with Jay, a child of Trackton, and his son, Bernardo, and follow them from Texas to Colorado. Important is what Jerome, Mark, Rebecca, and Bernardo share in common: Mark and Rebecca picked up some German from their nanny, Bernardo and Jerome are both bilingual in Spanish, and all four gained experience making decisions, understanding consequences, budgeting, solving problems, and setting goals by participating in community organizations that gave them identities, and perhaps more importantly responsibilities, beyond student and son or daughter.

For those of us working in college classrooms, when we meet Lisa Dobbs in chapter 4, we are reminded of how unfamiliar and alienating such spaces are for some of our students. "'The college classroom was the scariest place I'd ever been,'" recalls the woman who grew up in Roadville and relocated to Texas with her two sons after divorcing her alcoholic and abusive husband (68). We also meet Lisa's sister, Sally, now living in Minnesota with her husband and two daughters. When we join the families and Heath on their summer vacation, we sit in as the two women review their own transcripts and activity logs, we listen and identify with them as they discuss the difficulties of managing Sunday dinners, time on the weekends for families to spend together, and the propensities of parents and children to escape to personal technologies during down time.

We continue on with the stories of Zinnia Mae (Jerome's birth mother) and her other three children in the fifth chapter, also meeting Sissy, her husband Red, and their two children. Sissy's brother Tony was one of the first members of the Trackton community to go away to college. However, where Tony came from, it was unfriendly to lead conversation away from the community's knowledge-base, thus, talking about faraway places, people, and things was not only unfamiliar but unknown. Heath explains that such inexperience was particularly felt when these students were asked to contribute "critical perspectives," "comparative analysis," and "persuasive arguments" in their writing (99).

In chapters 6 and 7, we meet more of the descendants of the Piedmonts, continuing to observe changes in family life and learning how the third generation of the Piedmonts' activities outside of school and home prepared and shaped them to be the people they would become (something I was eager to read about and happily satisfied when I did in the "Epilogue"). The large-scale results of Heath's study feature prominently here. Heath found that changes in children's play and playthings inhibited them once they entered schools, causing "trouble in academic subjects that required the understanding of concepts of change" and "difficulty with texts heavy with concepts they could not readily reduce to labels or short phrases" (126). By the end of chapter 7, we are confronted fully with the impacts of cell phones, videogames, Wikipedia, and YouTube, causing Heath to give explicit attention to multimedia writing on pages 142 and 143. Leaning on the wisdom of a twelve-year-old—"'if I can't see it, I can't get it'" (143)—she advocated for "representational models" that combine both visuals and words to support learning, particularly writing.

The closing chapter unites the narratives of the people whose lives we have followed throughout the book as well as the many other narratives that make Heath's work so important. One finding is that children are not acquiring the scheduling skills we might think their growing participation in extracurricular activities would imbue them with and are often unable to site the details of the upcoming week let alone the upcoming months. As scheduling dominates the lives of parents and children, time for "extended" and "deliberative" talk is decreasing (162). Heath argues that without such kinds of talk happening in the home or elsewhere, children will grow into adults without a sense of the consequences of their actions, an understanding of sequences of events, and inexperienced with "conditionals or hypotheticals" that support "self-monitoring and planning" (163).

The weight of *Words at Work and Play*'s importance hits us when Heath explains: "My audio recordings in family life enable me to compare how the same family across two, sometimes three, generations spent Saturday mornings with their two-year-old or twelve-year old" (19). We wonder how she has possibly managed a slim 200-something-page book, and we forgive the sometimes confusing backwards and forwards of its narrative—from the 1970s to the 1990s to 2007, from personal narratives to statistics representative of the wide-scale social and economic changes that paralleled her research. Heath's book is an important read for a range of teachers, like parents, who are the earliest educational guides in children's lives, and more traditional teachers as well that will have to adjust their expectations of students as patterns of language in the home limit young children's capabilities of envisioning, planning, and then executing the ideas in their heads. One of the most striking characteristics of Heath's research is its dependence upon teens to perform as co-researchers and co-interpreters, encouraging teachers and researchers alike to instill more trust and greater responsibility in their seemingly inexperienced students and participants. For composition researchers and teachers, *Words at Work and Play* reminds us that learning to write is a multilayered process, one we cannot fully understand when we conduct our research solely in schools and focus exclusively on texts, and one we can never teach if we don't consider our students as people who have lives and identities outside of our classrooms.

St. Louis, MO

Feminist Rhetorical Practices: New Horizons for Rhetoric, Composition, and Literacy Studies, by Jacqueline Jones Royster and Gesa E. Kirsch. Carbondale: Southern Illinois UP, 2012. 180 pp.

Reviewed by Heather Ostman, SUNY Westchester Community College

In *Feminist Rhetorical Practices: New Horizons for Rhetoric, Composition, and Literacy Studies*, Jacqueline Jones Royster and Gesa E. Kirsch offer a comprehensive review and analysis of thirty years' worth of research and practice in feminist rhetorics. The authors view feminist rhetoric as a range of practices best understood within a matrix of four methodological strategies: the critical imagination, strategic contemplation, social circulation, and globalization. Taken together, these four strategies construct a new framework for analysis of feminist rhetorical practices, one which enables them to rework—and subvert—traditional rhetorical approaches. The authors offer a lens for examining the rich multiplicity of rhetorical practices today: traditional, non-traditional, and emergent—a revision based in the "ethics of care and hope," in which the inclusivity and recovery of lost or unrecognized voices are central priorities to "responsible rhetorical action"(136).

From the outset, and with the clear intention of asserting an ethical standpoint, Royster and Kirsch quickly abandon the notion that the term "feminist rhetorical practices" applies to rhetoric articulated only by women. Instead, the authors offer an interdisciplinary lens for viewing various rhetorical practices, both inclusive of traditional approaches as well as non-traditional approaches, and with the acknowledgment that there are other approaches, representative of written and non-written rhetoric, still to be included. To this end, Royster and Kirsch divide *Feminist Rhetorical Practices* into four parts, beginning with part 1, "A Call for Action in Research, Teaching, and Learning"; then part 2, "Re-visioning History, Theory, and Practice"; followed by parts 3 and 4, "Recasting Paradigms for Inquiry, Analysis, and Interpretation" and the "Conclusion," respectively.

The authors contextualize their analysis in part 1 by opening with reflective accounts of their own encounters with traditional rhetoric. In their narratives, Royster and Kirsch anchor their relationships to traditional rhetorical approaches by identifying themselves in terms of race, gender, and nationality. They document their experiences by noting significant rhetorical texts that shaped them as scholars and rhetors, including related works such as Carol Tavris's *Mismeasure of Women*, a historical account of the ways predominant academic disciplines undermined women, or as Kirsch notes, "set out to prove women's inferiority" (5). Her point thus emphasizes the urgency of *Feminist Rhetorical Practices*: traditional rhetorical models consciously and unconsciously prioritized the voices and research of privileged white men. Royster's personal narrative underscores the necessity of analyzing and broadening traditional rhetorical approaches. She recounts her frustration with researching less traditional subjects—in her case, African American women—and explains that she found herself asking: "Why is it that I have to learn about remarkable African American women whom I'm coming to know and admire inside a circle of women friends and colleagues (mostly African American), rather than inside traditional classrooms and other anointed academic structures?" (8). Together, the authors' disappointment with traditional rhetorical practices have led them to assemble this comprehensive review of texts dedicated to prioritizing women's voices and rhetorics, as well as the multiplicity of ways modern scholars can approach them. Finally, and perhaps most importantly, the authors demonstrate models for understanding and practicing feminist rhetorics by incorporating the four categorical strategies that organize the text into their own narratives.

The rest of part 1 and the following chapters in part 2 identify work that points to "tectonic shifts" in the field of Rhetoric. The authors argue that feminist practices have already begun to transform the rhetorical "landscape" and "have also been instrumental in expanding the scope and range of factors that we now perceive as significant in determining the highest quality of excellence in both performance and professional practice" (13). These chapters, like nearly all of the chapters, offer what are in essence selective bibliographies that support the authors' claims, as they seek to demonstrate that feminist rhetorical practices have not only changed the scholarly landscape in the last thirty years, they have necessitated a new framework for perceiving and understanding rhetorical practices in general.

Particularly in parts 3 and 4, Royster and Kirsch apply the four categorical approaches they outline at the beginning of the text to their survey of rhetorical work. Critical imagination, strategic contemplation, social circulation, and globalization provide lines of inquiry that overlap and interweave to create a matrix for understanding the multiplicity of rhetorical practices that exist and anticipate the potential for those still to come. Critical imagination, as a method of inquiry, they argue, may expose gaps in understanding created by traditional rhetorical practice, even as this understanding relies on traditional rhetorics to create a foundation for analysis. On the other hand, strategic contemplation searches directly for marginalized rhetorics and prioritizes reflective process in research and "allows scholars to observe and notice, to listen to and hear voices often neglected or silenced, and to notice more overtly their own responses to what they are seeing, reading, reflecting on, and encountering during their research processes" (86). Social circulation seeks to reframe feminist discourse work in a way that broadens rhetoric as an all-inclusive, human endeavor. Within this third category, the authors begin to demonstrate the "recent" shift away from traditional rhetorical approaches, and they suggest that social circulation might be best understood "with a disruption of the dichotomies associated with rhetoric being defined within what has been considered historically to be the public domains of men" (98). Globalization provides a fourth strategy, one which underscores the continual need for practitioners and students of rhetoric to stay vigilant to the world beyond what they know, to be cognizant of the voices from around the world, and to recognize the multiplicity of rhetorics as relevant to their own specific work.

Within the matrix of these four strategies, Royster and Kirsch argue that feminist rhetorical practices have become central to studies in Rhetoric, Composition, and Literacy (RCL). They view a convergence among the fields of rhetorical studies, feminist studies, and global studies within RCL, "showing evidence of a growing commitment to shift rhetorical studies away from traditional, imperialist perspectives of rhetorical performance and knowledge to a more democratic and more inclusive one that recognizes transnational constructions of rhetorical enterprises, not just Western ones" (111). Furthermore, the conclusion in part 4 outlines a new vision of RCL, one that acknowledges and builds upon this convergence. The authors refashion the traditional framework for researching and understanding rhetorical work and present a well-articulated argument for the diversity of interrogation strategies founded within an ethics of care and hope, which recognizes the importance and relevance of rhetorics different from one's own.

Royster and Kirsch's *Feminist Rhetorical Practices* is a comprehensive text, spanning thirty years' worth of work in feminist rhetorical studies and solidifying the place of that work as a central component in RCL today. The world has changed, they argue; compositionists cannot ignore the global nature of their work. Feminist rhetorical practices offer a re-visioning of that work to accommodate the diversity and complexity that characterize RCL. The authors' own expansive knowledge and research in traditional and non-traditional rhetorics ground this study, and because they offer scores of resources, the text is very appropriate for students and scholars of RCL who are actively researching feminist rhetoric and new rhetorical approaches. One especially useful component of the study is the sections that make deliberate "pedagogical connections." Since most compositionists are teachers, more of these sections would have provided a bonus in an already important book. But for instructors who are teaching a diverse student body, and that is most composition instructors these days, *Feminist Rhetorical Practices* offers a new vision for the field of Rhetoric, one that is inclusive of diverse voices, and one that opens the possibility for further inquiry and exploration with a clear shift away from the exclusivity of traditional rhetorical approaches.

Valhalla, NY

Illness as Narrative, by Ann Jurecic. U of Pittsburg P: Pittsburg, 2012. 168 pp.

Reviewed by Erin Trauth, Texas Tech University

Illness has unequivocally shaped society—our health and condition of mind and body often dictate the ways we live, think, and write about ourselves. In *Illness as Narrative*, Ann Jurecic examines how contemporary writers "compose" illness throughout history. In this in-depth study, she includes narratives which make meaning of "at risk, in prognosis, and in pain" (4). While personal accounts of illness were once harbored, the illness narrative has emerged as a prominent force in public personal accounts. While the genre is indeed prominent, illness narratives pose a unique issue in the critical realm. In six thoughtful chapters, she closely observes how readers have responded to these narratives, and ultimately asks how illness narratives—those deeply personal and painful accounts of confusing and frightening experiences—fit into literary studies as a genre for critical examination. By channeling the works of Bruno Latour, Veena Das, and Susan Sontag, among many others who show an overall dissatisfaction with "critical detachment" (98), Jurecic seeks to chart out ways to renew what Ricoeur calls criticism's "willingness to listen" (27) when dealing with the illness of others.

In chapter 1, Jurecic traces the rise of illness narratives whilst bringing forth questions about the fragile matter of critical work on illness narratives. She describes how events such as the changing role of the patient and the explosion of HIV/AIDS gave life to the practice of making meaning of illness through the written word. While illness narratives began to proliferate, the ways in which critics can examine them became problematic. Jurecic asks: "How can we define critical practices that are grounded in everyday life, practices that are rigorous, compelling and, at the same time, socially engaged and thoughtfully empathic?" (17). How does one "combine a willingness to suspect with an eagerness to listen" (Felski 22 qtd. in Jurecic 17) while responding critically to personal accounts of inconceivable disease and pain? *Illness as Narrative*, then, works to understand how critical readings of such works function in a way that is dually critical yet considerate.

In chapter 2, Jurecic describes how authors make personal meaning of life "at risk" (18) in risk narratives, focusing on examples of those conceiving of life through narrative while "in prognosis" (21), before prognosis with a genetic risk of developing disease (26), and through "literary risk" (29), or those accounts narrated as literary autobiographies. While the approaches of the authors vary, Jurecic traces the emergence of the memoir, claiming that it "is no accident that the age of the memoir emerged with the age of statistics" (21). She cites Lennard J. Davis and Kathleen Woodward, who describe the ways the use of statistics in risk assessment of health issues creates both a "normalcy" and an "otherness"—Woodward asserts that statistics functions as a type of "biopower, which controls bodies and populations" (20). Jurecic then proceeds to examine several contemporary narratives about risk from authors of varying backgrounds, such as Stephen J. Gould and David Rieff, in the end creating an understanding of how both writers and readers parley with existing narratives in order to make meaning of statistical risk.

Chapter 3 focuses on the problems of responding to the pain of others, as it is incredibly complex to do so when analyzing the work of writers living fully embodied, social lives (66). Jurecic first declares that "pain is everywhere" (43) in literature; the paradox, of course, is that pain is communicable for some writers, but not for others. For some critics, communicating pain is simple beyond the limitations of language—how can we truly "feel" one's reality of such a torturous experience? Elaine Scarry's influential work on pain asserts, "physical pain does not simply resist language but actively destroys it" (44). Questions regarding the many notions of pain and how to communicate them are the focus of this chapter—memoirists have continually questioned how to make readers receptive to their personal recollections of horrifying bodily experiences. Further, how do we judge the work of writers who attempt to communicate the intricate depths of pain? Jurecic explores the work of a range of writers, including Duadet and Manto, among others, to show how writers have worked to encourage readers to be "rigorous and responsive, to exercise reason and emotion, to be willing to suspect and listen, to acknowledged what is not known, and also what is" (66) when dealing with the complexities of pain narratives.

In chapter 4, Jurecic focuses primarily on the work of Susan Sontag, the prolific writer of *Illness as Metaphor*. Jurecic claims that Sontag has "done more than any other single writer to bring attention to how literature documents and shapes the cultural meaning and experience of illness, pain, and suffering" (67). Jurecic examines one core analogy of Sontag's *Illness as Metaphor* as one of the "most misread or misinterpreted metaphors" present in contemporary work on illness (68). She then focuses on several of Sontag's works on illness and suffering, centering closely on the "evidence of uncertainties that underlie her performance of certainty" (68). Sontag's work aligned at times with critics skeptical of determining meaning and other times with humanist critics who understood the performative function of illness narrative; Jurecic ultimately uses Sontag's work in this realm to represent the central struggle of those who write, read, or criticize work on suffering.

Chapter 5 centers on theory's "aging body"—or the aging progress of theorists and its impacts on critical work—at first tracing the initial role of the critic as one who must show "disinterestedness" (Arnold qtd. in Jurecic 92). Jurecic problematizes the critic's true function and the attitudes that surround such work in the context of illness narratives. She considers the work of Stephen Greenblatt, citing work which shows "evidence of the divide between theoretically informed critical practice" (94) and illness narratives. Jurecic reminds readers of writers' calls for listening. Michel Foucault, Jurecic asserts, is a prime example of how "mortal illness" can impact critical interests. As he died from AIDS, Foucault "faced his actual death by thinking about how lives and selves can be made into works of art" (101). His impending death, Jurecic explains, "prompted a reconsideration of the relationship between social, historical, and cultural coercions, on the one hand, and the possibility of composing the self through the reflection and caution on the other" (102). Jurecic also discusses the work of Judith Butler, Eve Kofsofsky Sedgwick, and Jean-Dominique Bauby, among others, in the end exerting a warning of caution and sensitivity to those who criticize the writing of others who faced unbearable pain and evidence of human's fragile mortality.

In chapter 6, Jurecic explores Sedgwick's notion of "paranoid practices" in critical work (113). She uses Anne Fadiman's work on medical suffering as a case study for examining whether practices which are "not governed by trust or suspicion... attentive—perhaps even reparative—... can be taught" (114). She explains that in Fadiman's illness narrative (as is the case with many) "the ailing body points to culture, pain points to philosophy, language points to consciousness, and all point to what is still to be learned about our fragility, our mortality, and how to live a meaningful life" (131).

As a whole, Jurecic's text is successful in exploring contemporary works on pain and illness and the critical response they elicit. *Illness as Narrative* seeks to draw wider attention to the illness narrative and to argue for new approaches to both literary criticism and teaching narrative in a way which balances the fragility of human life—it delivers. She asks that we consider why writers compose stories of illness, how readers receive them, and how both use these narratives to make meaning of human anguish, encouraging a practice that's both critical and *compassionate* in an otherwise often-distrustful critical context. In a time where illness pervades society more than ever before, *Illness as Narrative* is timely, considerate, and thought provoking—it is a helpful review of writing about illness and critical response to such narratives, one that reminds us that, in the end, we are all mere mortals ourselves.

Lubbock, TX

Announcements

Composition Forum

The Research Exchange Index, or REx, is designed to collect information about local, national, and international writing research conducted in unpublished and published studies. REx is also designed to solve a longstanding problem in writing studies: access to a wealth of information difficult to research across publications and difficult to find because it remains in institutional reports, programs, classrooms, or departments.

As a database about the processes of a research study, entries are different than articles about the studies that might be published in journals or books; therefore, entering data in REx not only doesn't infringe on any copyright, but, once made public, actually serves to promote work by authors/editors. Your contribution will become part of a peer-reviewed digital publication. After the collection deadline (May 1st, 2013), REx editors will review all entries for clarity and completeness of information, contacting researchers for further information as needed. Once the review process is complete, the edited entries will be included in the searchable REx database. REx editors will introduce the database with a scholarly essay that contextualizes contemporary writing research, offers an overview of database contents, and points to current and emerging research trends indicated by your studies.

From the first edition onward, REx will provide a historical snapshot of writing research, and it will offer a resource for planning future studies. For example, REx might be used to:

- generate aggregatable data about one or more types of contemporary writing research;
- demonstrate gaps in our knowledge of contemporary writing;
- provide models for research studies at new sites;
- indicate areas of future study;
- locate archives for historical studies of twenty-first-century writing; and
- discover potential collaborators or sites for collaborative studies.

With individual teacher-scholars' participation, REx will provide a rich and comprehensive profile of what research in "writing studies" is and is becoming. Start your entry by going to http://researchexchange.colostate.edu/index.cfm

Contributors

Peter Goggin is Associate Professor of English, co-director of the PhD in Rhetoric, Composition, Linguistics, and sustainability scholar for ASU's Global Institute of Sustainability. He has published on literacy and sustainability, and his work has appeared in numerous journals. He is founder/director of the annual Western States Rhetoric and Literacy conference.

A. Abby Knoblauch is an Assistant Professor of composition and rhetoric at Kansas State University where she teaches undergraduate and graduate courses in feminist rhetorics and pedagogies, rhetorical theory, teacher development, pop culture and the teaching of writing, and expository writing.

Timothy Oleksiak is a doctoral candidate in the Department of Writing Studies at the University of Minnesota, Twin Cities.

Tim Peeples, Professor of Professional Writing and Rhetoric, and Associate Provost for Faculty Affairs at Elon University, has taught first-year through advanced writing and rhetoric courses and served in a range of WPA positions. Tim's research focuses on the re-production of rhetorical space through rhetoric and administration.

Paula Rosinski, Associate Professor of Professional Writing and Rhetoric and Writing Center Director at Elon University, has taught a range of writing classes including first-year writing, multimedia writing and style and editing. Paula's research focuses on multimodal rhetoric and the transfer of rhetorical knowledge between self sponsored and academic writing.

Jamie White-Farnham earned her PhD in English, specializing in Writing & Rhetoric, at the University of Rhode Island in 2011. She is currently Assistant Professor and Writing Coordinator at the University of Wisconsin-Superior. Jamie thanks Bob Schwegler and Chuck Morgan at URI for their collegiality while teaching Writing 302.

Ryan Shepherd is a PhD student, teaching associate, and assistant director of the Writing Programs at Arizona State University. His work with Facebook and other digital platforms has been presented at Computers and Writing 2012, The Council of Writing Program Administrators 2012, and Western States Rhetoric and Literacy Conference 2011.

Rhetoric & Writing PhD Program

Preparing Rhetoric and Composition Faculty for over 30 Years

Since its founding in 1980, Bowling Green State University's program has prepared more than eighty graduates for faculty careers in rhetoric and composition. Students and faculty in the Rhetoric & Writing PhD Program are committed scholar-teachers who utilize a range of approaches—rhetorical, cultural, empirical, technological—that characterize rhetoric and composition in the twenty-first century.

Some highlights of the Rhetoric & Writing PhD Program:
- Eight core courses in history, theory, computer-mediated writing, research, scholarly publication, and composition studies as a discipline, plus electives in rhetoric and composition and related areas of scholarly interest to students.
- Professional development involving mentoring, collaboration, a monthly colloquium series, and post-prelim groups emphasizing dissertation work and the job search.
- Varied assistantship assignments (FYW, intermediate writing, writing center, faculty research, editorial work, program administration, community outreach, etc.) and competitive non-service fellowships in the fourth year of funding.
- Four-year graduation rate typical for full-time students.
- 100% placement rate among program graduates.

Rhetoric & Writing PhD Program
http://www.bgsu.edu/departments/english/rcweb/index.html
Facebook Group: BGSU Rhetoric & Writing

Program Director, Sue Carter Wood
carters@bgsu.edu
English Graduate Office: 419-372-6864

DEPARTMENT OF WRITING STUDIES — UNIVERSITY OF MINNESOTA

Study at a research-intensive university with an internationally recognized faculty in one of the longest established rhetoric & scientific and technical communication programs in the country. In addition to our rich history, we have a new commitment to Writing Studies as a field involving research and teaching about global, social, and the digital dimensions of writing.

M.A. and Ph.D. Degrees in Rhetoric and Scientific and Technical Communication
Our program combines theory and research in all aspects of writing, rhetoric, and technical communication. The Ph.D. is in high demand; all of our graduates have placed in academic or industry positions.

M.S. and B.S. Degrees in Scientific and Technical Communication and the Technical Communication Certificate
Designed for working professionals and other students whose primary goal is a career in the field of technical communication.

To find out more visit www.writingstudies.umn.edu

Graduate Study at Arizona State University
DEPARTMENT OF ENGLISH

MA Rhetoric and Composition
PhD Rhetoric, Composition, and Linguistics

FACULTY

Patricia Boyd | Alice Daer | James Gee | Maureen Daly Goggin (Chair)
Peter Goggin | Mark Hannah | Elisabeth Hayes | Kathleen Lamp | Elenore Long
Paul Kei Matsuda | Keith Miller | Ersula Ore | Shirley Rose | Doris Warriner

The Department of English at ASU has created a diverse and energetic intellectual atmosphere within which to pursue graduate studies. Boasting one of the largest, most productive faculties in the western United States, the department is highly regarded for its professional development and mentoring programs, which prepare students for successful careers in academia and beyond.

english.clas.asu.edu/graduate

STUDY ENGLISH AND EDUCATION

Joint PhD Program in English and Education

UNIVERSITY OF MICHIGAN

SCHOOL OF EDUCATION

DEPARTMENT of ENGLISH
LANGUAGE AND LITERATURE

Bringing together the best of research and scholarship from the traditional English discipline in combination with the strong pedagogical focus of the education field, this interdisciplinary program draws on top-flight resources to provide a satisfying and rich doctoral experience. To date, all of our graduates have taken tenure-track faculty positions in education and English departments in colleges and universities.

This PhD program is designed for students who hold master's degrees in English or education and who have teaching experience. Among the strengths of our program is the supportive and engaging community of scholars, including both students and faculty, and the flexibility we offer to students to pursue their individual interests. These interests have included rhetorical theory, literacy studies, new media composition, applied linguistics, English language studies, and writing assessment; our faculty are happy to work with you to craft a program centered on your interest.

Phone: 734.763.6643
Email: ed.jpee@umich.edu

soe.umich.edu/jpee

An MLA Resource for Teaching Writing with Literature

Integrating Literature and Writing Instruction

First-Year English, Humanities Core Courses, Seminars

Edited by **Judith H. Anderson** and **Christine R. Farris**

"If some instructors question literature's place in first-year writing programs, then this volume is available to respond to those concerns and to show how the use of literature may stimulate the analysis that eventually appears in students' essays."

—*Rocky Mountain Review*

"[This book] provides vivid examples of ways in which thoughtful and committed teachers have found literature to be a valuable tool, even for nonmajors."

—*George Levine*
Rutgers University

Now available

vi & 336 pp.

Cloth 978-0-87352-948-8
$40.00

Paper 978-0-87352-949-5
$25.00

Join the MLA today and receive 20% off the listed price.

Modern Language Association

Phone orders 646 576-5161 ■ Fax 646 576-5160 ■ www.mla.org

How does the MLA work for you?

Promotes the study of language and literature

Publishes your scholarship

Hosts an annual convention where you can share your work

Compiles the *Job Information List*

Creates opportunities for scholarly interaction—look for the new MLA Commons in winter 2013

The Modern Language Association is a community of nearly 30,000 members dedicated to strengthening the study and teaching of language and literature. The MLA makes it possible for you to

- research career and job market information
- read reports and surveys issued by the MLA on the job market, enrollments, evaluating scholarship, and the state of scholarly publishing
- benefit from public outreach activities, including the popular MLA Language Map
- download the Academic Workforce Advocacy Kit, a tool for helping improve conditions for teachers and students
- read FAQs about MLA style

Become an MLA member at **www.mla.org** and receive the following benefits:

- subscriptions to *PMLA* and the *MLA Newsletter*
- priority convention registration
- online access to the *Job Information List* for ADE- and ADFL-member departments
- access to directories of members and departmental administrators

Three easy ways to join:

- Visit www.mla.org.
- E-mail membership@mla.org to request a membership packet.
- Call 646 576-5151.

MLA BOSTON 2013

The MLA Annual Convention 3–6 January 2013 in Boston

featuring the presidential theme Avenues of Access

The largest gathering of teachers and scholars in the humanities now meets in January. Other changes include

- new features, including more roundtables and workshops
- more collaboration and discussion
- more free time in the evenings
- special presentations featuring renowned thinkers, artists, and critics in conversation
- local excursions for registrants
- regular *Twitter* updates during the convention

2013 members receive reduced rates and special discounts for the 2013 convention in Boston. Visit www.mla.org/convention for more information.

Follow the MLA Annual Convention on *Twitter* at www.twitter.com/mlaconvention.

Modern Language Association | MLA

www.mla.org

Now Available in the MLA series
Options *for* Teaching

Teaching Early Modern English Prose

Susannah Brietz Monta and Margaret W. Ferguson, eds.

"This volume is full of wonderful, promising, intriguing suggestions, which I will gladly borrow for my own teaching."

—*Debora Shuger
University of California
Los Angeles*

To gain a full understanding of the literature and history of early modern England, students need to study the prose of the period, which requires as much analysis and attention as the drama and poetry of the time.

The essays in this MLA Options for Teaching volume consider the broad cultural questions raised by prose and explore prose style, showing teachers how to hone students' writing skills in the process.

Now available.
x & 386 pp.
6 x 9
Cloth 978-1-60329-052-4
$40.00
Paper 978-1-60329-053-1
$25.00

Join the MLA today and receive 20% off the listed price.

Phone orders 646 576-5161 ■ Fax 646 576-5160 ■ www.mla.org

New Releases . . .

The WPA Outcomes Statement—A Decade Later
Edited by Nicholas N. Behm, Gregory R. Glau, Deborah H. Holdstein, Duane Roen, and Edward M. White. 344 pages. $32 (paperback); $65 (cloth); $20 (digital).

The WPA Outcomes Statement—A Decade Later examines the ways that the Council of Writing Program Administrators' Outcomes Statement for First-Year Composition has informed curricula, generated programmatic, institutional, and disciplinary change, and affected a disciplinary understanding of best practices in first-year composition.

Writing Program Administration at Small Liberal Arts Colleges
Jill M. Gladstein and Dara Rossman Regaignon
   290 pages. $32 (paperback); $60 (cloth); $20 (digital)

Writing Program Administration at Small Liberal Arts Colleges presents a research study of the writing programs at one hundred small, private liberal arts institutions. Using grounded theory's mixed methods approach, the book presents a detailed picture of the structures that deliver, support, and lead writing instruction at these institutions.

Also Just Released . . .

Rewriting Success in Rhetoric and Composition Careers
   Edited by Amy Goodburn, Donna LeCourt, and Carrie Leverenz.

and with the WAC Clearinghouse . . .

Writing Programs Worldwide: Profiles of Academic Writing in Many Places
   Edited by Chris Thaiss, Gerd Bräuer, Paula Carlino, Lisa Ganobcsik-Williams, and Aparna Sinha

International Advances in Writing Research: Cultures, Places, Measures
   Edited by Charles Bazerman, Chris Dean, Jessica Early, Karen Lunsford, Suzie Null, Paul Rogers, and Amanda Stansell

www.parlorpress.com

www.ingramcontent.com/pod-product-compliance
Lightning Source LLC
Chambersburg PA
CBHW031630160426
43196CB00006B/356